The PRINCE2® Practitioner

Struggling to apply the principles of PRINCE2 in practice?

Need guidance on adapting the process for smaller projects?

The PRINCE2® Practitioner provides the solution. This practical reference, matching the details and requirements of the 2009 PRINCE2 manual, contains new and updated real-life examples and case studies, highlights the links between related components and processes and gives clear guidance on how to fine-tune the method to help you manage projects successfully, whatever the context and size.

As an affordable alternative to expensive training, this best selling handbook by PRINCE2 expert Colin Bentley is an indispensable addition to your project management bookshelf and a companion to the *PRINCE2® for Beginners* book. If you have passed the PRINCE2 exams, this handbook will help you keep your knowledge and skills up to date to maintain registered status, and enable you to apply the theory of PRINCE2 to everyday project work after certification.

Colin Bentley has been a project manager since 1966, working as a consultant to many international firms such as The London Stock Exchange, Microsoft Europe, Tesco Stores and the BBC. Bentley has worked with PRINCE2, PRINCE and their predecessor, PROMPTII, since 1975. He wrote the original PRINCE2 manual and, until 2009, was the author of all revisions to the manual. He was the Chief Examiner for all examination papers in PRINCE2 until his retirement in 2010.

The PRINCE2® Practitioner

From practitioner to professional

Third edition

Colin Bentley

LONDON AND NEW YORK

First published 2006 as PRINCE2™ Revealed
Second Edition 2010
by Butterworth-Heinemann, an imprint of Elsevier

Third edition 2015
by Routledge
2 Park Square, Milton Park, Abingdon, Oxon OX14 4RN

and by Routledge
711 Third Avenue, New York, NY 10017

Routledge is an imprint of the Taylor & Francis Group, an informa business

© 2015 Colin Bentley

PRINCE2® is a registered trade mark of AXELOS Limited.
The Swirl logo™ is a trade mark of AXELOS Limited.

The right of Colin Bentley to be identified as author of this work has been asserted in accordance with sections 77 and 78 of the Copyright, Designs and Patents Act 1988.

All rights reserved. No part of this book may be reprinted or reproduced or utilised in any form or by any electronic, mechanical or other means, now known or hereafter invented, including photocopying and recording, or in any information storage or retrieval system, without permission in writing from the publishers.

Trademark notice: Product or corporate names may be trademarks or registered trademarks, and are used only for identification and explanation without intent to infringe.

British Library Cataloguing in Publication Data
A catalogue record for this book is available from the British Library

Library of Congress Cataloging in Publication Data
Bentley, Colin.
[Prince 2 revealed]
The Prince2 practitioner: from practitioner to professional / Colin Bentley. — Third edition.
pages cm
"First published 2006 as PRINCE 2 Revealed."
Includes bibliographical references and index.
1. Project management—Data processing. 2. Electronic data processing—Structured techniques. I. Title.
HD69.P75B464 2015
658.4'04028553--dc23
2014035780

ISBN: 978–1–138–82410–2 (hbk)
ISBN: 978–1–138–82411–9 (pbk)
ISBN: 978–1–315–74092–8 (ebk)

Typeset in Optima
by Florence Production Ltd, Stoodleigh, Devon, UK

Printed and bound in Great Britain by
TJ International Ltd, Padstow, Cornwall

Contents

List of figures vii
Preface ix

1 Introduction 1

2 An Overview of PRINCE2 3

3 Business Case 17

4 Organization 25

5 Plans 47

6 Progress 63

7 Quality 77

8 Risk 87

9 Change 103

10 Starting up a Project (SU) 121

11 Initiating a Project (IP) 139

12 Directing a Project (DP) 159

13 Controlling a Stage (CS) 171

14 Managing Product Delivery (MP) 189

15 Managing a Stage Boundary (SB)	197
16 Closing a Project (CP)	211
17 Tailoring PRINCE2 to the Project Environment	221
Appendix A Product Descriptions	*227*
Appendix B Project Management Team Roles	*257*
Appendix C Product-based Planning	*271*
Appendix D Quality Review	*283*
Appendix E Risk Categories	*295*
Index	*299*

Figures

2.1	The seven PRINCE2 principles	4
2.2	Business, user and supplier interests	7
2.3	PRINCE2 themes	10
2.4	PRINCE2 processes	12
2.5	A typical flow through the PRINCE2 processes	13
4.1	Business, user and supplier interests	25
4.2	Four layers of management	27
4.3	Project management team structure	30
4.4	Small project team structure	44
5.1	The PRINCE2 hierarchy of plans	48
5.2	The planning steps	53
8.1	The five steps in the management of risk	90
8.2	Summary risk profile	92
8.3	Risk action selection	93
8.4	Mapping risk management	99
10.1	Starting up a Project	122
11.1	Initiating a Project	139
12.1	Directing a Project	159
13.1	Controlling a Stage	171
14.1	Managing Product Delivery	189
15.1	Managing a Stage Boundary	197
16.1	Closing a Project	211
C.1	PRINCE2 product symbols	272
C.2	Product Flow Diagram	272
C.3	Product-based Planning steps	273
C.4	Product Breakdown Structure	274
C.5	A hierarchical top-down structure	275

C.6	An ellipse to indicate a product made by another project	276
C.7	A box indicating a temporary Product Description	276
C.8	Product Breakdown Structure mind map	277
C.9	Product Flow Diagram	278
C.10	Example of a Product Breakdown Structure	280
C.11	Example of a Product Flow Diagram	281
D.1	Quality review	286
D.2	Quality review preparation	287
D.3	Quality review follow-up	288
Cartoon 1	Responsibility	28
Cartoon 2	Project mandate	123
Cartoon 3	Quality Management Strategy	141

Preface

THE METHOD

This book presents the 2009 revision of PRINCE2, a structured project management method. Experience shows us why a good project management method such as PRINCE2 is needed if our projects are to be well managed and controlled.

The book is intended for those who wish to: (a) advance to the Practitioner level of PRINCE2; (b) dig deeper into the method to fully understand it and be able to tailor it to each new project's needs.

PRINCE® is a registered trademark of Axelos Limited.

PRINCE2® is a registered trademark of Axelos Limited.

Chapter 1

Introduction

PRINCE® is a registered trademark of Axelos Limited.

PRINCE2® is a registered trademark of Axelos Limited.

This book is a complete description of the PRINCE2 project management method. The method is owned by Axelos Limited, and has been put into the public domain, so there is no fee to be paid for its use. (If you want to make money from the method, for example, by offering training, products or consultancy, you need to be registered with Axelos Limited.)

This book is an in-depth explanation of PRINCE2 for those readers who want to proceed to the Practitioner level and beyond. It covers the whole method and provides insights into areas in the official manual that need further explanation.

Chapter 2

An Overview of PRINCE2

2.1 PROJECT PERFORMANCE ASPECTS

There are six aspects of project performance that always need to be managed:

- Costs: Estimating how much a project will cost is always a problem, followed by controlling efficiency and effectiveness to ensure that this cost is not exceeded.
- Time: How long will the project take? How effective will resources be? Have you made allowances for meetings, training, holidays, learning cycles?
- Quality: More important than getting cost and time right is getting the quality right. Do you know what quality the customer wants? Is that level of quality realistic in view of other constraints, such as time and cost? Have you allowed enough time and resources to achieve that quality?
- Scope: How precisely are the requirements known? Have you got an agreed cut-off point for finalizing requirements? Have you got a change control procedure in place to avoid 'scope creep'? Does the customer understand that, after you have agreed a price and time frame, any changes to the specification must be paid for? If the customer's detailed knowledge of the requirements is going to evolve slowly, is the cost and time needed to provide the changing requirements also allowed to 'evolve'?
- Risk: Have you reviewed the project for risks at the outset? Are you regularly reviewing risks? Do you have a risk management procedure in place? Do you know what level of risk the customer is willing to accept?

- Benefits: Are there valid reasons for doing the project? Does the outcome fit with company strategy? Are the claimed benefits realistic? Do you have measurements of the situation now, before the outcome is delivered, in order to measure the achievement of benefits?

PRINCE2 contains the processes and themes that will keep these aspects of project performance under control.

2.2 PRINCIPLES OF PRINCE2

There are seven principles on which PRINCE2 is founded, and these principles are unique to the PRINCE2 method (Figure 2.1).

Principles are characterized as:

- Universal: They apply to every project, any type, any size.
- Self-validating: They have been proved by use over many years.
- Empowering: They give users of the method the ability to shape the management of the project.

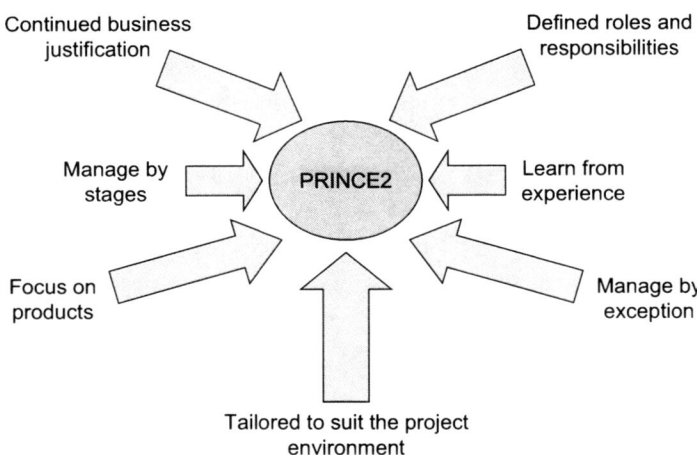

FIGURE 2.1 The seven PRINCE2 principles

An overview of PRINCE2

The seven PRINCE2 principles are:

- Continued business justification;
- Learn from experience;
- Defined roles and responsibilities;
- Manage by stages;
- Manage by exception;
- Focus on products;
- Tailor to suit the project environment.

2.2.1 Continued business justification

(A project should be driven by its Business Case)

PRINCE2 emphasizes that a project should be driven by a viable Business Case. The existence of the Business Case should be proved before the project is given the go-ahead, and should be confirmed at all major decision points during the project. It should also be documented. (If a product fails to deliver all the expected benefits, those who originally claimed the benefits would be there may suffer from amnesia!) Remember, the benefits and their value should be defined by the customer (Senior User) at the outset. It is also the Senior User's task to measure the achievement of the benefits after the end product has been in use for an agreed length of time.

So:

- You shouldn't start a project unless there is a sound Business Case for it.
- Make sure that the potential benefits are realistic and measurements of the current situation have been documented.
- At regular intervals in the project you should check that the project is still viable.
- Stop the project if the justification has disappeared.

The Business Case:

- Should be documented and approved;
- Drives the decision-making processes;

- Ensures that the project remains aligned to the business objectives and benefits being sought.

Even projects that are compulsory require justification – there may be several options available that yield different costs, benefits and risks.

Justification for a project may change, but it must remain valid.

2.2.2 Learn from experience

Project management should never be 'reinventing the wheel'. Those involved in the project may have previous experience; there will be earlier projects in the company from which lessons can be learned, and there are other sources of valuable lessons (e.g. the internet, suppliers, sister companies, and, of course, this book!) that can be used in the project.

Lessons should be sought at the beginning of a project (in the process *Starting up a Project* – see chapter 10), learned as the project progresses and passed on to other projects at the close. A Lessons Report should be issued at the end of a stage, without waiting until the end of the project, if a useful lesson is learned that could help other projects.

2.2.3 Defined roles and responsibilities

Project management is different to line management.

Projects require a temporary organization for a finite timescale for a specific business purpose. Managing the project staff can be a headache for a Project Manager. A project is temporary and may include staff who report to different line managers or even work for other organizations. The project may require a mixture of full-time and part-time resources. So how do we ensure that everyone knows who is responsible for what?

An explicit project management team structure is required. Good communication depends on people knowing not only what their own responsibilities are but also the responsibilities of others.

An overview of PRINCE2

The roles and responsibilities are divided into three groups, the interests of which must be represented in any project (Figure 2.2). These are:

- Business;
- User;
- Supplier.

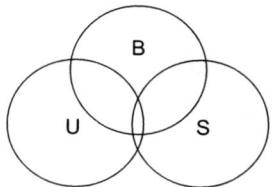

FIGURE 2.2 Business, user and supplier interests

PRINCE2 provides an organization structure that engages everyone involved: the business, user and supplier interests. Within the structure there are defined roles and responsibilities for every member of the project management team. The chosen people agree to a role description and sign their acceptance of that role. Roles can be split or combined, depending on the size of the project.

2.2.4 Manage by stages

This comes from two different thoughts:

1) If the Project Board is, in PRINCE2 terms, ultimately accountable for the project, and as PRINCE2 doesn't like the idea of regular progress meetings, there must be some key points in a project when the Project Board needs to review progress and decide if it wants to continue with the project – i.e. that the project is still viable;
2) Very often a project will last longer and contain more detail than can be planned for with any accuracy at the outset.

Based on these thoughts, PRINCE2 divides a project into stages. PRINCE2 has a Project Plan, an overview of the whole project, but the Project Manager only plans the next stage in detail – i.e. only as much of the project as can be accurately judged – and the Project Board only approves one stage at a time, reviewing the status at the stage end and deciding whether to continue or not. One check that the Project Board can make when assessing its confidence level in the next Stage Plan (see section 5.2.2) is how close to reality the last Stage Plan was.

The number of stages depends on the size, complexity and risk content of the project.

At the end of each stage, a plan is presented, together with an updated view of the Business Case, the Project Plan, the risks and suggested tolerances for the next stage. Thus senior management can review progress so far and decide from the information presented to them whether or not to authorize the next stage.

2.2.5 Manage by exception

PRINCE2 recognizes four levels of authority in a project. Authority is delegated from one management level to the next. Each management level is allocated tolerances within which they can continue without the need to refer to the next higher level of management. This is what is meant by *management by exception*. There are six tolerance limits:

1) Time: ± an amount of time on the target completion dates.
2) Cost: ± amounts of planned budget.
3) Quality: ± degrees off a quality target; for example, a product that weighs a target 10 kg, with an allowed −50 g to +10 g tolerance.
4) Scope: permissible variation of the plan's products; for example, mandatory requirements ± desirable requirements.
5) Risk: limits on the plan's exposure to threats; for example, the risk of not meeting the target date against the risk of overspending.
6) Benefit: ± degrees off an improvement goal; for example, 30 per cent to 40 per cent staff saving.

An overview of PRINCE2

To cut down on unnecessary meetings or problem referrals, PRINCE2 has the principle of allowing each management level to continue its work as long as there is no forecast that the tolerance limits for that level will be exceeded. Only when there is a forecast of a tolerance being exceeded does the next higher level of authority need to be consulted.

2.2.6 Focus on products

A PRINCE2 project focuses on the definition and delivery of products, and in particular their quality requirements. Planning, controls and quality needs are all product based.

2.2.7 Tailor to suit the project environment

PRINCE2 is tailored to suit the project's environment, size, risk, complexity, importance and the capability of the people involved. Tailoring is considered before the project begins: roles may be split or combined; processes and documents may be combined; it may be agreed that some reports can be oral; and some decisions made by phone or email, rather than at meetings.

2.3 STRUCTURE OF THE PRINCE2 METHOD

There are three parts to the structure of the method itself:

- Themes;
- Processes;
- Techniques.

The method has a number of *themes* to explain its philosophy about various project aspects, why they are needed and how they can be used. This philosophy is implemented through the processes.

The method offers a set of *processes* that provide a controlled start, controlled progress and a controlled close to any project. The processes explain what should happen and when it should be done.

The method offers only a few *techniques* and the use of most of them is optional. You may already have a technique that is satisfactorily covering a need. The exception to this is the Product-based Planning technique. This technique is a very important part of PRINCE2. Its understanding and use bring major benefits and every effort should be made to use it.

2.4 THEMES

FIGURE 2.3 PRINCE2 themes

Figure 2.3 shows the PRINCE2 themes positioned around the central process model.

The themes of PRINCE2 are shown in Table 2.1.

TABLE 2.1

Business Case	PRINCE2 emphasizes that a viable Business Case should drive a project. Its existence should be proved before the project is given the go-ahead and it should be confirmed at all major decision points during the project. Claimed benefits should be defined in measurable terms, so that they can be checked after delivery of the product.
Organization	The project management team structure, with definitions of the roles, responsibilities and relationships of all staff involved in the project. PRINCE2 describes the roles, which can be combined or shared depending on the size and complexity of the project.
Plans	PRINCE2 offers a series of plan levels that can be tailored to the size and needs of a project, and an approach to planning based on products rather than activities.
Progress	A set of controls that facilitate the provision of key decision-making information, allowing the organization to pre-empt problems and make decisions for problem resolution. For senior management, PRINCE2 controls are based on the concept of management by exception; i.e. if a plan is agreed, let the manager get on with it unless something is forecast to go wrong. A project is split into stages as an approach to defining the review and commitment points of a project to promote sound management control of risk and investment.
Risk	Risk is a major factor to be considered during the life of a project. PRINCE2 defines the key moments when risks should be identified and reviewed, outlines an approach for the analysis and management of risk, and tracks these risks through all the processes.
Quality	PRINCE2 recognizes the importance of quality and incorporates a quality-based approach to all the management and technical processes. It begins by establishing the customer's quality expectations and follows these up by laying down standards and quality inspection methods to be used, and checking that these are being used.
Change	This contains two complementary activities: managing changes and managing the products. PRINCE2 emphasizes the need for change control and this is enforced with a change control technique plus identification of the themes that apply the change control. Tracking the components of a final product and their versions for release is called configuration management. There are many methods of configuration management available, and PRINCE2 does not attempt to invent a new one – it defines the essential facilities and information requirements for a configuration management method and how it should link with other PRINCE2 themes and techniques.

2.5 THE PROCESSES

The steps of project management are described in seven processes, which are summarized in Figure 2.4. The processes describe the chronological flow of project management through a project.

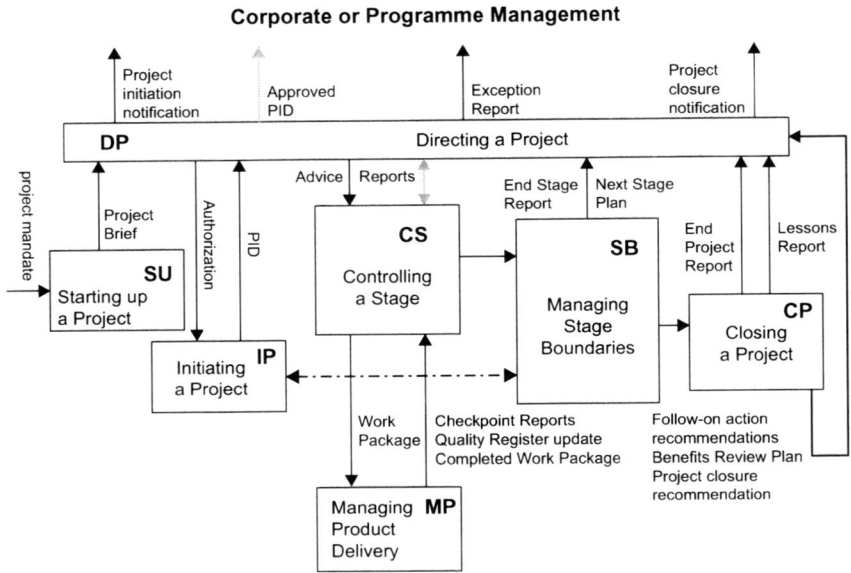

FIGURE 2.4 PRINCE2 processes

Any project using the PRINCE2 method will need to address each of these processes in some form. However, the key to successful use of the process model is to tailor it to the needs of the individual project. Each process should be approached with the question "How extensively should this process be applied on this project?"

A typical flow through the processes in a project is shown in Figure 2.5.

The *Directing a Project* process has been split into its five parts to show the points at which they are used.

An overview of PRINCE2

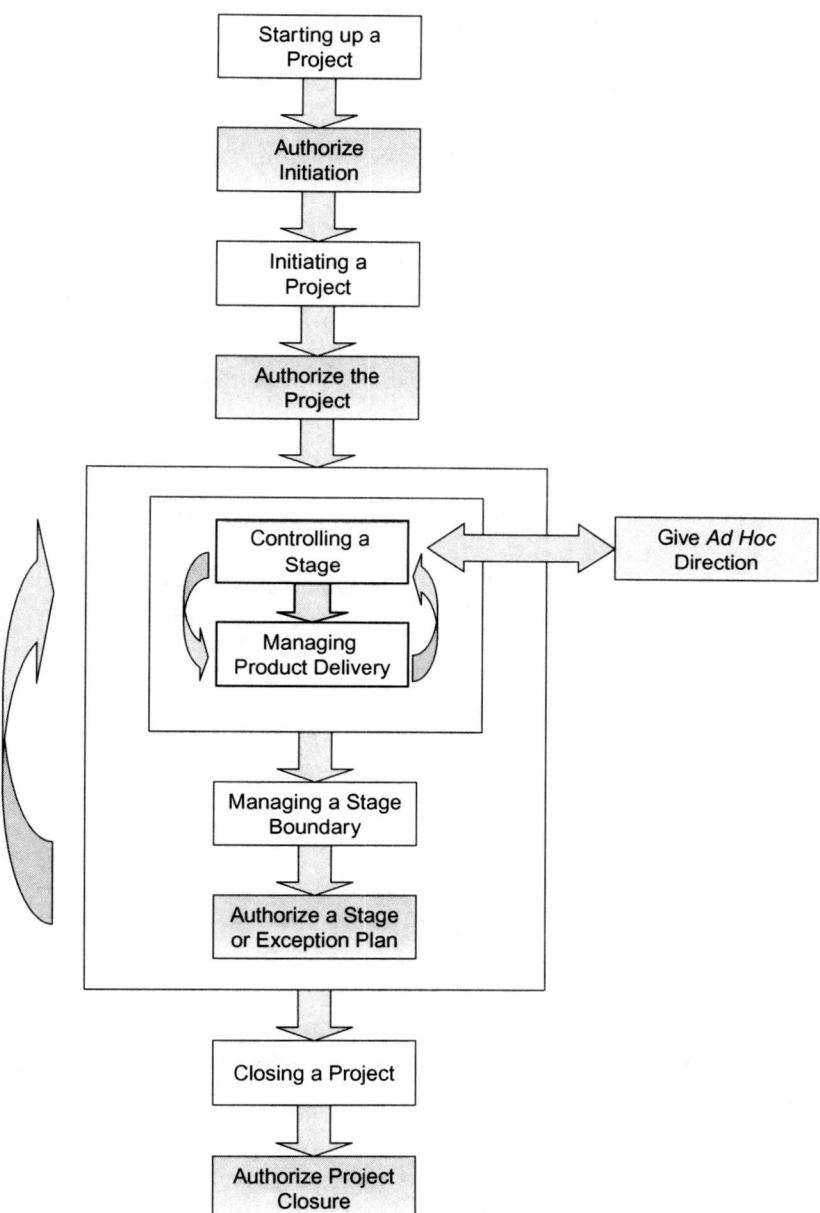

FIGURE 2.5 A typical flow through the PRINCE2 processes

2.5.1 Directing a Project (DP)

This process is aimed at the senior management team, the key decision makers, responsible for the project. They are usually very busy people and should be involved only in the decision-making process of a project. PRINCE2 helps them achieve this by adopting the principle of *management by exception*. The *Directing a Project* process covers the activities of this senior management team (the Project Board) throughout the project, from project start-up to project closure, and has five major steps:

- Authorizing the preparation of a Project Plan and Business Case for the project;
- Approving the project go-ahead;
- Checking that the project remains viable at key points in the project life cycle;
- Monitoring progress and giving *ad hoc* advice as required;
- Ensuring that the project comes to a controlled close.

2.5.2 Starting up a Project (SU)

This is intended to be a very short pre-project process with five objectives:

- Ensuring that the aims of the project are known;
- Designing and appointing the project management team;
- Deciding on the approach to do the work that will be taken within the project;
- Agreeing the customer's quality expectations;
- Planning the work needed to draw up the PRINCE2 'contract' between customer and supplier.

2.5.3 Initiating a Project (IP)

This process prepares the information to determine whether there is sufficient justification to proceed with the project, establishes a sound management basis for the project and creates a detailed plan for as much of the project as management are in a position to authorize.

The management product created is the Project Initiation Documentation – the baseline against which both project progress and success will be measured.

2.5.4 Controlling a Stage (CS)

This process describes the monitoring and control activities of the Project Manager involved in ensuring that a stage stays on course and reacts to unexpected events. The process forms the core of the Project Manager's effort on the project and is the process that handles day-to-day management of the project development activity.

Throughout a stage there will be many cycles of:

- Authorizing work to be done;
- Gathering progress information about that work;
- Monitoring and controlling changes;
- Reviewing the situation;
- Reporting;
- Taking any necessary corrective action.

The process covers these activities, together with the ongoing work of risk management and change control.

2.5.5 Managing Product Delivery (MP)

This process acts as a control mechanism so the Project Manager and specialist teams can agree details of the work required. This is particularly important where one or more teams are from third-party suppliers and are not using the PRINCE2 method. The work agreed between the Project Manager and the Team Manager, including target dates, quality and reporting requirements, is called a Work Package.

The process is the responsibility of the Team Manager and covers:

- Planning the team's Work Package;
- Ensuring that the Work Package allocated to the team is authorized and agreed;
- Ensuring that the work is done;

- Ensuring that products meet the agreed quality criteria;
- Obtaining acceptance of the finished products;
- Reporting on progress and quality to the Project Manager.

2.5.6 Managing Stage Boundaries (SB)

The objectives of this process are to:

- Plan the next stage;
- Update the Project Plan;
- Update the Business Case;
- Update the risk assessment;
- Report on the outcome and performance of the stage that has just ended;
- Obtain Project Board approval to start work on the next stage.

If the Project Board requests the Project Manager to produce an Exception Plan (see section 5.2.4 for an explanation), this process also covers the steps needed for that.

2.5.7 Closing a Project (CP)

The process covers the Project Manager's work to request Project Board permission to close the project either at its natural end or at a premature close decided by the Project Board. The objectives of this process are to:

- Note the extent to which the objectives set out at the start of the project have been met;
- Confirm the customer's satisfaction with the delivered products;
- Confirm that maintenance and support arrangements are in place (where appropriate);
- Make any recommendations for follow-on actions;
- Ensure that all lessons gathered during the project are annotated for the benefit of future projects;
- Report on whether the project management activity itself has been a success or not;
- Prepare a plan to check on achievement of the final product's claimed benefits.

Chapter 3

Business Case

3.1 PHILOSOPHY

Every project should be driven by a business need. If the project has no justification in terms of the business, it should not be undertaken. If the justification disappears, the project should be stopped. If there is a change to the justification, the Business Case should be revised and a judgement made on the continued viability of the project.

The Business Case is a vital project management tool. It should be considered before any project is commissioned, ideally at a higher level such as the strategy group, and certainly as part of any feasibility study.

In a customer/supplier environment it is likely that both parties will have their own Business Case: the customer looking for benefits to be obtained from the result of the project; the supplier looking to make a profit from the development work. PRINCE2 concentrates on the customer's Business Case.

3.2 HOW?

An outline Business Case should be included in the project mandate and, as a minimum, should include reasons why the project should be undertaken. If it is not, then a Business Case should be added as part of developing the Project Brief. The full Business Case is created during the initiation process and forms part of the Project Initiation Documentation.

If a project is part of a larger programme, its justification will point to the Business Case of the programme. In such a case, the project may have no business justification itself, but contribute to achievement of the programme Business Case. In this case, the project Business Case will refer back to the continuing need for the project within the perceived needs for the programme.

3.3 WHO?

The official PRINCE2 manual can seem quite confusing on the responsibilities for the Business Case and who does what and when. Here is a set of bullet points that, hopefully, will clarify the various issues:

- In some cases there may be a predefined Business Case in the project mandate set out by corporate management, or programme management if the project is part of a programme.
- The Business Case is the responsibility of the Executive from the start of a project until it closes. If there isn't an outline of the Business Case in the project mandate, it is the Executive's job to get it.
- The Senior User role is responsible for specifying to the Executive what the benefits will be and providing measurements of today's situation against which benefit realization can be measured once the products are in use.
- Once the project finishes, responsibility for the Benefits Review Plan passes to corporate or programme management.
- The Senior User(s) will be asked by corporate or programme management to provide measurements of benefits realization according to the Benefits Review Plan.
- Different benefits may take different lengths of time to appear. Therefore, there may be more than one benefit review.

3.4 WHEN?

The Business Case should be formally reviewed at the start of a project, and again at stage boundaries and at project closure. It should also be reviewed when major change requests are made to determine if the requested changes would have an impact on it. It should be monitored continuously throughout the project.

3.5 CONTENT

3.5.1 Reasons

This is a narrative description of the justification for undertaking the project.

3.5.2 Business options

What were the business options considered to solve the problem? What is the selected option and the reasons for its selection?

PRINCE2 suggests that business options should be considered under three headings:

- The 'do nothing' option: The first option always to be considered is to do nothing and to simply carry on as before; i.e. consider the costs that will be avoided, the benefits that will be lost, and whether the company will be able to cope if it does not 'do something'.

It is important to remember that the 'do nothing' option should be calculated by assessing the implications of staying with the current mode of operation for the anticipated life of the new product, service or system.

- The 'do something' option: This option estimates the implications of implementing a variety of solutions that need to be made in a similar way and over a similar time period to the 'do nothing' option above.
- The 'do the minimum' option: This option considers the bare minimum that could be done to solve the business problem.

Choosing between the three options is a matter of weighing the benefits and savings against the costs.

It should be made clear at this point that business options are not the same as the project approach; e.g. the business problem might have been a fall in profits in a subsidiary company. In this example, the options might have been:

- do nothing;
- close down the subsidiary;
- trim the workforce;
- improve the marketing of the subsidiary's products.

In this example, if the last option were selected, the project approach would be how to deliver the improved marketing.

3.5.3 Expected benefits

This is a description of what the expected benefits are, plus the estimated benefit figures over the life of the product. Benefits should be defined in terms that are measurable:

- at the start of the project; and
- when the final product is in use.

3.5.4 Negative consequences

Are there any disadvantages of the proposed business solution? (The PRINCE2 manual uses a non-English word 'dis-benefits' for this.)

3.5.5 Costs

They are the estimated development and running costs for the product.

3.5.6 Timescale

This is the estimated duration of the project and the timescale required before the benefits can be realized.

Business Case

3.5.7 Major risks

This is a summary of any major risks, their likely impact and the contingency plans (including their cost) to respond to the risks should they occur.

3.5.8 Investment appraisal

This considers what would happen if the project was not done – none of the costs would be incurred and the benefits would not be accrued. This is the 'do nothing' option and is used as the benchmark against which the predicted costs and benefits of the chosen option are measured.

3.5.9 If part of a programme

If the project is part of a programme, the programme will often provide the Business Case and the project simply contributes to it.

3.5.10 Specialist help

In large or very important projects the participation of a specialized business analyst may be needed to prepare the investment appraisal. This help may come from a central Project Support office or an external centre of expertise.

3.6 BENEFITS REVIEW PLAN

The concept of justifying a project through a Business Case is meaningless unless at some time there is a measurement of whether the claimed benefits have been achieved. The approach to confirming benefit achievement is to:

- Identify the benefits;
- Identify objective measures of benefit achievement;
- Assemble measurements of the current situation against which the improvements will be compared;
- Decide how, when and by whom benefits will be measured.

The Senior User(s) specifies the benefits and must later demonstrate to corporate or programme management that the forecast benefits that formed the basis of project approval have been realized. This may involve a commitment beyond the life of the project as it is likely that many benefits will not be realized until after the project has closed. This is a problem, because after the project closes, the 'temporary organization' is disbanded. So who will carry out any measurement activities, and does the project need to set aside money to pay for the measurement exercise?

PRINCE2 overcomes this dilemma by creating a Benefits Review Plan. This takes the claimed benefits in the Business Case and defines the timing, measuring methods and responsibilities of one or more benefit reviews. (Remember, some benefits may be achieved within the life cycle of the project.) The realization of benefits may be measured at different times; e.g. some after a month, others after three months and a final set after six months.

The Benefits Review Plan is first created by the Project Manager in the initiation stage and is submitted to the Project Board for approval as part of seeking project authorization. The Benefits Review Plan is updated towards the end of each stage with any benefits achieved and the plan is revised for any remaining reviews whether within or beyond the life of the project.

The Executive is normally responsible for ensuring that benefits reviews are planned, but for projects in a programme environment, the project's Benefits Review Plan will be produced and executed by the programme. For projects that are not part of a programme the responsibility for benefits reviews will transfer from the Executive to corporate or programme management as the project closes (as the reviews will need to be funded and resourced).

As the Benefits Review Plan may be managed by corporate or programme management, PRINCE2 recommends that it is kept separate from the Project and Stage Plans.

The post-project benefits review(s) will require corporate or programme management to ask the Senior User(s) to provide evidence of the benefits gained in comparison to those benefits promised when justifying the cost and risk of the project when it was authorized. The post-project benefits review(s) will also review the performance of the project's products in operational use and identify if there have been any side effects (beneficial or adverse) that may provide useful lessons for other projects.

3.7 LINKS

A basic Business Case should appear in the project mandate, or be developed as part of preparing the Project Brief.

There is a major link with the initiation stage, in which the Project Manager should finalize the Business Case before the Project Board decides whether the project should be undertaken.

The Business Case should be revised at the end of each stage as part of *Managing a Stage Boundary* (see chapter 15) and also in the event of raising an Exception Plan. This feeds into the end stage assessment, which is the review by the Project Board in *Authorize a Stage or Exception Plan* (see section 12.3), as part of its decision on whether to continue with the project.

The impact on the Business Case is assessed for each major issue as part of the activity *Capture and examine issues and risks* (see section 13.4).

Achievement of the Business Case is finally judged when implementing the Benefits Review Plan after project closure.

The implications of risk management should be linked to the Business Case; i.e. which benefits are at risk; the costs of what risk countermeasures may affect the benefits; which risks, if they occur, may affect the timescale of realizing the benefits.

3.8 IF IT'S A LARGE PROJECT

The Business Case is likely to take some time to prepare. There should have been at least the outline of a Business Case in the project mandate that triggered the project. Creating the full Business Case is likely to take some time in a large project, so don't be rushed through initiation by customers who are yelling "Just get on with it!" They are the ones who will be asking "Is it worth it?" halfway through the project or at the end.

3.9 IF IT'S A SMALL PROJECT

Don't ignore the philosophy that there should be business justification for every project. A lot of small projects undertaken without business justification can waste as much time as one large project. Carrying out a short, informal Business Case appraisal may be satisfactory, but the Executive should still be convinced that a genuine Business Case exists.

Chapter 4

Organization

4.1 PHILOSOPHY

The *Organization* theme supports the principle of defined roles and responsibilities.

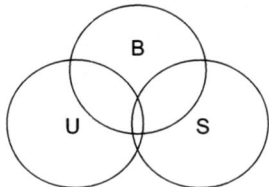

FIGURE 4.1 Business, user and supplier interests

PRINCE2 recognizes that three interests must always be represented in the decision-making body of a project. The acronym for this is B/U/S (Figure 4.1):

- The business;
- The user;
- The supplier.

The business interest covers the funding of the project, ensuring a match with company strategies and the benefits of the project from the outcome. The user interest represents those who will use or be affected by the final product(s). The supplier interest covers the resources that will build the products.

The organization for a PRINCE2 project is also based on a customer/supplier relationship. The customer is the person or group who wants the end product, specifies what it should be and, usually, pays for the development of that product. The supplier is whoever provides the resources to build or procure the end product.

This is true even if the customer and supplier work for the same company. If this is the case they may still, for example, report to different lines of management, have different budgets and therefore have different views of the finances of the project. The customer will be asking "Will the end product save me money or bring in a profit?", whereas the supplier will be asking if the provision of appropriate resources will earn a profit.

Establishing an effective organizational structure for the project is crucial to its success. Every project needs direction, management, control and communication. Before you start any project you should establish what the project organization is to be. *You need to ask the questions even if it is a very small project.* Answers to these questions will separate the real decision makers from those who have opinions, will identify responsibilities and accountability and will establish a structure for communication. Examples of the questions to ask are:

- What is the Project Manager's authority and who sets those limits?
- Who is providing the funds?
- Who has the authority to say what is needed?
- Who is providing the development resources?
- Who will manage the project on a day-to-day basis?
- How many different sets of specialist skills are needed?
- Who will establish and maintain the required standards?
- Who will safeguard the developed products?
- Who will know where all the documents are?
- What are the limits to each individual's authority?

4.2 FOUR LAYERS OF MANAGEMENT

When designing what the project organization should be, the PRINCE2 philosophy is to consider the four layers of management (Figure 4.2). The project management team structure allows for the

Organization

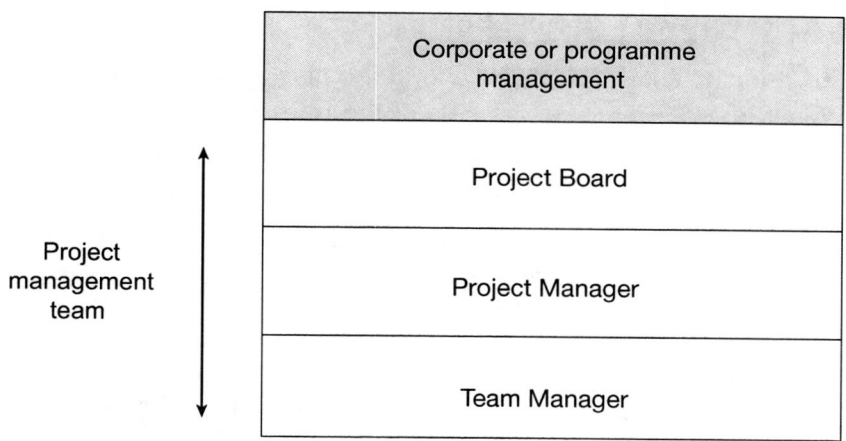

FIGURE 4.2 Four layers of management

possible inclusion of the four layers of management; however, whether they are all needed depends on the specific project, but that should be a decision you take when you understand the PRINCE2 philosophy and can compare it to the needs of a specific project.

4.2.1 Layer one – Corporate or programme management

A project may be part of a larger programme or it may be a major investment for a corporation, a key part of that company's strategy. What I am saying is that a project may be of concern to the very top level of management in the corporation. This would be the top layer in Figure 4.2. This layer is concerned with the business strategy. This layer provides a vision of what the company should look like and what it should be doing in the future. It has to co-ordinate all the ongoing projects to change the company to fit the vision that they have for it. There will come a point when the people in this layer say "Hang on, we haven't enough time to handle all the detail, we need to delegate." So for each project they appoint a Project Board to act on their behalf within certain constraints. I will address these constraints in the *Progress* theme.

4.2.2 Layer two – Project Board

This thinking takes us to layer two in the diagram; a layer called the Project Board. This layer consists of the roles needed to take those decisions that are too big for the Project Manager's authority level.

CARTOON 1 Responsibility

Examples of questions the Project Board would ask are:

- Does the Project Manager fully understand what they are looking for?
- Does the project look like a good way of spending its money?
- Is the proposed solution in line with company strategy?
- Is the project within tolerance of its planned time frame and/or budget? Should it continue or should the project be closed?
- Does the Project Board want to pay for this major change request?
- Is the Project Board prepared to accept the product being offered by the Project Manager?
- Does the product meet the Project Board's requirements?

4.2.3 Layer three – Project Manager

Layer three is the Project Manager role; i.e. the day-to-day planning, monitoring and control of the project. The work of this role is

Organization

reasonably easy to understand, but very often the Project Manager is not the person providing the funds. The bigger the project, the more likely it is that the Project Manager will have to go to a higher level of management for decisions and commitments on costs, the specification of what is needed, the resources required to do the job and acceptance of products developed by the project.

4.2.4 Layer four – Team Managers

Simple examples of projects that might need Team Managers are where the skill sets needed are so varied and/or the numbers of resources are so large that no one person has the ability or time to manage the whole thing. Geography may also be a factor in deciding whether you need Team Managers. If the developers are in groups some distance away from each other, it is very difficult to manage them all personally. Another situation is where the solution is to be provided by a third party. The external supplier will then want to manage its own resources.

4.3 OVERVIEW

To fulfil the philosophy, PRINCE2 has a project management team structure (Figure 4.3).

It is good to have a generic project management structure that can be tailored to any project. Without knowing anything about a project's size or complexity we can understand the same organizational terms and, by fitting names to these, understand quickly who does what. But with one structure for all sizes of project, it is important that it is flexible; a structure that can be suitable for large as well as small projects. The only way in which we can do this is to talk about *roles* that need to be filled, rather than jobs that need to be allocated on a one-to-one basis to individuals. In order to be flexible and meet the needs of different environments and different project sizes, the PRINCE2 structure defines roles that might be allocated to one person, shared with others or combined according to a project's needs. Examples are given later in the chapter.

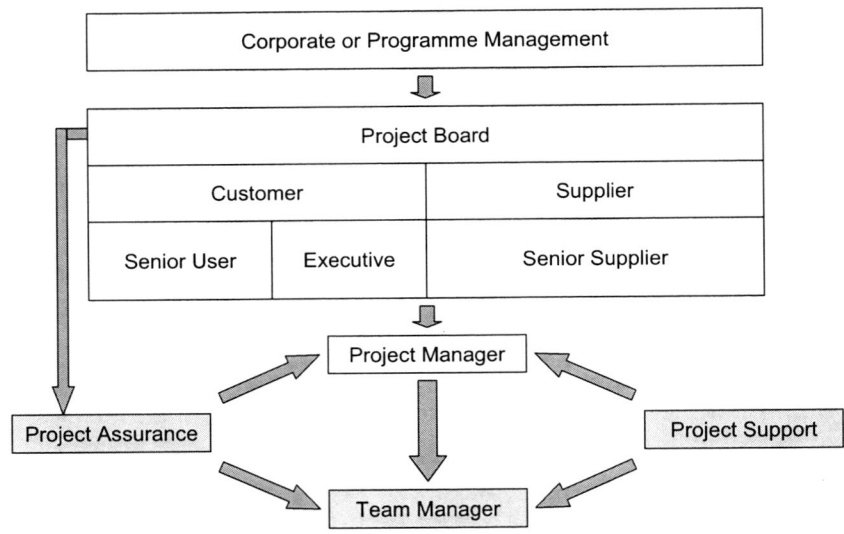

FIGURE 4.3 Project management team structure

Corporate or programme management hand the decision-making for a project to the Project Board. However, because the Project Board members are busy in their own right and haven't the time to look after the project on a day-to-day basis, they delegate this to the Project Manager, reserving the key stop/go decisions for themselves. If they are too busy or do not have the current expertise, they can appoint someone to a Project Assurance role to monitor an aspect of the project on their behalf. A typical example here would be the participation of a company's quality assurance function on behalf of the Senior User(s) or the Senior Supplier. (Note: they would take a Project Assurance role as far as PRINCE2 is concerned, not quality assurance.) Another example of the Project Assurance role would be a role for internal audit.

Depending on the project environment or the Project Manager's expertise, he or she might need some support. This might be purely administration tasks, such as filing, travel planning or note taking, but it also includes specialist jobs such as configuration management or expertise in the planning and control software tool that is to be used on the project.

4.4 PROJECT BOARD

4.4.1 General

The Project Board is appointed by corporate or programme management to provide overall direction and management of the project. The Project Board is accountable for the success of the project and has responsibility and authority for the project within the limits set by corporate or programme management.

It follows that members of the Project Board have to be managers with adequate authority for the resources that have to be committed.

The Project Board is the project's 'voice' to the outside world and is responsible for any publicity or other dissemination of information about the project.

4.4.1 Specific responsibilities

The Project Board approves all major plans and authorizes any major deviation from agreed Stage Plans. It is the authority that signs off the completion of each stage as well as authorizes the start of the next stage. It ensures that required resources are committed and arbitrates on any conflicts within the project or negotiates a solution to any problems between the project and external bodies. In addition, it approves the appointment and responsibilities of the Project Manager and any delegation of its Project Assurance responsibilities.

The Project Board is ultimately responsible for Project Assurance, and ensuring that the project remains on course to deliver the desired outcome of the required quality to meet the Business Case defined in the project contract. According to the size, complexity and risk of the project, the Project Board may decide to delegate some of this Project Assurance responsibility. (Project Assurance is defined in more detail in section 4.10.)

Responsibilities of specific members of the Project Board are described in the following sections.

4.5 EXECUTIVE

4.5.1 General

The Executive is ultimately responsible for the project, supported by the Senior User(s) and Senior Supplier. The Executive has to ensure that the project is value for money, maintain a cost-conscious approach to the project and balance the demands of business, user, and supplier.

Throughout the project the Executive 'owns' the Business Case.

The Executive is responsible for overall business assurance of the project; i.e. that it reflects company strategy, remains on target to deliver products that will achieve the expected business benefits and will complete within its agreed tolerances for budget and schedule.

The Executive's business assurance functions are to:

- Validate and monitor the Business Case against external events and against project progress;
- Keep the project in line with customer strategies;
- Monitor project finance on behalf of the customer;
- Monitor the business risks to ensure that these are kept under control;
- Monitor any supplier and contractor payments;
- Monitor changes to the Project Plan to see if there is any impact on the needs of the business or the project Business Case;
- Assess the impact of potential changes on the Business Case and Project Plan;
- Constrain user and supplier excesses;
- Inform the project of any changes caused by a programme of which the project is part (this responsibility may be transferred if there is other programme representation on the project management team);
- Monitor stage and project progress against the agreed tolerances.

If the project warrants it, the Executive may delegate some responsibility for the above business assurance functions to a Project Assurance role.

4.6 SENIOR USER(S)

The Senior User(s) is responsible for the specification of the needs of all those who will use the final product(s), user liaison with the project team and for monitoring that the solution will meet those needs within the constraints of the Business Case.

The role represents the interests of all those who will use the final product of the project, those for whom the product will achieve an objective or those who will use the product to deliver benefits. The Senior User(s) role commits any required user resources and monitors products against requirements. This role may require more than one person to cover all the user interests. For the sake of effectiveness the role should not be split between too many people.

If it becomes obvious that a large number of user managers should have a representation in the Senior User(s) role, they can be formed into a User Group and appoint one of the group to represent them on the Project Board as the Senior User.

4.7 SENIOR SUPPLIER

The role represents the interests of those designing, developing, facilitating, procuring and implementing the project products. The Senior Supplier is responsible for the quality of all products supplied by the suppliers. The role must have the authority to commit or acquire supplier resources required.

In more complex projects more than one person may be required to represent the suppliers. As with the Senior User(s) role, you do not want too many suppliers on the Project Board, as this may outnumber and overwhelm the Executive and Senior User(s) roles. An alternative is to appoint the company's purchasing manager as Senior Supplier. This person would then be the link to all suppliers via contracts – but their communication needs should not be forgotten.

4.8 PROJECT MANAGER

The Project Manager has the authority to run the project on a day-to-day basis on behalf of the Project Board within the constraints laid down by the Board. In a customer/supplier environment the Project Manager will normally come from the customer organization.

The Project Manager's prime responsibility is to ensure that the project produces the required products, to the required standard of quality and within the specified constraints of time and cost. The Project Manager is also responsible for the project producing a result that is capable of achieving the benefits defined in the Business Case.

4.9 TEAM MANAGER

This role leads a team to implement a Work Package. The allocation of this role to one or more people is optional. Where the project does not warrant the use of a Team Manager, the Project Manager takes the role.

The Project Manager may find that it is beneficial to delegate the authority and responsibility for planning the creation of certain products and managing a team of technicians to produce those products. There are many reasons why it may be decided to employ this role:

- Size of the project;
- Particular specialist skills or knowledge needed for certain products;
- Geographical location of some team members;
- Preferences of the Project Board.

The Team Manager's prime responsibility is to ensure production of those products defined by the Project Manager to an appropriate quality as defined in the products' Product Descriptions, in a timescale and at a cost acceptable to the Project Board. The Team Manager reports to and takes direction from the Project Manager.

The use of this role should be discussed by the Project Manager with the Project Board and, if the role is required, planned at the outset of the project. This is discussed later in the *Starting up a Project* (see chapter 10) and *Initiating a Project* (see chapter 11) processes.

Often maintenance work includes making small improvements or correcting faults in an operational product. Such work is normally covered by an annual budget and therefore doesn't need a Business Case for each piece of work. It doesn't need a Project Board – maybe there is a panel supervising how the budget is spent – and probably has only one stage. In PRINCE2 terms this type of work can often be done as a Work Package. If it needs a small team to handle the work, it can be managed by a Team Manager.

4.10 PROJECT ASSURANCE

4.10.1 General

The Project Board members do not work full time on the project; therefore, they place a great deal of reliance on the Project Manager. Although they receive regular reports from the Project Manager, there may always be questions at the back of their minds, such as:

- Are things really going as well as we are being told?
- Are any problems being hidden from us?
- Is the solution going to be what we want?
- Are we suddenly going to find that the project is over budget or late?

All of these questions mean that there is a need for the project management team to monitor all aspects of the project's performance and products independent of the Project Manager. These are the Project Assurance functions.

These Project Assurance functions are part of the role of each Project Board member. According to the needs and desires of the Project Board, any of these Project Assurance responsibilities can be delegated, as long as the recipients are independent of the Project Manager and the rest of the project management team. Any appointed Project Assurance roles assure the project on behalf of one or more members of the Project Board.

(Note that Project Assurance roles are often only delegated. The Project Board member retains accountability. Any delegation should be documented.)

It is not mandatory that all Project Assurance roles be delegated. Each Project Board member decides if and when their Project Assurance role needs to be delegated. Each of the Project Assurance roles delegated may be assigned to one individual or shared by a team. It may be for the entire project or only part of it. The person(s) filling a Project Assurance role may be changed during the project at the request of the Project Board member. This is usually done according to the skills needed by the Project Assurance role at that time in the project.

Any use of Project Assurance roles should be planned in the initiation stage. There is no stipulation on how many Project Assurance roles there must be. Project Assurance has to be independent of the Project Manager; therefore, the Project Board cannot delegate any of its Project Assurance responsibilities to the Project Manager.

If a company has an active quality assurance function, it may insist on representation in every project. In PRINCE2 terms the quality assurance department would take all or part of a Project Assurance role. This could, for example, include verification that the Project Board is performing its functions correctly.

4.10.2 Specific

- Maintenance of thorough liaison throughout the project between the supplier and the customer.
- Ensuring user needs and expectations are being met or managed.
- Ensuring risks are being controlled.
- Adherence to the Business Case.
- Constant reassessment of the value-for-money solution.
- Ensuring a fit with the overall programme or company strategy.
- Involving the appropriate people in writing Product Descriptions.
- Planning for the right people to be involved in quality checking at the correct points in the product's development.
- Ensuring that staff are properly trained in the quality checking procedures.
- Ensuring that the quality review/quality checking procedures are being correctly followed.

Organization

- Correctly dealing with quality checking follow-on actions.
- Ensuring that an acceptable solution is being developed.
- Ensuring that the project remains viable.
- Ensuring that the scope of the project is not 'creeping upwards' unnoticed.
- Maintaining focus on the business need.
- Ensuring that internal and external communications are working.
- Ensuring that applicable standards are being used.
- Observing any legislative constraints.
- Observing the needs of business interests (e.g. security).
- Adhering to quality assurance standards.

4.11 PROJECT SUPPORT

The provision of any Project Support on a formal basis is optional. It is driven by the needs of the individual project and Project Manager. Project Support could take the form of advice to one or more related projects on project management tools and administrative services, such as filing or the collection of actual data. Where set up as an official body in a company, Project Support can act as a repository for lessons learned and a central source of expertise in specialist support tools.

One support function that must be considered is that of configuration management. Depending on the project size and environment, there may be a need to formalize this and it quickly becomes a task with which the Project Manager cannot cope without support. (See chapter 9 *Change* for details of the work.)

4.12 LINKS

4.12.1 Controls

There are many links between the roles in the project management team structure and the controls they exercise. The following are fully described in the *Controls* theme. This is just a summary.

Layer one – Corporate or programme management

Corporate or programme management control the Project Board. They exercise control in a number of ways:

- They are responsible for the original terms of reference for the Project Board (the project mandate) and therefore control the statement of what the project is to deliver, the scope and any constraints.
- They can define the overall targets of the project in terms of delivery dates and budget.
- They provide the Project Board with the limits of cash and time at a project level beyond which the Project Board must return to them for a decision on what to do.
- They appoint the Executive (very often a member of corporate or programme management) to head the Project Board.
- They have the power to appoint other members of the Project Board, if they wish to do so.
- They indicate what reports they want, and at what frequency, from the Project Board.

Layer two – The Project Board

- The Project Board has to approve that the project contract (Project Initiation Documentation), that was drawn up by the Project Manager, is in line with the terms of reference handed down to them.
- Within the project limits set by corporate or programme management, the Project Board sets limits of time and budget deviation for each stage of the project. The Project Manager cannot go beyond those limits without fresh authority from the Project Board.
- The Project Board commits the budget and resources needed for each stage. This means that Project Board members need to be at managerial status in order to make these commitments. Their managerial level and authority will depend on the size and importance of the project. Having a Project Board member who has to go back to a line manager for the authority to commit to a plan simply delays the decision-making process and passes it to

managers who may not have the same level of commitment to the project, interest in or knowledge of the project's objectives. (And if these line managers then want to pass the decision on to their line managers, heaven knows when a decision will be made.)
- The Project Board has to approve the products of one stage before the Project Manager can move into the next stage.
- The Project Board has to approve any change to the original specification. This is more fully discussed in the *Change* theme (chapter 9).
- A project cannot close without the Project Board confirming that it is prepared to accept the results.
- The Project Board stipulates what reports it wants from the Project Manager, their content and frequency.
- The Project Board can appoint people to an independent Project Assurance role to monitor various aspects on its behalf.

Layer three – The Project Manager

The Project Manager agrees all work with Team Managers (or if that role is not used, with the individual team members):

- The Project Manager can set tolerance limits for a team's work beyond which it cannot go without the Project Manager's approval. These limits are set within those handed down by the Project Board for the stage.
- The Project Manager receives a regular report on each team's progress – the Checkpoint Report.
- The Project Manager can monitor the quality of work being produced by reference to the Quality Register.
- The Project Manager is responsible for the Project and Stage Plans and monitors progress against these.

Layer four – The Team Manager

- The Team Manager plans the team's work and agrees it with the Project Manager.
- The Team Manager holds regular checkpoint meetings with the team.

4.12.2 Plans

- The Project Manager creates and maintains the Project and Stage Plans.
- If there is a need for a recovery plan, the Project Manager creates this.
- Team Managers create Team Plans where required.

4.12.3 Risk

- The Project Manager maintains a Risk Register.
- The Project Board and corporate or programme management are responsible for the identification of risks external to the project.
- The Project Manager is responsible for the identification of internal risks.
- An owner is appointed from the project management team to keep an eye on each risk.

4.12.4 Quality

- The Executive is responsible for the quality of the Business Case, at the outset and as the project progresses.
- The Senior User(s) role is responsible for defining the expected business benefits, the quality of the original specification, for any user acceptance testing and for confirming that the solution's design and development continue to meet the user needs.
- The Senior Supplier role is responsible for the quality of the developed products.
- A company's independent quality assurance function may be represented on a project as part of the Project Assurance function.

4.12.5 Change control

Having agreed at the end of initiation what the project will deliver, it is important that the Project Board has to agree to any changes to this. However, there are projects where there may be large volumes of changes. During initiation the Project Board should decide if it will have the time to consider all requests for changes and off-specifications. If not (or it doesn't have the expertise to judge them), the Project Board can decide to appoint a Change Authority.

Change Authority

The Change Authority will consist of one or more people to whom consideration of changes is delegated. The Change Authority is normally given a change budget to pay for any approved changes with two restrictions:

- A maximum amount to be spent on a single change before the issue is referred to the Project Board;
- A maximum amount to be spent in a single stage before referring to the Project Board.

The Project Board decides who should sit on the Change Authority. Common choices are the Project Manager, those with Project Assurance roles, a user committee or a combination of these.

The Configuration Management Strategy can be used to establish severity ratings for changes. Depending on the severity, the change could be directed to:

- Corporate or programme management;
- The Project Board;
- A Change Authority; or
- The Project Manager.

These change authorities should be written into the appropriate job descriptions. For projects within a programme, programme management will define the authority level of the Project Board to approve changes.

4.13 CHANGES TO THE PROJECT MANAGEMENT TEAM

Ideally people appointed to a role on the project management team should stay in that role throughout the project's life. In particular, the Executive and Project Manager should stay for the whole duration.

This is not always possible. For example, the armed forces usually rotate their personnel every three years. If the project happens to be one that will take longer than that, there are often serious problems such as:

- Losing the Executive who has been the driving force behind the project;
- Bringing on a new Senior User(s) who has different ideas or wants changes to put their personal mark on the project;
- Swopping the Project Manager for someone who doesn't identify with the project in the same way.

There may, however, be good reasons for changes. A project moving out of a design phase into development may need different or additional Senior Suppliers; the skill set needed for Project Assurance may change as the project moves through its technical work; someone may leave the company. The PRINCE2 project management team structure and well-defined job descriptions should help to smooth out any difficulties caused by personnel changes.

A Stage Boundary provides a useful opportunity for personnel changes. The end stage procedure checks for any changes, and the End Stage Report, current and next Stage Plans provide a useful batch of progress information for any newcomers.

4.14 DO'S AND DON'TS

- Don't just use the generic structure slavishly. Use common sense and tailor the structure, when necessary, to the project.
- Don't drop responsibilities, but do move them to another role if that makes more sense for the project in hand.
- Do make sure that all responsibilities are given to an appropriate role.

4.15 IF IT'S A LARGE PROJECT

The larger the project the more likely it is that the project organization structure will need a person to fill each role. In fact the role of Senior

User may have to be shared between two or three people to get a representative view of the user needs. It would be sensible to control the number of people filling this role. I have seen projects with fifteen people clamouring to have a share of this role. The phrase that always comes to mind at such times is "It will take us half an hour to get the coffee order." If you are faced with lots of 'volunteers' for the role, make sure they are decision makers, not opinion holders; and organize them into a user committee, which meets and appoints a spokesperson to represent them all. The user committee can instruct the spokesperson on what they are to ask for, then get feedback from the spokesperson after any Project Board meetings.

Similarly a large project might have lots of suppliers. I do not recommend large numbers of them to share the Senior Supplier role. Two or three might be workable as a maximum, but it shouldn't be allowed to get out of hand. If there are lots of external suppliers, organize the contracts so that there is a main supplier who is responsible for the minor suppliers. Another possibility here is to appoint the company's purchasing manager to the role and make that person accountable for obtaining the supplier resources. Let me emphasize that a key part of each role is accountability for quality. The Senior User role is accountable for the quality of the specification. The Senior Supplier role is accountable for the quality of the products supplied as part of the solution. Make sure that you have someone in the roles who picks up this accountability.

There will normally be only one person as Executive. Remember the Executive is the key decision maker. The other roles advise and support the Executive. The Executive is always the person in charge of the purse strings. There may occasionally be projects where the supplier puts up some of the development cash. In such circumstances the supplier would quite correctly take a share of the Executive role. The division and balance of the decision-making would need to be carefully thought out in such cases.

Large projects are more likely to need to appoint people to the Team Manager role. This may be because the project is using external contractors, has people working in different geographical areas or is using a mix of skills beyond the Project Manager's scope.

4.16 IF IT'S A SMALL PROJECT

Let's take an example. Your boss wants you to organize the department's Christmas lunch for, say, 100 members of staff at one of six restaurants in town. Common sense says you don't want a huge number of people in the project management structure. Your boss is paying, so he or she is the Executive. The boss is also defining, or at least approving the arrangements, and so will also take the Senior User role. In terms of supplier the major resource used is going to be you. Who can commit your time? Right, the boss again, so your Project Board consists of your boss. In terms of Project Assurance, no doubt your boss is capable of checking that personally, so no extra people needed there. You will probably do most, if not all of the work yourself, so no need for Team Managers. You might get someone to write to the restaurants or ask the members of staff what their choice of menu is, but that would be the extent of the 'team' that you would need. The remaining question is whether you need any support and in a small project such as this, the answer is likely to be "No". So although we began by considering the full project organization structure, we end up with a structure that looks like that in Figure 4.4.

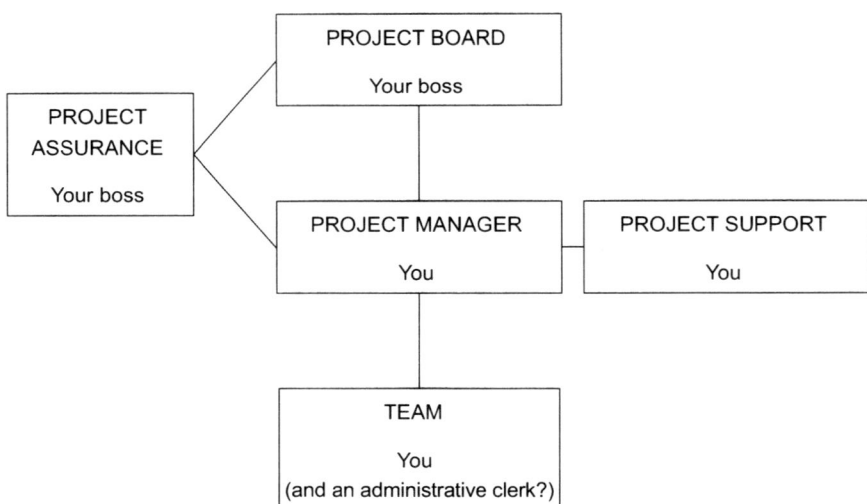

FIGURE 4.4 Small project team structure

All responsibilities are covered without unnecessary numbers or people being involved in their management.

There are two important things to remember:

- Use your common sense. Remember that roles can be combined and ask yourself the question "OK, who can make that commitment on behalf of the project?"
- However small the project may be, you can't drop any of the roles or their responsibility and accountability. All you can do is move these to another role.

Chapter 5

Plans

5.1 OVERVIEW

It is impossible to control a project without a plan, because without a plan you don't know whether you are ahead of the game, on target or way behind schedule. A plan gives you:

- Targets;
- A view on whether the targets are achievable;
- A view on the products needed to meet the targets;
- The work needed to create the products;
- The time needed to create each product;
- The resources and skills needed to do the work;
- Any equipment required by the resources;
- The sequence in which the products are required;
- A basis for work allocation;
- The ability to see product development matched with the resources across a time frame;
- A view of any risks inherent in the resources used and timing of the plan;
- A communication device for all those involved in the plan.

A plan is, however, only a statement of intent. Because something is in the plan does not necessarily mean that it is cast in concrete. There will always be uncertainties.

This chapter looks at the question of planning for a project.

5.2 HIERARCHY OF PLANS

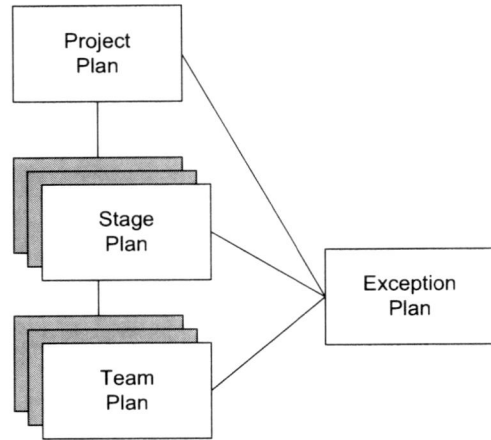

FIGURE 5.1 The PRINCE2 hierarchy of plans

Different levels of management within the project require different levels of detailed plans to discharge their responsibility. For instance, the Project Board and Project Manager need to assess the continuing viability of the project and therefore require a plan of the total project in overview.

The Project Manager needs to apply control to the project on a day-to-day basis and therefore requires a detailed plan – a Stage Plan – with activities broken down to a small number of days covering the next period of, say, a few weeks. This is OK as long as there is a longer-term view available in less detail – i.e. the Project Plan.

Similarly, if our project uses several teams, the Team Manager will need a detailed plan for the work of the team members. Again it would be sensible to limit this to a short period of time.

Also, if the original plan goes wrong, we need to create a new plan and get it approved by the Project Board (Figure 5.1).

5.2.1 Project Plan

The Project Plan, a mandatory plan in PRINCE2, is created at the start of the project as part of the Project Initiation Documentation. The Project Board does not want to know about every detailed activity in the project. It requires a high-level view. This allows the Project Board to know:

- How long the project will take;
- How much it will cost;
- What the major deliverables or products will be;
- Roughly when these will be delivered;
- What people and other resources will have to be committed in order to meet the plan;
- How control will be exerted;
- How quality will be maintained;
- What risks are there in the approach taken.

The Project Board will control the project using the Project Plan as a yardstick of progress, and it provides the Business Case with the costs and timescale.

It is worth remembering the Business Case at this point. The Business Case details (among other things) the costs of development and operation of the completed product. The predicted development costs are taken from the Project Plan. Therefore, this plan is essential to the decision as to whether the proposed system is a viable proposition in business terms. Don't forget, if the Project Plan changes, the Business Case changes.

5.2.2 Stage Plan

Stage Plans are also mandatory. Unless a project is very small it will be easier to plan in detail one stage at a time. Another part of the philosophy that makes stage planning easier is that a stage is planned shortly before it is due to start, so you have the latest information on actual progress so far available to you.

Having specified the stages and major products in the Project Plan, each stage is then planned in a greater level of detail. This is done just before the end of the previous stage.

The procedure at stage planning time involves taking those major products in the Project Plan that are to be created during that stage, and breaking these down to further levels of detail until you have reached a level where you can estimate the time and resources required with reasonable accuracy.

Given that each stage is planned at the end of the preceding one, the planner should now have a clearer view of:

- What has to be produced;
- How well the people perform;
- How accurate previous estimating has been.

5.2.3 Plan narrative

The Project and Stage Plans should have a narrative section. Suggested headings for the narrative are as follows:

- Project (and stage) identification.
- The plan level; e.g. project or stage.
- Summary of the plan and its background.
- Plan description.
- Intended implementation approach.

How do you intend to implement the plan? Is there anything in the Gantt chart that might need explaining? Some examples might be:

- You are not starting work on product X as soon as you could because you are waiting for the release of staff from another project.
- The time given for construction work looks shorter than normal because we are taking current product Y and modifying it.
- The time required for testing work looks longer than normal because we will be testing the product in a hazardous environment.

Plans

- Any constraints or objectives that have affected the plan.
- Quality plan: The activities and resources you may have added to check quality.
- Plan assumptions: The plan may assume the use of certain specific resources. Without the availability of these resources, the Project Manager may wish to adjust the plan.

On what assumptions is the plan based? Examples of assumptions are the actual staff to be allocated, and getting help or products from other sources at given times. It is essential to list your assumptions. If the Project Board accepts the plan, the Board is accepting your assumptions as reasonable. If your plan goes wrong because an assumption turns out to be incorrect, the Project Board can't throw rocks at you because it agreed with the assumptions.

It also gives the Project Board the chance to say if it knows anything about the assumptions that would make them invalid. An example here would be where you create a plan based on the assumption that good old Fred will be your senior technician. If the Senior Supplier knows that he or she has already committed Fred to another project, you can be told and replan. If no one knew of your assumption and you went ahead with the plan, fell behind and came up with the lame excuse "I would have been all right if you had given me Fred", no one is going to be too impressed:

- Plan prerequisites: Prerequisites are similar to assumptions but they must be in place on day one of the plan (and stay in place!) in order for the plan to succeed; e.g. trained staff, equipment and workplace arrangements.
- External dependencies: If the success of the plan depends on elements or products that are beyond the Project Manager's control, such as deliveries by suppliers or other projects, these would be identified here.
- Risks: This might be a copy of the entire Risk Register, or the Project Board may ask to see only the high probability/high impact risks and the actions you have taken or plan to take.
- Tolerance: What tolerance levels are agreed for the plan?
- Reporting: The methods, recipients, frequency and formats for reporting during the life of the plan may have been laid down by

the Project Board as part of the Project Initiation Documentation, but may vary according to the duration of a stage. Whatever is the case, they should be stated as part of the plan's text.

5.2.4 Team Plan

Team Plans are optional. Their use or otherwise is dictated by the size, complexity and risks associated with the project.

Team Plans are made at the lowest level of detail and should specify activities down to the level of a few days, perhaps ten at most. Team Plans are needed when internal or external teams are to do portions of the work. Part of the Project Manager's job is to cross-relate these plans to the Project and Stage Plans. If the Team Plan is produced by an external supplier, the Project Manager may not be able to insist that the plan is produced to PRINCE2 standards.

Although the hierarchy of plans may suggest that Team Plans are created after the Stage Plan, in fact, they need to be done in parallel. The Project Manager cannot guess how long a team will take to deliver a Work Package when preparing a Stage Plan. Team Plans and the Stage Plan must be done together, as one affects the other. The Stage Plan says when a Team Plan can start; the Team Plan says when the Work Package will be delivered, ready for the Stage Plan to move to the next set of products.

5.2.5 Exception Plan

Finally, there is the Exception Plan. This is produced when a plan is predicted to exceed the tolerances agreed between the planner and the next higher level of authority. The Exception Plan takes over from the plan it is replacing and has the same format.

If a Stage Plan is forecast to deviate, the Project Board may ask the Project Manager for an Exception Plan to replace the remainder of the current Stage Plan. If the Project Plan threatens to fall outside its tolerances, corporate or programme management would decide whether to ask for an Exception Plan to replace the remainder of the Project Plan.

Plans

If a Team Plan is forecast to deviate beyond tolerances, the Project Manager may modify the Work Package as long as it is within stage tolerances. If this cannot be done within stage tolerances, then the stage is in exception and the Project Manager must follow the process described above.

5.3 THE PRINCE2 APPROACH TO PLANNING

The PRINCE2 approach to planning:

- Defines the levels of plan needed for the project;
- Decides what planning tools and estimation methods will be used;
- Identifies the products whose delivery has to be planned;
- Identifies the activities needed to deliver those products and the dependencies between them;
- Estimates the effort needed for each activity;
- Allocates the activities to resources and schedules the activities against a time frame;
- Analyses the risks inherent in the plan;
- Adds explanatory text to the final plan.

The PRINCE2 planning philosophy is that all plans should start by identifying the products that will be produced by or are required for that plan (Figure 5.2).

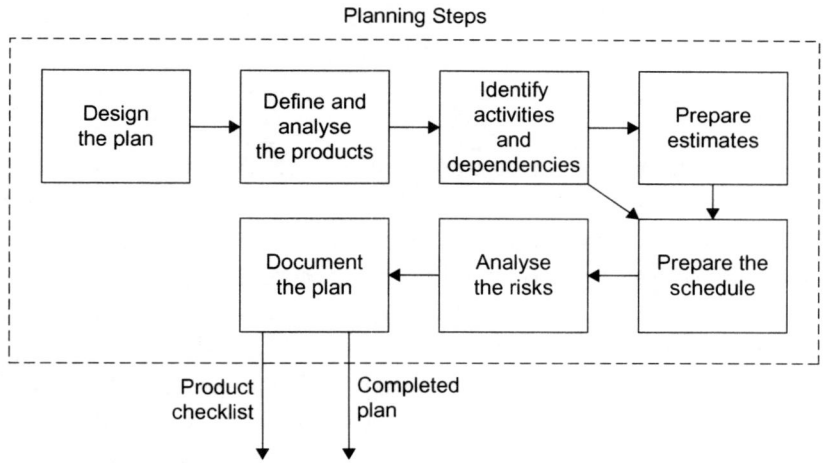

FIGURE 5.2 The planning steps

5.3.1 Design a plan

- Decide on how many levels of plan are needed by the project.
- Identify any planning tools to be used.
- Identify the method(s) of estimation to be used.

This activity is carried out only once per project, before the first plan is created. It defines the standards to be used in all future plans. The result should be a consistent set of plans.

How?

- Decide on what levels of plan are needed for the project; i.e. Project Plan, Stage Plans, Team Plans.
- Ascertain if the organization or programme uses a particular planning tool as standard.
- Identify what estimating methods are available and suitable for the project.
- Ensure that the estimating method chosen contains allowances for issue analysis, telephone calls, *ad hoc* meetings, different learning curves, experience, etc.
- Discuss with the Project Board the format in which plans should be presented.
- Discuss with the Project Board whether there should be a change budget set aside.
- Discuss with the Project Board whether there should be a separate allowance for any anticipated contingency plans.

In practice

Where the project is part of a programme, the programme will have made most of these decisions and it is just a question of finding out what the standards are. Beware of overcommitting a resource, especially yourself. No one is 100 per cent efficient. There will inevitably be interruptions, such as telephone calls, *ad hoc* meetings and non-project work which demand your time. These should be allowed for in your estimate of how much time people can commit to the work in your plan. Even the most efficient of experienced workers is unlikely to devote more than 70 per cent of their time to planned work. At least 50 per cent of a Project Manager's time should be spent in managing. The Project Manager of a large project should not contemplate doing any of the specialist work at all. As an exercise, make a note of where the time is spent in a typical day. Use the information to guide you in how to plan your time.

For small projects

A really small project may not need a planning tool, but a little thought should be given to the other steps before diving in and assuming you can hold it all in your head. The comments about how efficient people are still holds true for the smallest project.

5.3.2 Define and analyse products

PRINCE2 uses a Product-based Planning technique to define and analyse a plan's products. In general terms this technique:

- Identifies the products whose delivery has to be planned;
- Describes each of the products in terms of purpose, composition and quality criteria and ensures that these descriptions are agreed by all concerned;
- Identifies the sequence of delivering the products and the dependencies between them.

The Product-based Planning technique is fully explained, including an example, in Appendix C.

By defining the products and their quality requirements everyone can see and understand the required plan result. It means that whoever has to deliver a product knows in advance what its purpose is, to what quality it has to be built and what interfaces there are with other products.

In practice

The Product-based Planning technique is a key point in PRINCE2. If you are not doing this step, then you are not really using PRINCE2. It is an ideal method of involving users, specialists and Project Assurance roles in the creation of a plan without having the normal problems of 'design by committee'.

For small projects

It is very tempting in small projects to assume that use of Product-based Planning is not needed. Experience has shown me that it is very easy to forget a product, realize that you have done things in the wrong order or fail to consider a quality requirement when you dive in and 'just do it'. It doesn't take much time to do the Product-based Planning step and it will always pay dividends.

5.3.3 Identify activities and dependencies

This step:

- Identifies all activities necessary to deliver the products;
- Defines the dependencies between the activities, based on the dependencies shown in the Product Flow Diagram.

For Stage and Team Plans the Product Flow Diagram may still be at too high a level for the purposes of estimation and control. This optional activity allows a further breakdown based on the Product Flow Diagram until each activity defined should only last a handful of days.

How?

- Consider if a product in the Product Flow Diagram is too big to estimate the time needed to complete it, or would need such a large effort that it would be difficult to control against that estimate.
- Where a product is too big, break it down into the activities needed to produce it. This should continue down to the level where an activity is less than, perhaps, ten days' effort, ideally no more than five days.
- Where a product has been broken down into several activities, put the activities into their correct sequence.
- Review the dependencies between products and refine them to give dependencies between the new activities. For example, where Product Flow Diagram dependencies went from the end of one product to the start of the next, is there now an opportunity to overlap, or start some activities on a product before all the activities on its preceding product have been done?

Plans

In practice

You may decide not to do this step, but simply extend the previous step down to the level where you have all the detail you need for your plan. This was originally included because all planning tools used Work Breakdown Structures and assumed you would be working with activities and tasks. This process was inserted as a bridge from PRINCE2's product approach. Other people found it convenient to use this process to draw a line below which Product Descriptions were not needed.

For small projects

Following the above comments, this process will usually not be needed for a small plan.

5.3.4 Prepare estimates

This step:

- Identifies the types of resource needed for the plan;
- Estimates the effort for each activity/product.

How?

- Examine each activity/product and identify what resource types it requires. Apart from human resources there may be other resources needed, such as equipment. With human resources, consider and document what level of skill you are basing the estimate on.
- Judge what level of efficiency you will base your estimates on, and what allowance for non-project time you will need to use.
- Estimate the effort needed for each activity/product.
- Understand whether that is an estimate of uninterrupted work, to which the allowances must be added, or whether the estimate already includes allowances.
- Document any assumptions you have made; e.g. the use of specific named resources, levels of skill and experience, or the availability of user resources when you need them. Check the assumptions with those who have such knowledge, such as the Senior Supplier and Senior User(s).

In practice

The organization may already have estimating guidelines for standard types of product. This should be particularly true for standard PRINCE2 management and quality products. For example, the amount of time needed to write an End Stage Report, Highlight Report, and to prepare and hold a quality review should be known.

For small projects

Beware of giving an estimate for the project before you have gone through this process. It seems easy to give a figure off the top of your head for a small project. But once given, the Project Board will hold you to this. It is amazing how many forgotten activities, unchecked assumptions and ideas that people are 100 per cent effective lie waiting to be discovered by this process – even in the smallest of projects.

5.3.5 Prepare the schedule

This step:

- Matches resources to activities/products;
- Schedules work according to sequence and dependencies;
- Adjusts the schedule to avoid people being over- or underused;
- Negotiates a solution with the Project Board for problems such as too few resources, too many resources or inability to meet fixed target dates;
- Calculates the cost of the resources used in the plan.

A plan can only show whether it can meet its targets when the activities are put together in a schedule against a time frame showing when activities will be done and by what resources.

How?

- Draw a planning network.
- Assess resource availability. This should include dates of availability as well as what the scale of that availability is. Any known information on holidays and training courses should be gathered.

Plans

- Allocate activities to resources and produce a draft schedule.
- Revise the draft to remove as many peaks and troughs in resource usage as possible.
- Add in management and quality activities or products (Stage and Team Plans only).
- Calculate resource utilization and costs.

In practice

This may be the point when you transfer the plan to your planning tool.

For small projects

You may not need a planning tool. You should remember to add time and effort for any quality and management products.

5.3.6 Analyse the risks

This step checks the draft plan for any risks in it.

You should not commit to a plan without considering what risks are involved in it and what impact the plan might have on risks already known.

How?

- Look for any external dependencies. These always represent one risk, or more, as they might not arrive on time or might be of poor quality, or be wrong in some other way.
- Look for any assumptions you have made in the plan, for example, the resources available to you. Each assumption is a risk.
- Look at each resource in the plan. Is there a risk involved? For example, a new resource doesn't perform at the expected level; a resource's availability is not achieved; or the tools or technology to be used are unproven.
- Take the appropriate risk actions. Where appropriate, revise the plan. Make sure that any new or modified risks are shown in the Risk Register.

In practice

Depending on the size of the Work Package, analysing the risks is a continuous, cyclic process. The emphasis is on being aware of the status of the team members' work and keeping the Project Manager up to date on that status.

For small projects

Where the project is too small to have Team Managers, the Project Manager will carry out the risk analysis.

5.3.7 Document the plan

This step adds text to explain the plan.

A plan should not be simply a diagram, Gantt chart or a tabular list of products and target dates. Plans should have a narrative section.

Suggested headings for the narrative are:

- Plan description.
- Quality plan.
- Plan assumptions.
- Plan prerequisites.
- External dependencies.
- Risks.
- Tolerances.
- Reporting.

How?

- Agree tolerance levels for the plan.
- Document what the plan covers, the approach to the work and the checking of its quality.
- Document any assumptions you have made.
- Add the planning dates to the Product Checklist (if used).
- Publish the plan.

In practice

The majority of the material for the text will evolve from the previous planning steps. Some of it will already be known because of local standards.

Plans

For small projects

Even if you don't have to publish a plan, you should still document the assumptions.

5.4 LINKS

There is a link between the structure of plans and the controls described in the *Controls* theme (see section 6.5). For example, at an end stage assessment the Project Board will examine the performance of the current Stage Plan and be asked to approve the next Stage Plan. The Team Manager will prepare a Team Plan and agree this with the Project Manager as part of accepting a Work Package.

5.5 DO'S AND DON'TS

By all means use a planning and control tool. It is much easier to modify a plan electronically rather than reach for the eraser. But don't let the tail wag the dog. I have known project managers shut themselves in their office for two or three days a week, adjusting the plan to reflect the last set of timesheets. By the time they emerge, things have changed (slightly) again, and back they go to tune the plan again. By all means update the plan regularly with actuals, but then stand back and look at what the latest situation is telling you. If you have broken the plan down into sufficient detail, you should be getting warnings of slippage or faster progress than expected. Go out and have a word in the right ears. Can we recover? Can we take advantage of the progress? Is anyone struggling and in need of help? Project progress is often a case of swings and roundabouts. We have a good week followed by a bad week, or vice versa. By all means update the plan with actuals every week, but the plan itself should only be modified every two or three weeks on the basis of definite corrective actions that are needed to put the plan back on an even keel. Naturally, if an event comes along that we know will require a major change, don't wait. But a lot of small hiccups will sort themselves out if the team is aware that you know and have taken an interest in putting things right.

5.6 IF IT'S A LARGE PROJECT

You really will need to use a planning and control tool – a software package. There may already be a standard tool that you are expected to use. Think very carefully about whether you have the time to update it with actuals. In a large project it may well be worth delegating the maintenance of plans to Project Support. Do you have expertise in using the package? Can you afford the time to become an expert?

Many project managers struggle to create and update the plans themselves. Many of them have had to learn how to use the tool as they go along. In consequence they know about 10 per cent of the tool's capabilities, and are ignorant of many shortcuts and easier ways of doing things with the plan. The Project Manager's job is to generate the information to build the plan in the first place, use the updated plan as a guide to the status and look ahead for problems or risks.

5.7 IF IT'S A SMALL PROJECT

You may be prepared to put enough detail into the Project Plan to allow you to monitor and control the entire project. If so, no other plans are needed. But remember that in a small project you need to have broken down the creation of each product to a small handful of days, otherwise you will have insufficient detail against which to monitor progress. Balance this need for detail against the Project Board's desire to be able to see the entire project on one page.

Chapter 6

Progress

6.1 INTRODUCTION

Three of the PRINCE2 principles are supported by the *Progress* theme. These are:

- Management by stages;
- Management by exception;
- Continued business justification.

The purpose of the *Progress* theme is to define the points in a project at which control should be exercised, and to define the PRINCE2 responsibilities, documentation and procedures for monitoring progress at these points, and comparing actual progress against plans.

6.2 MANAGEMENT BY STAGES

A stage is a collection of activities and deliverables whose delivery is managed as a unit. As such, it is a subset of the project, and in PRINCE2 terms it is the element of work that the Project Manager is managing on behalf of the Project Board at any one time.

6.2.1 Number of stages

A PRINCE2 project must have at least two stages: initiation and the rest of the project. Initiation is always the first stage. It prepares the Project Initiation Documentation and submits it to the Project Board to ask for the project to be authorized.

The question of how many stages to break a project into depends on balancing a number of factors:

- How far ahead in the project is it sensible to plan?
- Which are the key decision points in the project?
- How risky is the project?

Too many short stages increase the administration overhead; too few lengthy stages reduce the level of Project Board control.

6.2.2 Links

The concept of stages links to end stage assessments by the Project Board.

There is also a link to risks. As mentioned before, the riskier the project, the shorter and more frequent the stages may be to enable a formal risk review to be done by the Project Board as part of the decision on whether to continue the project.

Another link is to the tolerance levels (described in section 6.3), which give the Project Board tighter control to set exception limits for the next stage than simply to have exception limits for the entire project.

6.2.3 Do's and don'ts

- Always have an initiation stage however short the project.
- Don't split a project into more stages than Project Board control requires.
- Don't have a stage that is longer than you can comfortably plan in detail. Remember, a Stage Plan is going to be the Project Manager's main basis for control. This means that you need to get each piece of work that you hand out down to a few days. This will allow you to monitor whether the work is slipping or not. It is a fact of life that people only realize they will not finish on time when they get near the target date. If the pieces of work are twenty days or more in duration, then by the time the person tells you they will be late, it is usually too late to put any recovery actions in place.

6.2.4 If it's a large project

The stage-limited commitment is especially important for a large project with a rapidly changing environment that makes it almost impossible to develop an accurate plan for the total project at the outset.

6.2.5 If it's a small project

Even in a very small project with a Project Board of only one person, it is sensible to begin with an initiation stage. In a small project it may only take half an hour or so to get this understanding, but many projects get into trouble because of misunderstandings at the outset. It is very easy to make assumptions on what you think is needed – and get it wrong. If you start the project by heading off in the wrong direction, then you only need to be slightly wrong to waste a lot of time, money and effort. It is also easy for the Project Board to forget the original agreement and begin to think that something quite different was requested. Documenting the initial agreed objectives and scope and who was committed to do what can save the Project Manager from many arguments and headaches later on in the project.

6.3 MANAGEMENT BY EXCEPTION

Tolerance is the permissible deviation from a plan without the matter having to be referred to the next higher level of authority.

There are six elements of tolerance:

- Time;
- Cost;
- Quality;
- Scope;
- Risk;
- Benefit.

No project has ever gone 100 per cent to plan. There will be good days and bad days, good weeks and bad weeks. If the Project Board is going to 'manage by exception' it doesn't want the Project Manager running to it saying "I've spent a dollar more than I should today" or "I've fallen an hour behind schedule this week". But equally the Project Board doesn't want the project to overspend by a million euros or slip two months behind schedule without being warned. So where is the dividing line? What size of deviation from the plan is OK without going back to the Board for a decision? These margins are the tolerances.

The second philosophical point about tolerances is that we don't wait for tolerances to be exceeded; we forecast this occurrence so that the next higher level of authority has time to react and possibly prevent or reduce the deviation or exception.

Project tolerances should be part of the project mandate handed down by corporate or programme management. If they are not there, it is the Executive's job to find out from corporate or programme management what they are. The Project Board sets stage tolerances for the Project Manager within the overall project tolerances that they have received. The portion allocated to a stage should depend on the risk content of the work and the extent of the unknowns, such as technologies never used before, resources of unknown ability, tasks never attempted before.

The Project Manager negotiates appropriate tolerances for each Work Package with the Team Manager. Again, these will be sub-tolerances within the stage tolerances set for the Project Manager. As long as the plan's actual progress is within the tolerance margins, all is well. As soon as it can be *forecast* that progress will deviate outside the tolerance margins, the next higher level of authority needs to be advised.

6.3.1 Links

There are links to the *Controlling a Stage* (chapter 13) and *Managing Product Delivery* (chapter 14) processes that will bring any forecast deviation to the notice of the appropriate level of authority.

6.3.2 Do's and don'ts

What do we do if a project has such a tight deadline that our shortest plan can only just achieve that date, i.e. we are offered no time tolerance? We try to enlarge the cost tolerance. This would allow us to pay for overtime, extra resources, better equipment and better resource, or anything else that might save time if the target date was threatened.

If the converse was true and no cost tolerance was offered, we would ask for a greater time tolerance. This would allow us to not use overtime, drop some resources and use cheaper resources.

If both time and cost tolerances are tight, this is where we look at two other elements: scope and quality. For scope, we list everything we have to deliver in order of priority. Then if the going gets tough, we take the list to the customer and say "You can't have everything within the tolerances. What products can we drop?"

Quality is the dangerous aspect of tolerance. This is because quality reduction can happen without your knowing. If a team knows that it is under time and/or cost pressure, the easiest thing to do is relax on the quality checking, carry out fewer tests or let things slip through that they know aren't exactly right. Occasionally there may be quality concessions that can be made in order to stay within other tolerances, such as "You can have all the products, but you can't have the colours you wanted."

6.3.3 If it's a large project

It is very important to establish tolerances at all the levels described. The Project Manager should consider carefully any tolerances for scope and quality that may be called upon. Priorities for the various elements of the product need to be agreed at the beginning so that they can influence the sequence of design and development. There would be no point in trying to down-scope late in the project if all the minor 'nice-to-haves' have already been developed.

6.3.4 If it's a small project

There will probably be no Team Managers. In that case the Project Manager may still wish to allow a small tolerance for an individual's Work Package. The danger in telling an individual that they have a certain tolerance is that the tolerance becomes the expected target.

For example, if you tell a person that they have until Thursday to do a job with a tolerance of one day, in their mind the target becomes Friday. Some managers prefer to set tolerances but keep them to themselves.

6.4 CONTINUED BUSINESS JUSTIFICATION

At the end of each stage, the Project Board can stop the project if it considers that the project is no longer viable. For example, the organization's business needs may have changed to the point at which the project is no longer cost-effective. A project may also be cancelled if the estimated cost to complete the project exceeds the available funds.

6.5 PROJECT BOARD CONTROLS

The Project Board has five control points as defined in the *Directing a Project* process (see chapter 12):

- Authorize initiation;
- Authorize the project;
- Authorize a stage;
- Give *ad hoc* direction;
- Authorize project closure.

6.5.1 Authorize initiation

This is where the Project Board decides if the Project Brief and outline Business Case can sufficiently justify the initiation stage.

6.5.2 Authorize the project

This is where the Project Board decides if there is agreement on:

- What the project is to achieve;
- Why it is being undertaken;
- Who is to be involved and in what role;
- What the project is likely to cost;
- How and when the required products will be delivered.

This information is documented in the Project Initiation Documentation, which is then 'frozen', and used by the Project Board as a benchmark throughout the project and at the end to check the performance and deliveries of the project.

6.5.3 Authorize a stage

The reasons for breaking projects into management stages are to give the Project Board opportunities for conscious decision-making as to whether to continue with the project or not, based upon:

- A formal analysis of how the project is performing, based on information about results of the current stage;
- An assessment of the next Stage Plan;
- A check on what impact the next Stage Plan will have on the overall Project Plan;
- A check to confirm that the business justification for the project is still valid;
- A check that the required quality is being built into the products;
- Confirmation that the scope of the project has not changed;
- Confirmation that the risks facing the project are manageable.

Unless the project is broken into stages to provide suitable points at which to make the decisions, the Project Board cannot be fully in control of the project and its resources.

6.5.4 Give *ad hoc* direction

This Project Board activity contains three controls.

Requests for advice

The Project Manager may at any time ask for Project Board guidance on an issue that has been raised.

Highlight Reports

At a frequency defined by the Project Board in the Project Initiation Documentation, the Project Manager sends a Highlight Report to the Project Board to review progress and achievements in the current stage.

Exception Reports

If the Project Manager can forecast that the plan will end outside its tolerance margins, an Exception Report must be sent immediately to the Project Board, detailing the problem, options and a recommendation to solve the problem.

6.5.5 Authorize project closure

The final control point for the Project Board is to confirm that the project has done everything required, all completed products have been handed over and that the resources may now be released.

6.5.6 Links

There is a link to the setting of tolerances, particularly stage tolerances.

Another link is to the change control mechanism, because the Project Board makes the decision on whether changes are to be implemented or not.

6.5.7 Do's and don'ts

Do make sure that you obtain sign-off from the Project Board, confirming that the project *as defined in the Project Initiation Documentation* has been completed and that the end product has been accepted. However small the project has been, never assume that the end product has been accepted.

Don't allow the Project Board to let the project drift on by modifying the end product or creating extra products outside the scope of the initiation. Any such work thought up by the customer when you deliver what you believe to be the end product should form part of another project and another Project Initiation Documentation. You will not be able to measure the success of the project fairly if you allow time and cost to be added for work that is not covered in the Project Initiation Documentation. Remember, project success is measured against the Project Initiation Documentation *plus any approved requests for change*. It is your own Business Case that will suffer if you allow last minute 'wouldn't it be nice if' tinkering to creep in.

Progress

6.5.8 If it's a large project

All of these controls should be used and documented.

6.5.9 If it's a small project

Many of these controls can be done informally, but the Project Board should always consider what documentation of its decisions is needed in case things turn sour later.

6.6 PROJECT MANAGER CONTROLS

6.6.1 Risk Register

Risks are examined:

- Before starting the project (*Starting up a Project* and *Authorizing initiation*);
- Before commencing a new stage (*Managing a Stage Boundary* and *Authorizing the project*);
- As part of the analysis of any major change (*Capture and examine issues and risks*);
- Before confirming project closure (*Authorizing project closure*).

6.6.2 Issue Register

Having approved the objectives and products required in the project initiation, it is only right that the Project Board should have to approve any changes to them. Once requested changes have been estimated for the effort and cost of doing them, the customer has to decide on their priority, whether they should be done and whether the money to do them can be found. As for all the other decisions, this needs an assessment of the impact on the Project Plan, the Business Case and the risk situation.

6.6.3 Work Packages

A Work Package is an agreement between the Project Manager and a Team Manager (or an individual) to undertake a piece of work.

It describes the work, agreed dates, standards to be used, and quality and reporting requirements. No work can start without the Project Manager's approval via a Work Package, so it is a powerful schedule, cost and quality control for the Project Manager.

6.6.4 Checkpoint Report

This is a report from a Team Manager to the Project Manager. It is sent at a frequency agreed in the Work Package.

The information gathered in the Checkpoint Report is recorded for the Project Manager and forms the basis of the Highlight Report.

6.6.5 Quality Register

The Quality Register records every planned quality check, plus details of when it actually happened, who participated and what the results were. It provides the Project Manager with an overview of what is happening with regard to quality. Team Managers provide details of the actual quality checks and Project Support updates the Quality Register. It is also an ISO 9000 requirement that the customer can see a trail of the quality work carried out at any time.

6.6.6 Links

There is a link to chapter 4 *Organization* as part of 'who does what'.

There is a link to the work needed in the process *Starting up a Project* (see chapter 10).

There are links to the *Change* theme and configuration management.

There is a link to the Project Manager's Daily Log.

6.6.7 Do's and don'ts

Do check the need for all these points against the environment of the project.

Don't be misled by the comfortable feeling at the start of a project that everybody is committed and behind you. This is the direction from which back-stabbing occurs! That 'togetherness' feeling can evaporate as problems and/or changes come along. I used to work for a very cynical manager whose favourite phrase was "Don't plan for the honeymoon; plan for the divorce". In other words, if everything in the project was to go sweetly, the 'honeymoon' feeling would last and there would be little need for controls and documentation of who agreed to do what and why. But life has a way of changing, people change their minds, forget things and unexpected events occur. Just in case things turn sour you need to have the controls mentioned in this chapter available to you, and to be able to lay your hands on documentation to support why the project did what it did.

6.6.8 If it's a large project

All of these items should be considered for use. Their documentation and safe filing should also be considered as they will form a key part of the Project Manager's audit trail of why things happened and who decided what.

6.6.9 If it's a small project

Many of the controls can be done informally. There may be no teams or only individuals reporting direct to the Project Manager with no Team Managers appointed. This shortens the checkpoint control. The Project Manager would hold the checkpoint meetings with the team and write up the Checkpoint Report personally. (Remember that it may have been agreed to give the Checkpoint Report verbally.)

6.7 EVENT-DRIVEN AND TIME-DRIVEN CONTROLS

Some PRINCE2 controls are event-driven, others are time-driven. Table 6.1 shows which controls are time-driven and which event-driven.

6.7.1 Links

There will be entries in the Communication Management Strategy to describe how the Project Board, or at least the Executive, will keep corporate or programme management informed.

TABLE 6.1

	Event-driven	Time-driven
Project initiation	√	
Stages	√	
Management by exception	√	
End stage assessment	√	
Highlight Report		√
Exception Report	√	
Work Package	√	
Checkpoint Report		√
Risk Register	√	
Quality Register	√	
Issue Register	√	

A higher-level architecture group may prescribe the project approach where the project is part of a programme. It will have to conform to the same architecture as the other parts of the programme. The Project Board, especially the Senior Supplier, has to check this.

6.7.2 Do's and don'ts

Do keep reports and meetings to a sensible minimum. Try to avoid the monthly progress meetings where your project is one item on a crowded corporate or programme management agenda.

Do avoid appointing the Project Board from below, i.e. without reference to corporate or programme management. This only leads to mistrust of the Project Board by corporate or programme management. If this happens, any so-called 'decision' made by the Project Board will ping-pong between them and corporate or programme management for approval by the latter. What you are looking for is a Project Board that has the confidence of the management so that once the Project Board has taken a decision, you can move on.

6.7.3 If it's a large project

The controls and reporting should be documented and copies kept in the project files.

6.7.4 If it's a small project

A small project may not interest corporate or programme management. In this case the Executive will assume the role.

Chapter 7

Quality

7.1 PHILOSOPHY

The *Quality* theme defines the PRINCE2 approach to ensuring that the project will create and verify products that are fit for purpose.

The *Quality* theme supports the principles of *focus on products* and *define roles and responsibilities*.

7.2 QUALITY DEFINITION

PRINCE2 uses the ISO definition of quality:

> *"The totality of features and inherent or assigned characteristics of a product, person, process, service and/or system that bear on its ability to show that it meets expectations or satisfies stated needs, requirements or specifications".*

Many people get alarmed at the word 'inherent' and wonder if they have any control over whatever might be meant by this. A simple example is that if you are creating a wheel of some kind, an inherent characteristic would be that it should be round, which goes without saying.

7.3 THE QUALITY PATH

Part of the PRINCE2 quality philosophy is that quality is built into every phase of a product's specification and development and is not left to a check before final delivery.

TABLE 7.1

Step	Product	Process or technique
Ascertain the customer's quality expectations	Project mandate or Project Brief	Starting up a Project.
Document the customer's quality expectations and acceptance criteria	Project Product Description	Starting up a Project.
Write a Quality Management Strategy	Project Initiation Documentation	Initiating a Project.
Write a stage Quality Plan	Stage Plan	Managing a Stage Boundary.
Record planned quality activities	Quality Register	Managing a Stage Boundary.
Define an individual product's quality criteria	Product Description	Product-based Planning.
Explain the techniques, interfaces, constraints and configuration management requirements for each piece of work	Work Package	Controlling a Stage.
Report back on the quality work performed	Quality Register	Managing product delivery.
Check that quality work is being done correctly	Quality Register	Controlling a Stage.
Control changes	Issue Register	Change.
Keep track of changes to products	Configuration Item Records	Configuration management.

7.3.1 Customer's quality expectations

The customer's quality expectations should be made clear in the project mandate at the very outset of the project. If not sufficiently clear, the Project Manager should clarify the expectations when preparing the Project Product Description (during the *Starting up a Project* process – see chapter 10). The customer's quality expectations are often expressed in terms that are too broad to be measurable.

Types of quality expectation will vary according to the type of final product. Suggestions are:

- Major functions;
- Appearance;
- Personnel level required to use/operate the product;
- Performance levels;
- Capacity;
- Accuracy;
- Availability;
- Reliability (mean/maximum time to repair; mean time between failures);
- Running costs;
- Security;
- Ease of use;
- Timings.

Any thoughts or actions about quality in a project must start by finding out what the customer's quality expectations are. It is dangerous to assume that the customer will always want a superb quality product that will last forever. Have a look at the products in your local cut-price store and you will see what I mean. Let me quote you two different examples of customer quality thinking from projects in my past.

Example 1

A telecommunications company had bid for a packet switching system in Australia. They had been told they were the favoured supplier and their bid price looked good in relation to their competitors. Suddenly a bright young man employed by the Australian customer looked at the geography of the country and said to his bosses "Most of this system is going to be across the deserted middle of the country. It's going to be very expensive to fix any faults out there. Have we specified a high enough quality?" So the tender was recalled and when it re-emerged it contained a quality requirement that said all components (hardware and software) supplied had to have a mean time between failure of three years. This was backed up by heavy penalty clauses in the event of failure. The bidding telecommunications company looked at its original bid, which had included testing work 'to a commercial level' and realized that this was not enough. So lots more 'testing to destruction' was added to the price, plus back-up equipment to take over in case of failure, and so on. The price of their bid became so high that they lost the contract (but probably saved themselves money in the long run).

Example 2

The exploration arm of an oil company had a meeting with the data processing section to discuss the results of a seismic survey carried out in the mountains of a South American country. They had a very short time in which to analyse the results and decide if there were oil or gas reservoirs there. Their exploration contract had to be renewed or they would lose their favoured position. Their first quality need was for accuracy of analysis and, beyond that, they needed a fast turn around. They weren't worried about the result layout being 'user-friendly'. The product was to be used once and then thrown away.

There are big differences in the approaches to quality needed by these two projects.

7.3.2 Acceptance criteria

These turn the customer's quality expectations into measurable terms. 'Of good quality' may sound fine as an expectation, but how can it be measured?

A project's acceptance criteria are a set of measurable attributes of the final product. The PRINCE2 concept is that the acceptance criteria must be met before the user accepts the final product. However, some acceptance criteria cannot be measured until the final product has been operational for some time. Such criteria must be added to the Benefits Review Plan.

Acceptance criteria may be split into 'time zones'. Some must be fully met before the project can be closed, but for others, such as performance, there may be a series of improving targets that must be met after periods of operational use.

Acceptance criteria should also be prioritized in case there comes a time when one criterion can only be fully met at the expense of another one. For example, delivery on time versus having a product that is 100 per cent complete.

Expectations of performance, reliability, flexibility, maintainability and capability can all be expressed in measurable terms.

Acceptance Criteria must be suitable for the product, such as:

- Reference to meeting the customer's quality expectations;
- Target dates;
- Major functions;
- Capacity;
- Appearance;
- Availability;
- Development cost;
- Running costs;
- Maintenance;
- Ease of use;
- Timings;
- Personnel level required to use/operate the product.

7.4 THE PROJECT PRODUCT DESCRIPTION

This specialized form of a Product Description is created during the *Starting up a Project* process (Chapter 10), and may be refined during initiation. It is used in the *Closing a Project* process (Chapter 16) to check that the acceptance criteria have been met. It includes:

- the purpose of the final product;
- the set of major products of which it consists;
- the customer's quality expectations;
- acceptance criteria;
- project-level quality tolerances.

7.5 THE QUALITY MANAGEMENT STRATEGY

The next step is to decide how the project is going to meet the customer's quality expectations for the product. This is documented in a Quality Management Strategy, created in the *Initiating a Project* process (Chapter 11).

Other inputs to this should be the standards to be used to guide the development of the product and test its ability to meet the quality expectations. The supplier should have standards, but the customer may also have standards that it insists on being used, and such standards have to be compared against the expectations to see which are to be used. There may be gaps where extra standards have to be obtained or created. The customer has the last say in what standards will be used to check the products. There may also be regulatory standards to be met.

7.5.1 PRINCE2 and a company's Quality Management System

There may be confusion here between two uses of the initials QMS. In PRINCE2, this is the Quality Management Strategy, described in this section. The other use is for a company's Quality Management System, which is a document covering all the standards that a company needs for its functions, not only project management. PRINCE2 may form part of a company's Quality Management System where project management standards are defined.

7.5.2 Quality Management Strategy responsibilities

The Quality Management Strategy identifies the standards to be used and the main quality responsibilities. The latter may be a reference to a quality assurance function (belonging to either the customer or supplier, or both). There is a cross-reference here to the Project Board roles. These roles contain Project Assurance responsibilities, some of them affecting quality. If these have been delegated, there must be a match with the responsibilities defined in the Quality Management Strategy.

7.6 PROJECT ASSURANCE VERSUS QUALITY ASSURANCE

There is often confusion between these two terms.

Project Assurance refers to the Project Board's accountability for assuring that the project is conducted properly in all respects. This is, therefore, a responsibility within the project organization.

Quality assurance is the function within a company that establishes and maintains the Quality Management System for the whole company. Quality assurance activities are therefore outside the scope of PRINCE2 and the responsibility of corporate or programme management.

It is sensible to arrange for quality assurance independent of the project management team. Quality assurance provides a check that the project's direction and management are adequate for the nature of the project and that it complies with relevant corporate or programme management standards and policies.

7.7 QUALITY REGISTER

This is created in the *Initiating a Project* process (Chapter 11). It is a record of all planned quality activities and the results of those activities. A suggested structure is shown in Appendix A.26.

The Quality Register is updated during the *Managing a Stage Boundary* process (Chapter 15) when planning the next stage. Details of planned checks are added, which should include the planned date of the checks, plus any required resources known at this time. For example, at least the chairperson and presenter should be known for a quality review, and possibly some of the reviewers. When a Team Plan is created for a Work Package, other reviewers may be identified and these are also added to the Quality Register. When the quality check is done (*Execute a Work Package* – section 14.2), the actual date is added with details of how many errors were found and the target date for correction. Finally, the date of actual completion is added when the product is accepted.

7.7.1 The stage quality plan

Each stage has its own quality plan containing lower level detail than the Quality Management Strategy. This identifies the method of quality checking to be used for each product of the stage. The plan also identifies responsibilities for each individual quality check. For example, for each quality review the chairperson and reviewers are identified. This level of detail should be shown in the Quality Register. This gives an opportunity for those with Project Assurance roles to see each draft Stage Plan and to input their needs for checking and identifying the staff who should represent them at each check.

7.8 PRODUCT DESCRIPTIONS

Product Descriptions are created as part of Product-based Planning. A Product Description should be written for each major product to be produced by the project. In Appendix A, there are Product Descriptions for every PRINCE2 management product.

The Product Description should be written as soon as possible after the need for it is recognized. At the start, it may only be possible to create a skeleton of a Product Description to be completed as more information becomes available. Writing the full description helps the planner understand what the product is and how long it is likely to take to build it.

The Product Description is also the first place where we start thinking about the quality of the product, how we will test the presence of its quality and who we might need in order to test that quality.

It is very sensible to get the customer to write as much of the Product Description as possible, particularly the product's purpose, and quality criteria. This helps the customer define what is needed and is useful when delivering a product to be able to confirm that a product meets its quality criteria.

Product Descriptions form an important part of the information handed to a Team Manager as part of a Work Package.

Any time that a product approved by the Project Board has to be changed, the Product Description should also be checked to see if it needs an update.

7.9 QUALITY REVIEW

This is a method of checking a document's quality by a team review. The purpose of a quality review is to inspect a product for errors in a planned, independent, controlled and documented manner, and ensure that any errors found are fixed. It needs to be used with common sense to avoid the dangers of an over-bureaucratic approach, but with the intent to follow the procedures laid down (to ensure nothing is missed). The quality review procedure is fully explained in Appendix D.

Quality review documentation, together with the Quality Register, provides a record that the product was inspected, that any errors found were corrected and that the corrections were themselves checked. Knowing that a product has been checked and declared error-free provides a more confident basis to move ahead and use that product as the basis of future work.

7.10 LINKS

There is clearly a link to the project organization. If the customer or supplier has an independent quality assurance function, how can they neatly fit into the project organization? The answer is via the Project Assurance role. Both customer and supplier could appoint someone from their quality assurance function to carry out part of their Project Assurance role. This gives them access to the detailed planning, so that they can ensure that satisfactory testing with the correct participants has been planned. They can get feedback from these participants either directly or through the Quality Register about the results of quality work. The Project Assurance function can do a valuable job by checking that the Product Descriptions are correct.

Change control has a clear impact on quality. If uncontrolled changes are made, this is likely to destroy the quality of the project in terms of schedule and costs, as well as making it unclear what is being delivered. This means that there would be no connection between what was originally requested and what is finally delivered. In the same way configuration management has links to quality. If you do not keep control over what version of a product you are using, the quality is likely to suffer.

7.11 DO'S AND DON'TS

- Do treat the need for quality very seriously. The customer may, over time, forgive you for delivering late and may forgive you for coming in over budget; but the customer will never forgive you for delivering a poor quality product.
- Don't miss out on any of the quality steps.

7.12 IF IT'S A LARGE PROJECT

Quality is like carpet underlay. It enhances the feel and life of the product, but it is very difficult to put it in after the carpet has been laid. In a large project, you can't check everyone's work, so make full use of the Project Assurance role to check for you. Your job is to define the quality required, plan for it, monitor people who are checking for it and react quickly if there is a quality problem.

Where you have several teams working for you, ensure that the Project Assurance roles check the quality work intentions in the Team Plans and get customer representation in there, checking that the supplier is delivering good quality. Finding out during acceptance testing that a poor quality solution has been delivered is far too late, and all too often this leads to litigation, where only the lawyers win. Remember, the customer doesn't want large penalty payments. The customer wants a product that will meet the requirements.

7.13 IF IT'S A SMALL PROJECT

It is very easy to think that quality in a small project will look after itself. "It's such a small project we can check the quality when we've finished. Delivering a quality product from a small project is easy", they will say. "Only an idiot could get it wrong". Well, if you don't go through the quality steps mentioned above, it could be 'welcome to the idiot's club'.

Chapter 8

Risk

8.1 PHILOSOPHY

A risk is an event or combination of events that may or may not occur, but if they do they will have an effect on achievement of the project's objectives. This means that risk management is a prerequisite to the PRINCE2 principle of *continued business justification.*

A risk may be a threat or an opportunity.

Every project is subject to constant change in its business and wider environment. The risk environment is constantly changing too. The project's priorities and the relative importance of risks will shift and change. Assumptions about risk have to be regularly revisited and reconsidered, e.g. at each end stage assessment.

The purpose of the *Risk* theme is to identify, assess and control any uncertainties in order to improve the project's chances of success.

Risk management should be proactive and systematic.

8.2 RISK MANAGEMENT STRATEGY

Risks can arise at any time, but there are also defined moments when the risk situation should be examined. This describes the procedures to be used to identify, record, analyse and control risks. The strategy should cover both situations.

A Risk Management Strategy should be created for a project as part of *Initiating a Project* (chapter 11). Any corporate or programme risk management policies or guides should be sought out and checked for application to the project.

8.2.1 Risk tolerance

Another name for this is 'risk appetite'. An important piece of information required at the creation of the Risk Management Strategy is how much risk the Project Board is willing to take in the project. For example, a project to build a new chemical factory would have a very low 'risk appetite', whereas, in wartime, a project to capture a strategic bridge may have a very high 'risk appetite'.

Risk tolerance can be related to the other tolerance parameters: risk to completion within timescale and/or cost; risk to achieving product quality and project scope; and risks to achieving the benefits defined in the Business Case.

The organization's overall tolerance of exposure to risk must also be considered as well as a view of individual risks.

8.2.2 Risk Register

A project should record risk details in a Risk Register. Procedures for maintaining this are part of the Risk Management Strategy.

Details of the suggested contents of a Risk Register can be found in Appendix A.28.

Until the Risk Register is created during initiation, any discovered risks should be recorded in the Daily Log, and then transferred over on creation of the register.

8.2.3 Risk management times

PRINCE2 suggests that you:

- Carry out risk assessment at the start of a project. Make proposals on what should be done about the risks. Get agreement on whether to start the project or not. So risk assessment is done during the *Starting up a Project* process (risks in the project mandate, the initiation Stage Plan, the project approach, etc.). As there is no Risk Register yet, details of identified risks are kept in the Daily Log. Risk management is also done as part of the

Risk

Initiating a Project process. The Risk Register is now available, so any risks recorded in the Daily Log can be transferred.

- Appoint an owner for every risk. Build into a Stage Plan (or put a reminder in the Daily Log) the moments when the owners should be monitoring the risks. Check with the owners that they are doing the job and keeping the risk status up to date.
- Review every issue for its impact on existing risks or the creation of a new risk. Build the time and cost of any risk avoidance or reduction, for example, into your recommendation on the action to be taken.
- Review the risks at the end of every stage. This includes existing risks that might have changed and new risks caused by the next Stage Plan.
- Inspect the risks at the end of the project for any that might affect the product in its operational life. If there are any, make sure that you notify those charged with looking after the product. (Use the follow-on action recommendations for this.)

8.2.4 Risk responsibilities

The Project Manager has the responsibility to ensure that risks are identified, recorded and regularly reviewed. The Project Board has two responsibilities:

- Notify the Project Manager of any external risk exposure to the project;
- Make decisions on the Project Manager's recommended reactions to risk.

8.2.5 Early warning indicators

These are thresholds or levels of items that can be monitored to give advanced warning that a risk situation might be developing. Examples are:

- The number of issues being raised;
- The number of quality review errors;
- The amount of time behind schedule;
- The amount overspent.

8.3 THE RISK MANAGEMENT PROCEDURE

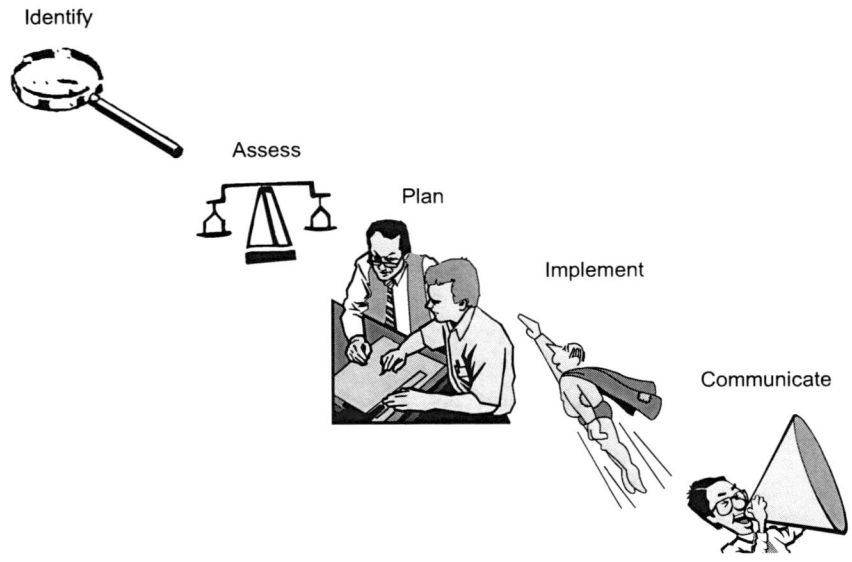

FIGURE 8.1 The five steps in the management of risk

The risk management procedure has five steps as shown in Figure 8.1:

- Identify;
- Assess;
- Plan;
- Implement;
- Communicate.

8.3.1 Identify risks

This step identifies the potential risks (or opportunities) facing the project. It is important not to judge the likelihood of a risk at this early time, but to:

- Identify critical parts of the project;
- Note potential sources of risk for these parts;
- Prepare early warning indicators for these;

Risk

- Identify risks and record them in the Risk Register;
- Review captured risks with stakeholders.

Risk cause, event and effect

It is easy to confuse a risk cause with its impact. PRINCE2 offers a useful way of expressing risks in an unambiguous manner. This breaks a risk into its three parts:

- Risk cause;
- Risk event;
- Risk effect.

An example of this way of defining a risk might be:

> "The new drink/drive laws (risk cause) might reduce the number of diners prepared to come to our country restaurant (risk event), which would badly effect our cash flow (risk effect)".

8.3.2 Assess

Risk assessment is concerned with the probability, proximity and impact of individual risks, taking into account any interdependencies or other factors outside the immediate scope under investigation.

- *Probability* is the likelihood of a particular outcome actually happening (including a consideration of the frequency with which the outcome may arise).
- *Proximity*: When considering a risk's probability, another aspect is when the risk might occur. Some risks will be predicted to be further way in time than others, and so attention can be focused on the more immediate ones. This prediction is called the risk's proximity. The proximity of each risk should be included in the Risk Register.
- *Impact* is the effect or result of a particular outcome actually happening. For example, occasional personal computer system failure is fairly likely to happen, but would not usually have a major impact on the business. Conversely, loss of power to a building is relatively unlikely to happen, but would have enormous impact on business continuity.

Summary risk profile

A graphic way of viewing risks is in a summary risk profile – an example is shown in Figure 8.2. This puts risks, using their unique identifiers, in a table of low to high probability and impact. In the example, the top right-hand corner contains risks with a high probability and high impact. The thick black line shows the risk tolerance level, so any risks to the right of that are beyond the risk tolerance levels. Such a table is a snapshot of known risks at a certain time and would need to be updated regularly. Updating it may show trends in known risks.

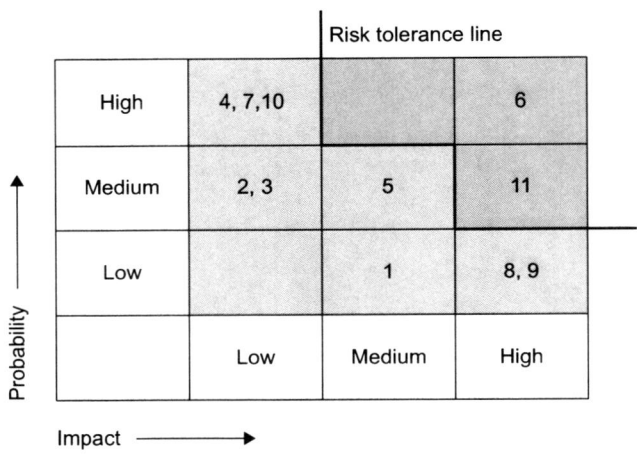

FIGURE 8.2 Summary risk profile

8.3.3 Plan

This involves selection of a risk response from a range of actions. For each possible action it is a question of balancing the cost of taking that action against the likelihood and impact of allowing the risk to occur (Figure 8.3).

The consideration has to be done in the light of the risk tolerances.

It can be useful to look at previous projects' Lesson Reports to see what risks were considered, what responses were selected and whether the responses were effective.

Risk

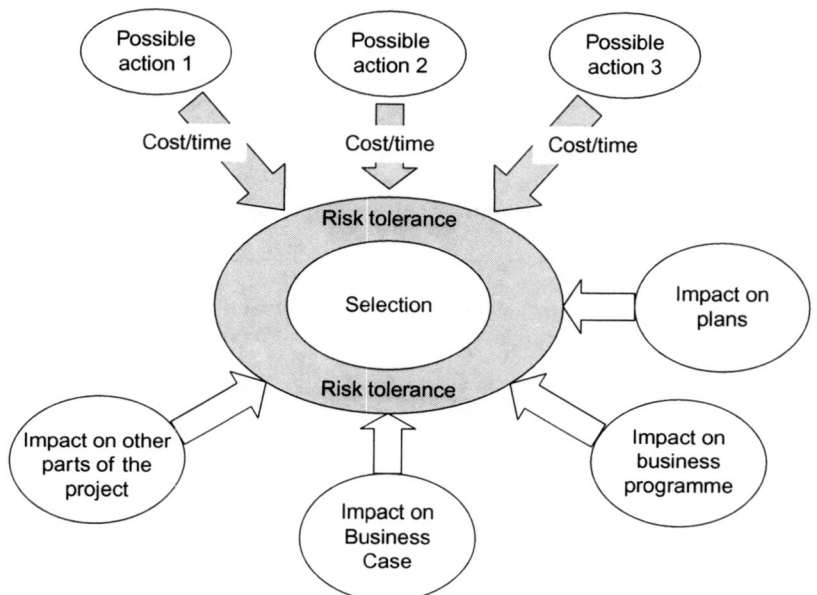

FIGURE 8.3 Risk action selection

The actions break into broadly five types of threat response, three types of response to opportunities and one type common to both threat and opportunity (Table 8.1).

Results of the risk planning are documented in the Risk Register. If the project is part of a programme, project risks should be examined for any impact on the programme (and vice versa). Where any cross-impact is found, the risk should be added to the other Risk Register.

8.3.4 Implement

Having made the selection, the implementation will need planning and resourcing, and is likely to include plan changes, new or modified Work Packages.

There must be mechanisms in place for monitoring and reporting on the risk actions.

Some of the actions may only be to monitor the identified risk for signs of a change in its status.

TABLE 8.1

Risk Responses

Avoid (threat)	Terminate the risk – by doing things differently and thus removing the risk, where it is feasible to do so. Countermeasures are put in place that either stop the threat or problem from occurring, or prevent it having any impact on the project or business.
Reduce (threat)	Treat the risk – take action to control it in some way where the actions either reduce the likelihood of the risk developing or limit the impact on the project to acceptable levels.
Transfer (threat)	This is a specialist form of risk reduction where the financial impact of the risk is passed to a third party via, for example, an insurance policy or penalty clause.
Accept (threat)	Tolerate the risk – perhaps because nothing can be done at a reasonable cost to mitigate it, or the likelihood and impact of the risk occurring are at an acceptable level.
Fallback (threat)	These are actions planned and organized to come into force as and when the risk occurs.
Share (threat or opportunity)	Both parties agree on the likely costs and share any savings or extra costs on either side of this figure.
Exploit (opportunity)	Take action to ensure the opportunity does occur and the positive impact is achieved.
Enhance (opportunity)	Work to improve the chances of the opportunity arising and enhancing the benefits gained from its occurrence.
Reject (opportunity)	A decision not to take the opportunity (at this time) because of other considerations.

Risk owner

It is good practice to appoint one individual to be responsible for monitoring each identified risk. This should be the person best placed to observe the factors that affect that risk. According to the risk, this may be a member of the Project Board, someone with Project Assurance duties, the Project Manager, Team Manager or a team member.

Risk actionee

This is a term used to describe a person assigned to carry out a risk response action.

8.3.5 Communicate

Risks owned at team level should be reported on in the Checkpoint Reports. The Project Manager includes some form of report on any significant risks in the Highlight Report. The End Stage Report also summarizes the risk status.

Where a risk actually occurs, an issue should be raised to trigger the necessary actions. There may also be open risks at the end of a project that should be passed to those operating and maintaining the product. This forms part of the follow-on action recommendations, part of the End Project Report.

Are there any risks and their actions that should be noted in the Lessons Log?

8.4 RISK BUDGET

A risk budget is a sum of money set aside at initiation time to cover responses to a project's threats and opportunities, such as fallback plans. Apart from the risks known at the start of a project, it is always prudent to make provision for risks that are as yet unknown.

8.5 ILLUSTRATIVE LIST OF RISK ANALYSIS QUESTIONS

This section contains an illustrative list of questions that a Project Manager may require to have answered for a particular project. It is based on the Office of Government Commerce (OGC) publication *Management of Project Risk*. Appendix E contains another set of risk analysis questions. It would be worth a Project Manager's time to read both lists and compile a list of questions relevant to a new project.

8.5.1 Business/strategic

- Do the project objectives fit into the organization's overall business strategy?
- When is the project due to deliver? How was the date determined?
- What would be the result of late delivery?

- What would be the result of limited success (functionality)?
- What is the stability of the business area?

8.5.2 External factors

- Is this project exposed to requirements due to international interests? (i.e. are there legal implications from overseas, or are foreign companies involved?)
- Could there be 'political' implications of the project failing?
- Is this project part of a programme? If so, what constraints are set for the project by that programme?

8.5.3 Procurement

- Has the supplier a reputation for delivery of high-quality goods?
- Is the contract sufficiently detailed to show what the supplier is going to provide?
- Are the customer's acceptance criteria clear to both parties?
- Is the contract legally binding/enforceable? (Consideration should be given to topics including ownership rights and liability.)

8.5.4 Organizational factors

- What consideration needs to be given to security for this project?
- Does the project have wholehearted support from senior management?
- What is the commitment of the user management?
- Have training requirements been identified? Can these requirements be met?

8.5.5 Management

- How clearly are the project objectives defined?
- Will the project be run using a well-documented approach to project management?
- Does this approach cover aspects of quality management, management of risk and development activities in sufficient depth?

- How well does the project team understand the chosen methodology?
- What is the current state of Project Plans?
- Is completion of this project dependent on the completion of other projects?
- Are the tasks in the Project Plan interdependent? (And can the critical path through tasks be identified?)
- What is the availability of appropriate resources? (What are the skills and experience of the project team? What is the make up of the project team?)
- Will people be available for training?
- How many separate user functions are involved?
- How much change will there be to the users' operation or organization?

8.5.6 Technical

- Is the specification clear, concise, accurate and feasible?
- How have the technical options been evaluated?
- What is the knowledge of the equipment? (For example, for IT this is the hardware/software environment.)
- Does the experience of the Project Manager cover a similar application?
- Is this a new application?
- What is the complexity of the system?
- How many sites will the system be implemented in?
- Is the proposed equipment new/leading edge? Is the proposed hardware/software environment in use already?
- Who is responsible for defining system testing?
- Who is responsible for defining acceptance testing?
- On what basis is the implementation planned?
- What access will the project team have to the development facilities?
- Will the system be operated by the user or specialist staff?
- Have requirements for long-term operations, maintenance and support been identified?

8.6 LINKS

At key points in a project, management of risk should be carried out (Figure 8.4).

8.6.1 Select the project approach and assemble the Project Brief

The project mandate may have referred to a number of risks facing the potential project; e.g. competitor action, impending or mooted legislation, company policy changes, staff reorganization or cash-flow problems. The preparation of the Project Brief should cause an early study of such risks. Creation of the project approach may also have introduced some extra risks. Any risks should be noted in the Daily Log until the Risk Register is created during initiation.

8.6.2 Authorize initiation

This is the first formal moment when the Project Board can examine any known risks (recorded in the Daily Log) as part of deciding whether project initiation can be justified. Pragmatically, the Project Manager should have discussed informally with Board members any known risks that seem to threaten the project viability.

8.6.3 Refine the Business Case – Focus on both business and project risks

The Project Manager examines risks again as part of preparing the Project Initiation Documentation. At this time the Project Plan will be created, and this may identify a number of project risks, such as unknown performance of resources, contractor ability and any assumptions being made in the plan. New risks may also come to light as a result of adding detail to the Project Brief. At the same time all existing risks are reviewed for any new information or change in their circumstances.

8.6.4 Authorize the project

The Project Board now has an updated Risk Register to examine as part of its decision on whether to go ahead with the project. As a result

Risk

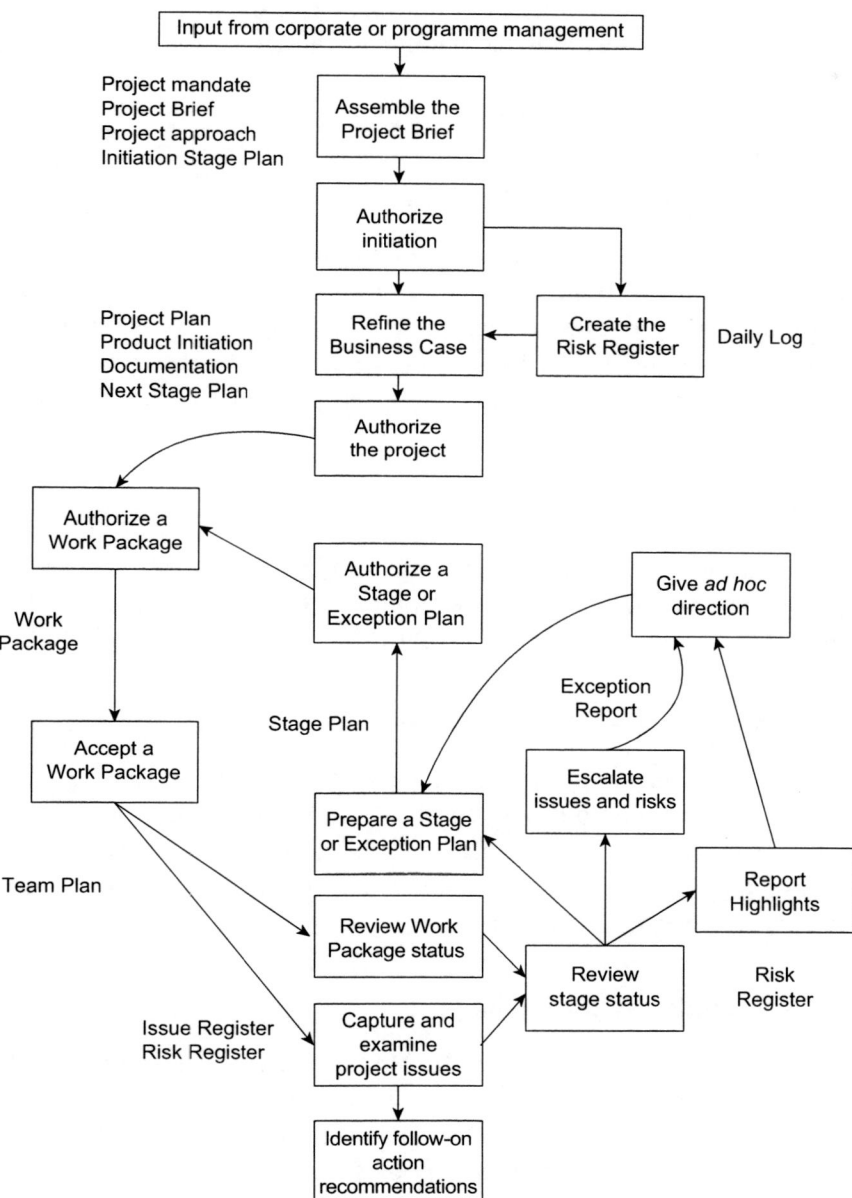

FIGURE 8.4 Mapping risk management

of refining the Business Case, a number of business risks may have been identified. Very often the 'owners' of these risks will be members of the Project Board, and they should confirm their ownership and the actions required of them.

8.6.5 Managing a Stage Boundary

Each time that a plan is produced, elements of the plan may identify new risks, modify existing ones or eliminate others. No plan should be put forward for approval before its risk content has been analysed. This analysis may lead to the plan being modified in order to take the appropriate risk action. The Risk Register should be updated with all such details.

8.6.6 Authorize a Stage or Exception Plan

Before authorizing a Stage or Exception Plan, the Project Board has the opportunity to study the risk situation as part of its judgement of the continuing viability of the project.

8.6.7 Authorize a Work Package

Negotiation with the Team Manager or team member may identify new risks or change old ones. It may require the Project Manager to go back and amend some part of the original Work Package or change the Stage Plan. Examples here are the assignee seeking more time or needing to change resources.

8.6.8 Accept a Work Package

This is the point when the Team Manager creates a Team Plan to ensure that the products of the Work Package can be delivered within the constraints of the agreed Work Package. As with any other plan, it may contain new risks or modify existing ones.

8.6.9 Capture and examine issues and risks

Assessment of a new issue may identify a risk situation. This may stem from either the technical impact analysis or the business impact

Risk

analysis. For example, the proposed change may produce a risk of pushing the stage or project beyond its tolerance margins.

8.6.10 Review the stage status

This brings together the Stage Plan with its latest actual figures, the Project Plan, the Business Case, open issues, the tolerance status and the Risk Register. The Project Manager (in conjunction with the Project Assurance roles) looks for risk situation changes as well as any other warning signs.

8.6.11 Escalate issues and risks

As well as issues, a risk change may cause the Project Manager to raise an Exception Report to the Project Board.

8.6.12 Report Highlights

As part of this task, the Project Manager may take the opportunity to raise any risk matters with the Project Board. Examples of this would be notifying the Board of any risks that are no longer relevant, warning about new risks and reminders about business risks that Board members should be keeping an eye on. (The suggested format of a Highlight Report is included in Appendix A.11.)

8.6.13 Give *ad hoc* direction

The Project Manager advises the Project Board of exception situations via the Exception Report. The Project Board has the opportunity to react with advice or a decision – for example, bringing the project to a premature close, requesting an Exception Plan or removing the problem. The Project Board may instigate *ad hoc* advice on the basis of information given to it from corporate or programme management or another external source.

8.6.14 Hand over products

At the end of the project a number of risks may have been identified that will affect the product in its operational life. These should be transferred to the follow-on action recommendations for the information of those who will support the product after the project.

8.7 DO'S AND DON'TS

The Project Manager should:

- Examine every plan for risks before publishing it;
- Appoint an owner for every risk;
- Try to delegate as many of these as possible. When writing up your Daily Log for actions to take next week, do look at the Risk Register to find owners who should be reporting on the status of risks.

The Project Manager should not:

- Forget to warn the Project Board of any risk deterioration that might go beyond the tolerance margins;
- Be shy about appointing a member of the Project Board as owner of a risk where it is appropriate.

8.8 IF IT'S A LARGE PROJECT

Some large organizations now employ a Risk Manager, an expert/consultant who advises all project managers on identifying and controlling risks.

It is sensible to set aside some time specifically to consider the risk situation. This will be a natural part of each Stage Boundary, but in a long project it is also worth setting this time aside, say, every two weeks.

8.9 IF IT'S A SMALL PROJECT

Risks are still an important factor.

Chapter 9

Change

The *Change* theme covers change control and configuration management, and touches on the principles of *manage by exception*, *focus on products* and *continued business justification*.

9.1 CONFIGURATION MANAGEMENT

9.1.1 Configuration management overview

Within the context of project management the purpose of configuration management is to identify, track and protect the project's products as they are developed.

Its objective is to achieve a controlled and traceable product evolution through properly authorized specifications, design, development and testing.

This objective is met by defining and ensuring the:

- Issue and control of properly authorized specifications;
- Issue and control of properly authorized design documents;
- Issue and control of properly authorized changes to the specification or design documents;
- Control of the various versions of a product and their relationships with its current state.

Configuration management is also the process of managing change to the elements that comprise a product. It implies that any version of the product and any revision of the components that make up the product can be retrieved at any time, and that the resulting product will always be built in an identical manner. Product enhancements and special variants create the need to control multiple versions and releases of the product. All these have to be handled by configuration management.

Configuration management is a discipline which:

- Records what components or products are required in order to build a product;
- Provides identifiers and version numbers to all products;
- Controls access and change to components of a product once they have been declared complete by the developer;
- Provides information on the impact of possible changes;
- Keeps information on the links between the various parts of a product; e.g. what components comprise a product, where component x is used, what the 'full product' consists of;
- Provides information on the status of products (configuration items) being developed, including who is responsible for the development;
- Is the sensible storage place for Product Descriptions;
- Gives project management the assurance that products are being developed in the correct sequence.

Configuration management holds a central position in project management. Product Breakdown Structures used in planning provide the identification information for the configuration items. The links allow the construction of the Product Flow Diagrams. They offer input and verification of the products required for a plan. You cannot adequately do change control without configuration management. Configuration management provides product copies and Product Descriptions for quality checks and keeps track of the status of the product. It provides the information to construct a release package, either a complete one or a partial one, and then records the issue of a release.

Configuration Item Records are valuable assets in themselves. Configuration management helps management know what its assets are supposed to be, who is responsible for their safekeeping and whether the actual inventory matches the official one.

Configuration management gives control over the versions of products in use, identifies products affected by any problems and makes it easier to assess the impact of changes.

Configuration management supports the production of information on problem trends, such as which products are being changed regularly or frequently, thereby assisting in the proactive prevention of problems.

Where the end product is to be used in more than one place, configuration management helps organizations to control the distribution of changes to these operational sites. Where there is any volume of changes, you will need to decide between putting together a 'release package' of several changes or issuing a complete new product. The latter may be a more controlled and cost-effective means of updating an operational product than sending out one changed product at a time. The decision and control mechanisms for this are part of configuration management.

Configuration management supports the maintenance of information on proven reliable releases to which products can revert in case of problems.

Because all products are under the control of configuration management once they have been developed, it makes it more difficult for them to be changed maliciously, thus improving security.

After any disaster, the data held in the configuration library helps to recreate a release by identifying the products required and their storage place.

9.1.2 Configuration management detail

Configuration management covers all the technical products of a project. It should also be used to record and store management and quality products, such as plans, quality check details and approvals to proceed. Whether management products are included or not depends on a number of factors such as:

- Effort involved;
- Resource availability;

- Capability of any other current method for handling management and quality products;
- Project Manager's preference;
- Availability of configuration management software.

Costs

There are the expected costs of staffing and training Configuration Librarians. If a central office (e.g. part of a Project Support office) has been set up to provide configuration management functions to a number of projects, there may be a need for a configuration manager.

If software is to be used to record and track the data, there will be the cost of its purchase or rental, any hardware bought to run it, plus the staff training. Having said that, it is very difficult to keep the comprehensive records required to do a complete job without a computer database and software. The costs here are far outweighed by the increase in speed, capacity and detail of information. The increase in speed of reaction by the Configuration Librarian probably reduces the number of librarians needed to cover all the site's products.

The need to go through the configuration management tasks may slightly slow down the handover of a finished item or the implementation of a change. But this penalty is very small when weighed against the risk and impact of operationally using a product or product that is from an incorrect release, or has not been checked out. Without it there is also the risk of more than one person changing a product simultaneously, resulting in all but the final change being lost.

Possible problems

If products are defined at too low a level, the Configuration Librarian may be overwhelmed by the amount of data to be fed into the library. This is a problem particularly where no configuration management software is being used.

If products are defined at too high a level, the information for impact analysis may be too vague and result in a larger than necessary product change being indicated; e.g. altering a whole set of products when only one product is affected.

Procedures must cater for emergency changes, where an emergency change is required in order to let the operational product continue.

Where configuration management is new, development staff may be tempted to view its controls as bottlenecks and bureaucracy. But it has been used in engineering for many years and is regarded in those circles as essential. It is also regarded as an essential part of any quality product; should you be looking for accreditation under standards such as ISO 9001. It is regarded as essential because of the control it gives, and experience over many years has shown its value and also the cost of the problems arising when it is not used.

When is it done?

A Configuration Management Strategy is required as part of the Project Initiation Documentation. This should state:

- What method is to be used;
- Who has the responsibility for configuration management;
- What naming convention will be used to identify products of this project;
- What types of product are to be covered;
- What types of status are to be used (e.g. 'allocated', 'draft available', 'quality checked').

Once a product has been identified as required, it should receive an identifier from the configuration management method. Sensibly, this should coincide with the creation of a draft Product Description.

Among the configuration management planning activities required are those to identify what baselines will be required (explained later on in this section), and for what purpose; which baselines exist concurrently and which cannot; and when baselines will be taken.

The status of a product should be tracked from the moment the Product Description is created.

Configuration Item Records

The detail to be kept about the products will depend to some extent on the complexity of the end product, the number of products, the resources available to keep the records and the information demanded by the maintenance and support groups. As a minimum each product should be identified by:

- The project identifier;
- The product identifier;
- The version number.

Baselines

Baselines are moments in a product's evolution when it and all its components have reached an acceptable state such that they can be 'frozen' and used as a base for the next step. The next step may be to release the product to the customer, or it may be that you have 'frozen' a design and will now construct the products.

A baseline is created for one of a number of reasons:

- To provide a sound base for future work;
- As a point to which you can retreat if development goes wrong;
- As an indication of the component and version numbers of a release;
- As a bill of material showing the variants released to a specific site (e.g. a foreign language version);
- To copy the products and documentation at the current baseline to all remote sites;
- To represent a standard configuration against which supplies can be obtained; e.g. purchase of personal computers for a group;
- To transfer configuration items to another library; e.g. from development to production; from the supplier to the customer at the end of the project.

Product Status Account

Product status accounting provides a complete statement of the current status and history of the products generated within the project or within a stage.

A use for a Product Status Account is that it allows a Project Manager to check that all stage products have been completed and approved at a stage end. Another use is for configuration auditing.

Configuration auditing

Configuration auditing checks whether the recorded description of products matches their physical representation and whether items have been built to their specification. There are two purposes of configuration auditing. The first is to confirm that the configuration records match reality. In other words, if my configuration records show that we are developing version 3 of a product, I want to be sure that the developer has not moved on to version 5 without my knowing and without any linking history to say why versions 4 and 5 have been created. The second purpose is to account for any differences between a delivered product and its original agreed specification. In other words, can the configuration records trace a path from the original specification through any approved changes to what a product looks like now? These audits should verify that:

- All authorized versions of configuration items exist;
- Only authorized configuration items exist;
- All change records and release records have been properly authorized by project management;
- Implemented changes are as authorized.

This is defined as an inspection of the recorded configuration item description and the current representation of that item to ensure that the latter matches its current specification. The inspection also checks that the specification of each item is consistent with that of its parent in the structure. In a sense, it can be regarded as similar to stock control – that is, whether the book description matches with that on the shelf. In addition, the audit should ensure that documentation is complete and that project standards have been met.

In engineering establishments, the aim of configuration auditing is to check that, in spite of changes that may have taken place in requirements and design, the items produced conform to the latest agreed specification and that quality review procedures have been performed satisfactorily. It verifies at successive baselines that the item produced at each baseline conforms to the specification produced for it in the previous baseline, plus any approved changes.

Configuration audits should be done:

- Shortly after implementation of a new configuration management system;
- Before and after major changes to the structure of the project's end product;
- After disasters, such as the loss of records;
- On detection of several unauthorized configuration items;
- Randomly.

Configuration audit checklist

Here is an example checklist for an audit. The following questions should be asked:

- Do the configuration records match the physical items?
- Are (randomly tested) approved changes recorded in the Issue Register? Are they linked to the appropriate products? Is their implementation controlled by the configuration management method?
- Does the configuration library accurately reflect the inclusion of any random products? Are there links to relevant Issue Reports?
- Are regular configuration audits carried out? Are the results recorded? Have follow-on actions been performed?
- Are (randomly tested) archived and back up versions of products retained and recorded in the correct manner?
- Are the recorded versions of products used in multiple locations correct?
- Do product names and version numbers meet naming conventions?
- Is configuration library housekeeping carried out in accordance with defined procedures?
- Are members of staff adequately trained?
- Can baselines be easily and accurately created, recreated and used?

Building a release package

At the end of a project the product which has been developed is released into production. For many installations this may be a simple matter. The product will run operationally in the same environment used for its development, and 'release' is nothing more than 'cutting the tape'.

But there can be many problems concerned with the move of development work over to live operation. The following are some of the questions that should be asked:

- How do we release details of how to build the product to a sister company on another site?
- How do we ensure that we only release products that have been thoroughly tested as part of the whole product?
- How do we create innumerable copies of the product (for example, for products produced by software houses or electrical component manufacturers) and guarantee that they will be identical?
- How can we change an operational product without the risk of it malfunctioning after the change?
- How can we keep a check on which of our customers or sites has what version of the product?
- How do we install a major enhancement of a product?
- If the people who developed the product are not to be the people who install the product, do the installers know how to do it?
- Do we issue the complete product for every update or just the changed components?
- Do we issue a complete new operating manual or only the changed pages?

The answer is in release control – another important job for the Configuration Librarian. The tasks for the Configuration Librarian are:

- Identify the products to be included in the release;
- Ensure that all the required products have reached a status which allows them to be released into live operation;
- Report on any required products which do not have a current approved status;
- Build a release package;
- List the changes since the previous release and the error reports or requests for change solved by the release;
- Distribute the release;

- Be able to recreate any baseline (i.e. past release) if a site reports problems on a release;
- Know which site has what version and variant of the product.

Control of releases

Each product release should have a release identifier of the same form as the version number described for a product (i.e. baseline number and issue number) which identifies:

- The level of functionality provide by the release – defined by the baseline number;
- The modification status of the release – defined by the issue number;
- The release configuration – by reference to the relevant baseline summary.

Revision of release and issue number

The release identifier should be revised:

- When the new release of the product provides changed functionality, the baseline number is incremented up to the next whole number (e.g. 2.1 becomes 3.0);
- When the new release of the product provides fault fixes only, the issue number is incremented by one (e.g. 1.4 becomes 1.5);
- Optionally, when the new release of the product consolidates many (e.g. 20) minor changes, the baseline number is incremented up to the next whole number.

Release package contents

A release should be accompanied by a release build summary. It should contain:

- The release name and identifier;
- The release date;
- The person/section/group with responsibility for the release. This will normally be the contact for any installation problems;
- A brief description of the release – whether it is a complete or partial release, what has caused the release, what is its purpose, the major benefits over previous releases;

Change

- A list of prerequisites for the installation of the release;
- A list of all the project issues answered by this release;
- A bill of material listing what is contained in the release. This should cover documentation and any procedures;
- Assembly steps;
- Assembly test steps;
- Any customization steps. If the release can be tailored in any way, this describes the possibilities and lists the steps to be carried out;
- Notification of any dates when support for previous releases will cease;
- An acknowledgement to be completed and returned by the assembler on successful completion of the assembly.

While current, a baseline cannot be changed. It remains active until it is superseded by the next baseline.

9.2 CHANGE CONTROL

Change is inevitable during the life of a project. No matter how well planned a project has been, having no control over changes will destroy any chance of bringing the project in on schedule and to budget.

9.2.1 Change Authority

As part of the Configuration Management Strategy the Project Board must decide if it wishes to delegate some authority for approving or rejecting requests for change or off-specifications. This depends on factors such as the number of requests expected, the technical nature of the requests and the availability of Project Board members to look at the requests.

The Project Board should define a scale of importance for changes, to identify those which should be handled by:

- Corporate or programme management;
- The Project Board;
- A Change Authority;
- The Project Manager.

If a Change Authority is appointed, it should be given a change budget, together with any constraints on its use, such as the maximum cost of a single change or maximum budget for a single stage.

9.2.2 Issues and types of issue

In PRINCE2 an issue is the formal way into a project of any inquiry, complaint or request. It can be raised about anything by anyone associated with the project; for example:

- A desired new or changed function;
- A failure of a product in meeting some aspect of the user requirements;
- A concern in the mind of someone connected with the project;
- A problem.

In other words, there is no limit to the content of an issue beyond the fact that it should be about the project.

All possible changes should be handled by the same change control procedure. Apart from controlling possible changes, this procedure should provide a formal entry point through which questions or suggestions also can be raised and answered.

All issues have to be closed by the end of the project or transferred to the follow-on action recommendations. The transfer of an issue to these recommendations can only be done with the approval of the Project Board.

9.2.3 Request for change

A 'request for change' records a proposed modification to the user requirements.

9.2.4 Off-specification

An off-specification is used to document any situation where the product is failing to meet its specification in some respect.

9.2.5 Problem or concern

An issue may be simply a question or general concern expressed by someone.

9.3 PROCEDURE FOR ISSUE AND CHANGE CONTROL

PRINCE2 provides a structured set of procedures to identify, analyse and control changes.

There are five steps in the change control procedure:

- Capture;
- Examine;
- Propose;
- Decide;
- Implement.

9.3.1 Capture

This is a brief analysis of the issue to determine its type and whether it should be handled formally or informally.

The purpose of this analysis is to:

- Ensure decisions on issues are made at the correct level – Project Manager, Project Board, or corporate or programme management;
- Protect the Project Board from having to make decisions on trivial matters as much as possible;
- Reduce the need for formal documentation as much as possible.

Issues that need to be managed formally are transferred to an Issue Report, given a unique identifier and entered on the Issue Register.

If an issue is a problem or concern, this may not require formal handling. The Project Manager may decide to deal with it directly. A note of the issue and action taken, if any, should be made in the Daily Log. If a later decision is made that the issue requires to be handled formally, it is transferred to an Issue Report and entered on the Issue Register.

9.3.2 Examine

Impact analysis is done to find out:

- What would have to change?
- What would be the impact on other products?
- The estimated time and cost;
- Any impact on quality;
- Any impact on the project scope;
- Any impact on the Business Case;
- Any impact on risks.

If the project is part of a programme, the issue should be analysed for any impact at that level. After this analysis, the priority of the issue should be re-evaluated. The Issue Register and Issue Report are then updated with all this information.

9.3.3 Propose

Alternative responses are considered and a selection made that balances the costs and risks of the response against the value of the change.

9.3.4 Decide

The Project Manager may be able to decide on minor issues if they can be handled within the Stage Plan. If so, permission for this should have been documented in the Configuration Management Strategy.

Remember that tolerances are not there to pay for requests for change.

Other Issue Reports should go to the Project Board or Change Authority for a decision. Where the selected response would cause an exception outside tolerances, an Exception Report would be escalated to the Project Board.

The Project Board's decision may be to:

- Implement the change. This means asking the Project Manager to create an Exception Plan;

- Delay the change to an enhancement project after the current one is finished;
- Defer a decision until a later meeting;
- Ask for more information;
- Cancel the request.

The decision should be documented on the Issue Report and in the Issue Register.

9.3.5 Implement

This will take the form of either a new or modified Work Package, or if an Exception Report was raised, the Project Board may request an Exception Plan (see section 5.2.4 for further details).

9.4 LINKS

There is a very strong link between change control and configuration management. They are inseparable. You can't have one without the other. It is sensible to give the same person or group responsibility for both elements.

Configuration management links to quality. If you lose control over which versions should be used, or release old versions of components, or allow the release of an untested change, the quality of the product will suffer.

There is another link with organization and the *Initiating a Project* process (see chapter 11). Before the project begins there should be a decision on how big the change control need is likely to be and what part of the project management team will administer change control. It may be a member of the team, possibly part time? Will an administrative clerk come in for half a day a week? Does it need a small group of specialist Configuration Librarians?

Another link is between *Starting up a Project* (see chapter 10), the organization, plans, and change control. At the outset of a project a decision is needed on whether a Change Authority is needed and how changes will be funded.

9.5 DO'S AND DON'TS

- Do relate the complexity of the configuration management method to the needs of the project.
- Don't underestimate the importance of configuration management. As stated at the beginning of the chapter, if there is more than one person working on the project and if there will be more than one version of a product, you need configuration management. Make sure that it's adequate for the job.
- Do think about the stability of the customer's specification before you dive into a project. The less stable it is, the more change control will be required and the higher the cost of authorized changes is likely to be.
- Don't underestimate the importance of change control. There is no project control without it.

9.6 IF IT'S A LARGE PROJECT

There may be many changes; so many that the Project Board cannot find the time to consider them all. They can choose to appoint a Change Authority: a group of people representing the Project Board. The Change Authority will meet at a frequency based on the volume of changes coming through. In order for the change control board to operate, the Project Board will allocate it a change budget and provide certain restrictions. These may be the maximum amount of the budget to be spent in one stage and the maximum amount of the budget that can be spent on one change. Any need to go beyond these boundaries would require reference back to the Project Board.

The Project Support office should be handling configuration management, probably using one of the software tools available on the market. If the customer already has a configuration management method in place to look after all products in live operation, the project should use the same method.

9.7 IF IT'S A SMALL PROJECT

Members of the team can probably do configuration management. I looked at a feasibility study where one of the analysts performed the

Configuration Librarian's job. It took about two hours of his time each week. There was a lockable filing cabinet in which the various versions of sections of the report were kept. Team members were responsible for telling the librarian when they wanted to move to a new version. The librarian checked the log and allocated the next version number, having first logged the reason for the change. These reasons had to be documented. Once a fortnight the analyst would take the configuration records round the office and check that there was a match between the records and the version numbers in use.

Change control will still be important.

Chapter 10

Starting up a Project (SU)

A PRINCE2 project is triggered by a project mandate, which is a request to provide a solution to a business problem. Ideally the project mandate should have the information required to form the Project Brief, but, as this is created before the project begins, there may have been no control over its content. Part of the work of the *Starting up a Project* process is to fill in any gaps (Figure 10.1).

10.0.1 What does the process do?

- Receives a project mandate.
- Confirms the existence of (or completes) adequate terms of reference for the project.
- Creates a Daily Log.
- Appoints the project management team.
- Identifies the type of solution to be provided – the project approach.
- Identifies the customer's quality expectations.
- Enters into the Daily Log any risks known already or discovered in the work of this process.
- Plans the initiation stage.

10.0.2 Why?

To establish:

- What is to be done;
- Who will make the decisions;

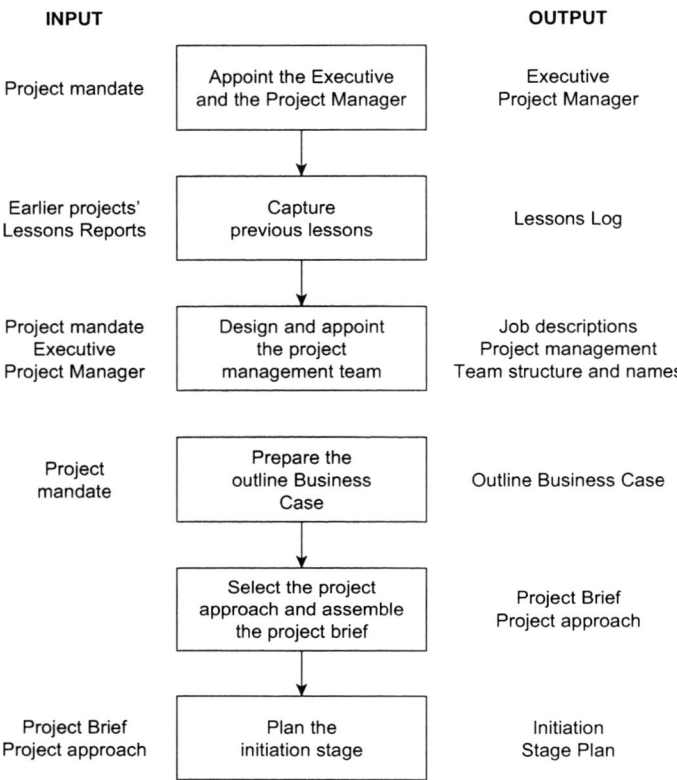

FIGURE 10.1 Starting up a Project

- Who is funding the project;
- Who will say what is needed;
- What quality standards will be required;
- Who will provide the resources to do the work.

10.1 APPOINT THE EXECUTIVE AND PROJECT MANAGER

10.1.1 Responsibility

Corporate or programme management and the Executive (once appointed).

Starting up a Project (SU)

CARTOON 2 Project mandate

10.1.2 What does the activity do?

- Appoints the Executive and Project Manager, and prepares and obtains signatures for their job descriptions.

10.1.3 Why?

Every project needs a sponsor, the key decision maker, but usually this person is too busy to manage the project on a day-to-day basis, so we also need a Project Manager to do the planning and control. We need to identify these two people before anything can happen (in a controlled manner) in a project.

10.1.4 How?

- Corporate or programme management identify the Executive to be responsible for the project.
- Either corporate or programme management, or the Executive, or both identify a suitable Project Manager.
- The Project Manager starts with the standard PRINCE2 role descriptions for their jobs. These are then tailored by discussion between the Executive and Project Manager.
- The tailored roles are documented, and both people sign two copies of their job descriptions. The individual keeps one copy, and the other is kept by the Project Manager for filing once the project filing system has been set up.

10.1.5 Information needs

TABLE 10.1

Management information	Usage	Explanation
Project mandate	Input	Basic information about the project's objectives.
Executive role description	Input	From the role description given in Appendix B.
Executive job description	Output	The standard role modified by the information in the project mandate, the person chosen and the project environment.
Project Manager role description	Input	From the role description given in Appendix B.
Project Manager job description	Output	The standard role modified by the information in the project mandate, the person chosen and the project environment.

10.1.6 In practice

The Executive:

- Holds the purse strings for the project;
- Ensures that the project meets company strategies;
- Ensures that there is always a valid Business Case in existence.

The Executive should have strong links with the senior management group responsible for this appointment. Ideally the person nominated should be a member of that group; for example, belongs to the programme management team. It is necessary to have a strong bond of confidence between corporate or programme management and the Executive because this person will be making key decisions on their behalf. If the higher level of management wants to check every decision made by the Executive, then this will slow down the whole project process. The relationship between the Executive and corporate or programme management should be similar to that between the Project Board and the Project Manager; i.e. "As long as work is progressing within laid down constraints, then get on with it. We will back you up."

10.1.7 For small projects

A small project is more likely to be stand-alone. There may be no corporate or programme management involved with the project. In this case the sponsor becomes the Executive by default and would appoint the Project Manager personally. Some of the Project Board roles can be combined, such as the Executive and Senior User roles. There may be no need for any Team Managers, because this role may be filled by the Project Manager. There may be no Project Support needed to assist the Project Manager, and one of the project team may be appointed as Configuration Librarian.

10.2 CAPTURE PREVIOUS LESSONS

10.2.1 Responsibility

Project Manager.

10.2.2 What does the activity do?

- Creates a Lessons Log.
- Looks for lessons from previous similar projects that might be relevant to this project.

10.2.3 Why?

It would be foolish to ignore lessons that might help the project.

10.2.4 How?

- Such sources as quality assurance, programme management and other experienced project managers may have lessons that could avoid problems or provide good advice.

- Once PRINCE2 has been used for several projects, there will be Lessons Reports from them that may be useful.

10.2.5 Information needs

TABLE 10.2

Management information	Usage	Explanation
Lessons Reports from previous projects	Input	Search for lessons that might be useful for the current project.
Lessons Log	Output	Useful lessons transferred from previous reports.

10.2.6 In practice

This depends on a number of factors: how experienced you are; how many Lessons Reports you can call on (probably not many if you are not working in a PRINCE2 environment); whether lessons are recorded by the Project Assurance group or a centre of expertise; how experienced your team members are, and so on.

10.2.7 For small projects

Don't be afraid to ask others. People who have run completely dissimilar projects may remember lessons that will be useful to you, such as "Build enough time in the plan for you to do your project management work as well as any technical work you personally have to do".

10.3 DESIGN AND APPOINT THE PROJECT MANAGEMENT TEAM

10.3.1 Responsibility

Executive and Project Manager.

Starting up a Project (SU)

10.3.2 What does the activity do?

- Proposes the other Project Board members.
- Discusses with the Project Board members whether they will need help to carry out their assurance responsibilities.
- Designs any Project Assurance roles to be delegated.
- Identifies candidates for any Project Assurance roles to be delegated.
- Identifies any required Team Managers – their names may not be known at this point, and can be added later.
- Identifies any Project Support requirements.

10.3.3 Why?

The complete project management team needs to reflect the interests, and have the approval of:

- Corporate or programme management;
- The users of the final product, those who will specify details of the required product;
- The supplier of that product.

Project Board members must decide whether they want independent checks on their particular interests in the project as the project progresses (the Project Assurance part of the role), or whether they can do this verification themselves.

The Project Manager has to decide if any administrative support is needed, such as planning and control tool expertise, configuration management, filing or help with specialist techniques.

10.3.4 How?

- Identify customer areas that will use or control the end product, the commitment required and the level of authority and decision-making that is suitable for the criticality and size of the project (Senior User).
- Identify who will provide the end product, and the level of commitment and authority required from them (Senior Supplier).

- Identify candidates for the roles.
- Check out their availability and provisional agreement.
- Check whether the Project Board members will carry out their own Project Assurance responsibilities.
- Identify candidates for any Project Assurance functions which are to be delegated.
- Check out their availability.
- Consider whether any Team Managers will be required.
- Decide if any Project Support will be required.
- Identify resources for any required support.
- The project management team design is presented to corporate or programme management for approval.
- The Project Manager and corporate or programme management discuss and agree each member's job description, based on the role descriptions found in Appendix B.

10.3.5 Information needs

TABLE 10.3

Management information	Usage	Explanation
Role descriptions	Input	Identify the responsibilities required of each role.
Project management team design	Output	Matching of the standard roles to the project's environment and needs. Presented for corporate or programme management approval.
Job descriptions	Output	Standard role descriptions tailored to the individuals selected for the project management team.

10.3.6 In practice

Corporate or programme management may have already defined some or all of the composition of the Project Board, particularly where the project is part of a programme.

If the project is part of a programme, the use of the programme's assurance and support functions may be imposed.

If the management of many different user areas are looking for Project Board representation, it may be more effective to form a user committee, whose chair represents all their interests on the Project Board. An alternative approach to having lots of suppliers sharing the Senior Supplier role is to appoint the user's purchasing manager as Senior Supplier. This person then controls the suppliers and commits their resources via a series of contracts.

In theory, the Project Board should decide on what action to take about Issue Reports. If the volume is likely to be high, the Board may choose to appoint a Change Authority to assess all issues on their behalf. This Change Authority might, for example, be the same body as those charged with Project Assurance, or may be a small group of representative user managers. If appointed, the Project Board should give a change budget to such a body. This is usually accompanied by a couple of constraints, such as "No more than £X spent on any one change" or "No more than £Y spent in any stage without reference to the Project Board".

10.3.7 For small projects

There may be no need to get approval from any higher level of authority than the Executive. There may be no Project Support functions. If Project Board roles are to be amalgamated, it may be sufficient to use the standard role descriptions listed in Appendix B of this book.

It would be normal practice for Project Board members to carry out their own Project Assurance. In very small projects the Executive and Senior User roles will often be combined. If a department is developing a product for its own use and all the project's resources are from that department, the Senior Supplier and Senior User may also be the same person as the Executive.

10.4 PREPARE THE OUTLINE BUSINESS CASE

10.4.1 Responsibility

Executive.

10.4.2 What does the activity do?

- Begins the preparation of the Business Case from information found either in the project mandate or requested from corporate or programme management. At this point only the reasons for the project may be known, but full financial justification for the project will be developed during initiation.

10.4.3 Why?

PRINCE2 believes that a small amount of time and resource, relative to the likely cost of the project, should be spent in ensuring that the expense of the project is justified.

10.4.4 How?

The Executive:

- Creates the outline Business Case, based on what is currently known about the project;
- Ensures understanding of the project reasons and objectives;
- Identifies how the project will contribute towards corporate or programme management objectives;
- Understands how the project will be funded;
- Learns from any previous lessons on business justification;
- Obtains. where necessary, approval of the outline Business Case from corporate or programme or management.

The Project Manager:

- Creates the Project Product Description;
- Identifies the customer's quality expectations;

Starting up a Project (SU)

- Agrees with the customer's acceptance criteria;
- Checks the feasibility of any target date or cost mentioned in the project mandate or outline Business Case;
- Captures any risks identified while obtaining this information in the Daily Log;
- Any significant risks are summarized as part of the outline Business Case.

10.4.5 Information needs

TABLE 10.4

Management information	Usage	Explanation
Lessons Log	Input	Lessons from earlier projects about preparing a Business Case.
Project mandate	Input	Should contain at least the reasons for the project.
Project Product Description	Output	Records the customer's quality criteria and acceptance criteria.
Daily Log	Updated	Updated with any risks identified during the activity.

10.4.6 In practice

At this early time, only the reasons for wanting the project may be known. You may be lucky and find that there was an earlier feasibility study that estimated some of the benefits, but beware – these are notoriously optimistic.

The Project Manager should remember that it is a responsibility of the Project Board, particularly the Executive, to produce the Business Case, not the Project Manager.

10.4.7 For small projects

There is always the temptation in small projects to assume that a Business Case is not necessary, and its creation a waste of time because it holds you back from getting on with the job. An outline Business Case usually takes only a few lines in a small project, but it is always worthwhile finding out the reasons for the project and doing a few common sense checks on the validity of these reasons. It prevents you from being embarrassed when corporate management ask "Why are you doing this project?"

Example

A long time ago when online computing was just beginning, a large computer company had an offline system that would break down data on futures sales into inventory demands on a number of factories. This was to avoid under- and overproduction of expensive components. A small team of programmers was assembled to produce an online version of the system. When the programs were completed, the sales chief was invited in, seated down in front of a terminal and asked to input a set of sales figures. This took almost an hour. The sales chief then asked how long it would be before the results would appear on the screen. The answer was "about four hours". When the figures were eventually ready, the sales chief had to scroll through about two hundred pages full of the data, which was not as quick as sifting through a printout. The project, although only small in terms of manpower, was a complete waste of time and effort and could have been easily avoided by checking the benefits in an outline Business Case.

10.5 SELECT THE PROJECT APPROACH AND ASSEMBLE THE PROJECT BRIEF

10.5.1 Responsibility

Project Manager.

10.5.2 What does the activity do?

Project Brief:

- Identifies all stakeholders; i.e. those with an interest in the project. Ensures their views are known on the information in the following bullet points;

Starting up a Project (SU)

- Confirms project objectives and desired outcomes;
- Confirms project scope (including any exclusions);
- Identifies any interfaces required of the project's products;
- Identifies project tolerances from programme or corporate management.

Project approach:

- Identifies the operational environment in which the solution must work when delivered;
- Decides on what kind of a solution (project approach) will be provided to fit into that environment to achieve the points made in the outline Business Case and the general method used to provide that solution;
- Identifies the skills required to implement the project approach;
- Identifies any timing implications of the project approach.

The main project approaches to be considered are:

- Build a solution from scratch;
- Take an existing product and modify it;
- Give the job to another organization to do for you;
- Buy a ready-made solution 'off the shelf'.

Finally, assemble the Project Brief.

10.5.3 Why?

The project approach will affect the timescale and costs of the project, plus possibly its control over scope and quality. This information should be made available to the Project Board in deciding whether to initiate the project.

A check should be made that the proposed project approach is in line with the customer/programme's strategy.

The Project Brief is the basis for the Project Board decision on whether to authorize initiation.

10.5.4 How?

- Identify any time, money, resource, operational support or later product extension constraints.
- Check for any direction or guidance on the project approach from earlier documents, such as the project mandate.
- Identify any security constraints.
- Check for any corporate or programme statement of direction which might constrain the choice of project approaches.
- Consider how the product might be brought into use and whether there are any problems which would impact the choice of project approach.
- Check the Lessons Log, current industry thinking and any new techniques or tools available for help with the project approach.
- Produce a range of alternative project approaches.
- Identify the training needs of the alternatives.
- Consider how the product might be brought into use and whether there are any problems which would impact the choice of project approach.
- Compare the alternatives against the gathered information and constraints.
- Prepare a recommendation.
- Compare the information available about the required project against the information required by the Project Board to approve project initiation.
- Gather any missing information.
- Incorporate the outline Business Case.
- Incorporate the Project Product Description.
- Incorporate the project approach.
- Incorporate the project management team structure and role descriptions (or point to where these can be found).
- Record any new risks or issues in the Daily Log.

10.5.5 Information needs

See Table 10.5.

Starting up a Project (SU)

TABLE 10.5

Management information	Usage	Explanation
Corporate statement of direction	Input	Provides any constraints on the project approach.
Project tolerances	Input	Set by corporate or programme management.
Project Product Description	Input	Forms part of the Project Brief.
Outline Business Case	Input	Forms part of the Project Brief.
Project management team	Input	Forms part of the Project Brief.
Project Brief	Output	Summarizes the objectives of the project.
Project approach	Output	Defines how the solution will be provided.

10.5.6 In practice

Be careful about how you go about this. Although the activity title suggests that you can sort out the project approach before doing the Project Brief, you need to do it the other way round. The Project Brief contains the objectives, scope, constraints, and you can't say how you will approach the provision of a solution before you know what the problem and objectives are.

The customer needs to think very carefully about the project approach. Preparation of the above information can avoid the customer being pushed into a project approach which is favoured by a supplier, but later turns out to have problems for the customer, such as lack of flexibility or maintenance difficulties.

Example

> The Swiss branch of a multinational was regularly falling many weeks behind centrally imposed cutover dates to new versions of a system used by branches in all countries. I was asked to look into the situation.

I discovered that, as the system didn't quite fit the local documentation needs of the Swiss branch, instead of adopting its manual procedures, the Swiss branch had accepted an offer from a local software house to modify the system in order to produce the required documentation. This was fine, but later the company realized that the software house had to be called in every time an update to the system was issued by headquarters. Eventually they realized that the changes were taking so long to do that their system was many weeks behind each centrally imposed cutover time. When I checked into the reasons why each update was taking longer, I found that, apart from the increasing complexity of modifying the already modified software, the software house now had only one programmer who understood the system, and she was six months pregnant and about to start her maternity leave!

In your case, there may have been an earlier feasibility study that looked at a number of different approaches for achieving the end objective and selected one that could be the basis for your project. If the project is part of a programme, a Project Brief may have already been provided, thus rendering this process unnecessary.

The Project Manager should informally check out the Project Brief with Project Board members to ensure there are no problems before formal presentation.

10.5.7 For small projects

There may be pressure on the Project Manager to 'get on with the job' and start with incomplete terms of reference. This should be resisted as it opens up the possibility of disagreement later on what the project was supposed to do (its scope). The Project Manager also needs to know how much the solution is worth in order to make appropriate judgements if changes occur later.

10.6 PLAN THE INITIATION STAGE

10.6.1 Responsibility

Project Manager.

Starting up a Project (SU)

10.6.2 What does the activity do?

- Produces a plan for the initiation stage of the project.

(If the initiation stage is to be of a significant size, the Project Manager should consider whether it would be sensible to use the *Controlling a Stage* and *Managing Product Delivery* processes – see chapters 13 and 14 – to control the work.)

10.6.3 Why?

Investigating and establishing the foundation of a project, then preparing a document to get approval to start the project, is important work that needs planning. Since initiation will consume some resources, the Project Board should approve the plan for it.

10.6.4 How?

- Examine the Project Brief and decide how much work is needed in order to produce the Project Initiation Documentation.
- Evaluate the time needed to create the Project Plan.
- Evaluate the time needed to create the next Stage Plan.
- Evaluate the time needed to refine the Business Case.
- Evaluate the time needed to perform risk analysis.
- Create a plan for the initiation stage.
- Submit the initiation Stage Plan for Project Board approval.

10.6.5 Information needs

See Table 10.6.

10.6.6 In practice

The initiation stage should normally be short and inexpensive compared to the cost and time of the whole project; e.g. 2–3 per cent of the whole project.

The Project Initiation Documentation is an extension of the Project Brief and includes details of the project management team and risk

TABLE 10.6

Management information	Usage	Explanation
Lessons Log	Input	There may be lessons to be learned about initiation and/or planning.
Project Brief	Input	Estimate the effort required to produce the initiation stage products. Assess from the project approach what initiation controls will be needed.
Daily Log	Input	Assess whether there are any risks that might affect initiation.
Initiation Stage Plan	Output	A detailed plan of the initiation work for presentation to the Project Board before it can authorize initiation.
Daily Log	Update	Assess whether the plan changes any risks or introduces new ones.

analysis, together with a refined Business Case and Project Plan. The initiation Stage Plan should show the effort and resources to generate the extra information and the plan for the next stage.

If informal communication with members of the Project Board is to be frequent during initiation, this can reduce the need for formal reporting.

10.6.7 For small projects

Initiation may only take a matter of an hour or two and therefore may not need a formal plan.

Chapter 11

Initiating a Project (IP)

All activities are the responsibility of the Project Manager (Figure 11.1).

11.0.1 What does the process do?

- Defines a strategy to cover the quality responsibilities, quality methods and tools to be used.

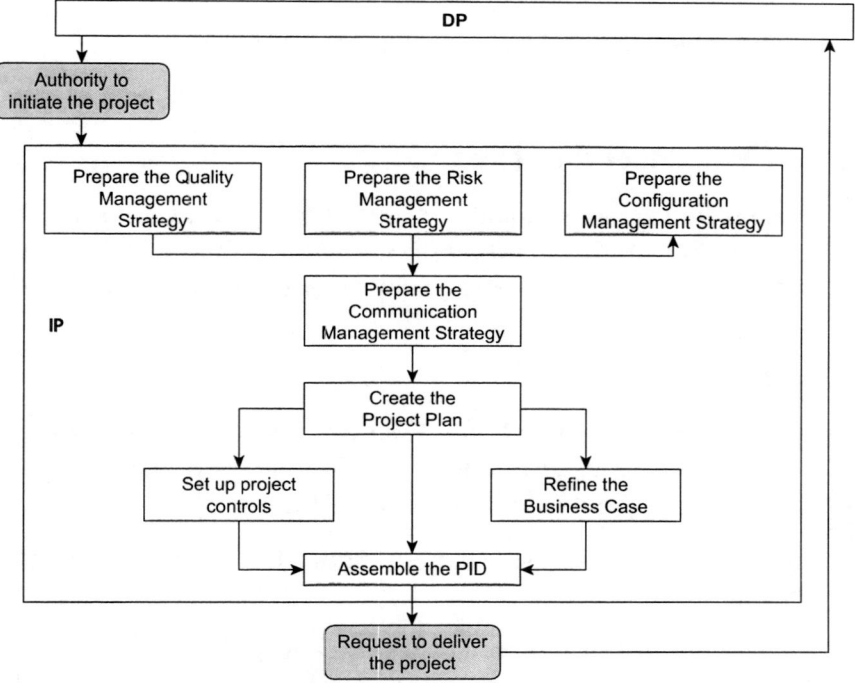

FIGURE 11.1 Initiating a Project

- Defines a strategy for how risks will be managed.
- Defines a strategy for how products and any changes to them will be controlled.
- Defines a strategy for communicating with all interested parties.
- Creates a high-level plan for the whole project.
- Identifies how the project is to be controlled.
- Expands and confirms the existence of a viable Business Case.
- Reassesses the risks facing the project.
- Prepares documentation to ask the decision makers to sign up to the project.
- Prepares the next Stage Plan.

11.0.2 Why?

All stakeholders with an interest in the project should reach agreement on what is to be done, and why it is being done, before major expenditure starts.

11.1 PREPARE THE QUALITY MANAGEMENT STRATEGY

11.1.1 What does the activity do?

- Takes the customer's quality expectations, the quality standards of both the customer and supplier, and the project approach, and defines how the customer's quality expectations will be achieved.

11.1.2 Why?

To be successful, the project must deliver a quality product, as well as meeting time and cost constraints. The means of achieving this quality must be specified before work begins.

Quality work cannot be planned until the customer's quality expectations are known.

The time and cost of the project will be affected by the amount of quality work that has to be done; therefore, quality planning must be done before a realistic Project Plan can be produced.

Initiating a Project (IP)

11.1.3 How?

- Verify that the customer's quality expectations are understood.
- Establish links to any corporate or programme quality assurance function.
- Establish what the customer's quality standards are.
- Establish the supplier's quality standards.
- Decide if there is a need for an independent quality assurance function to have representation on the project management team.
- Identify the quality responsibilities for the project's product of both the customer and supplier in their job descriptions.
- Establish how quality will be achieved.
- Create the Quality Management Strategy.
- Create the Quality Register.

11.1.4 Information needs

See Table 11.1.

11.1.5 In practice

For in-house projects there may be no doubt about the quality standards to be used, but where customer and supplier are from

CARTOON 3 Quality Management Strategy

TABLE 11.1

Management information	Usage	Explanation
Customer's quality expectations	Input	You can't plan to deliver a quality product until you know what the customer's expectation is.
Project approach	Input	This may affect your ability to control quality; for example, if you buy a product 'off the shelf'.
Customer's quality standards	Input	The customer may require the product to be built using their own standards.
Supplier's quality standards	Input	If the product is to be built – in part or in whole – by a supplier, you have to negotiate whether the product is built to the supplier's standards, the customer's, or some combination of the two.
Quality Management Strategy	Output	A document describing the standards to be used and quality responsibilities.
Updated job descriptions	Output	Job descriptions need updating to reflect the quality responsibilities.
Quality Register	Output	Set up to hold details of all planned quality activities, involved personnel, method to be used, dates and results.

different companies it is necessary to agree and document which standards will be used. In such circumstances it is important that the Project Manager specifies how the quality of the products from the supplier will be checked. Sensibly, this would be done by customer involvement in the supplier's quality testing.

11.1.6 For small projects

Even if the customer leaves the quality checking to the developer, there should be customer involvement in specifying the testing environment and the test situations with which the products should successfully cope.

Initiating a Project (IP)

11.2 PREPARE THE RISK MANAGEMENT STRATEGY

11.2.1 What does the activity do?
- Describes the procedure to be used in handling risks.
- Identifies risk responsibilities.
- Defines any tools and techniques to be used in the management of risk.
- Describes any risk reporting requirements.

11.2.2 Why?
Projects bring change, and therefore the possibility of risks is always present. Before a project begins, the method of identifying, analysing and controlling risks must be established.

11.2.3 How?
- Find out if there are any corporate or programme risk strategies, practices and standards that the project should use.
- Review the Lessons Log for any lessons that relate to risk.
- Check if the Daily Log already has any risk entries.
- Create a Risk Management Strategy for the project, including:
    o Procedures to cover identifying, evaluating, assessing, countering, monitoring and communicating the risk tools and techniques to be used;
    o Records to be kept;
    o Risk tolerances;
    o Responsibilities for risk activities.
- Check the Risk Management Strategy with Project Assurance to confirm that it meets the needs of the Project Board.
- Create the Risk Register.
- Transfer any risks currently recorded in the Daily Log to the Risk Register.

11.2.4 Information needs
See Table 11.2.

TABLE 11.2

Management information	Usage	Explanation
Lessons Log	Input	There may be lessons to be learned about managing risks.
Daily Log	Input	Existing risks.
Corporate or programme risk strategies	Input	If available, decide on their use in the project.
Risk Management Strategy	Output	Describe how risks will be identified and managed during the project.
Risk Register	Output	Record any risks transferred from the Daily Log plus any new risks identified when creating the strategy.

11.2.5 In practice

There will always be risks in projects, and when planning and monitoring it is useful to run through a checklist of typical risks that might occur.

11.2.6 For small projects

Risks will be encountered in even the smallest of projects. You may be happy to make a note of them in your Daily Log, rather than create a separate Risk Register, but a reminder is needed to check plans and other management products for potential risks. You may decide to act as risk owner for all risks, but a note should be made in the Daily Log to check on the status of each risk at an appropriate time.

11.3 PREPARE THE CONFIGURATION MANAGEMENT STRATEGY

11.3.1 What does the activity do?

- Defines where and how project management and specialist products will be stored, how they will be identified and how access to them will be controlled.
- Defines how changes will be controlled.

11.3.2 Why?

A project must maintain control over the management and specialist products created and used. Time and money can be wasted if people work from old versions that should have been withdrawn. A product should be protected against unauthorized changes.

Changes are inevitable in any project and, unless carefully controlled, can destroy plans, the scope of the project, quality and benefits, etc.

11.3.3 How?

- Review any corporate or programme configuration management standards that should be used. (Configuration management is fully explained in chapter 9.)
- Consider the project's needs for configuration management (in terms of the number of products there will be, project length and any security requirements).
- Check for any lessons about configuration management in the Lessons Log.
- Check the Risk Register for any risks concerning configuration management.
- Create a Configuration Management Strategy, including:
  o Product identification, control, what product statuses it is important to know;
  o How the accuracy of the records will be checked against the actual product states and versions;
  o Responsibilities – who will act as Configuration Librarian?
  o A change control procedure and records to be kept;
  o Change control responsibilities – whether there will be a Change Authority, or if one is needed.
- Create the Issue Register.
- Transfer to the Issue Register any current issues that were previously recorded in the Daily Log.
- Check the Configuration Management Strategy with Project Assurance to ensure it meets the needs of the Project Board.
- Create Configuration Item Records for the management products created so far.

11.3.4 Information needs

TABLE 11.3

Management information	Usage	Explanation
Lessons Log	Input	Any lessons to be learned about change control or configuration management.
Risk Register	Input	Any existing risks that might affect configuration management or change control.
Corporate or programme strategies	Input	If available, decide on their use in the project.
Configuration Management Strategy	Output	How changes will be identified and managed and how products will be controlled during the project.
Configuration Item Records	Output	For any management products created.
Issue Register	Output	All issues transferred from the Daily Log plus any new issues identified when creating the strategy.

11.3.5 In practice

There is a saying that if a project has more than one product or more than one person working in it, the project is already using configuration management; then, it is just a question of how well it is being done.

A company may have good, working procedures and, possibly, software in use in all its projects and in all operational products. In such a case the Project Manager may have to acknowledge and use the same procedures.

11.3.6 For small projects

You may not need – or be able to afford – a separate Configuration Librarian. You may allocate the job to one of the project team, but everyone on the project needs to understand about version control, how version numbers will be used and where old versions will be stored.

In one small project that I knew of – a project to create a design for a product – one of the systems analysts was appointed Configuration Librarian, in addition to their normal duties. Master copies and archived versions were stored in a filing cabinet. The other analysts were supposed to hand over a copy of their documents whenever they reached a point that could be 'frozen'. If further work was needed later, a copy would be taken with a new version number and the fact recorded by the librarian. Each week the librarian would check that the 'master' documents held in the filing cabinet were the same versions as those that were being worked on by the team. If not, the records were brought up to date.

11.4 PREPARE THE COMMUNICATION MANAGEMENT STRATEGY

11.4.1 What does the activity do?

- Defines the communication lines between the project management team and corporate or programme management, stakeholders, and any other interested parties.
- Defines the timing of all communications and their content.
- Identifies the responsibilities for each communication.

11.4.2 Why?

Good communication between the relevant parties is a major benefit to a project. It avoids delays and misunderstandings.

11.4.3 How?

- Research any corporate or programme standard communication needs, formats and timings.
- Check for any lessons about communication in the Lessons Log.

- Discuss with the Project Board both its requirements for communication and the project's requirements for information from the Project Board.
- Identify all stakeholders and discuss with them their communication needs. (Remember that the Project Board is the source of all decisions – not the stakeholders.)
- Check the Quality, Risk and Configuration Strategies for any communication needs.
- Create a Communication Management Strategy, including:
  o Procedures;
  o Formats;
  o Timings;
  o Responsibilities;
  o Tools and techniques.
- Check the strategy with Project Assurance to ensure that it will meet Project Board needs.
- If any risks or issues are created as a result of this work, update the appropriate register and/or the Daily Log.

11.4.4 Information needs

See Table 11.4.

11.4.5 In practice

There are many people who will identify themselves as stakeholders when in fact they are not, but want as much information as they can get to form part of their 'power base' as they attempt to climb the management ladder. There are also stakeholders who want to be decision makers, or at least opinion-givers. Always check the list with the Project Board and confirm that what the stakeholders want is genuinely needed.

Be careful of line management-oriented companies. Often a senior line manager only reluctantly gives decision-making power to a subordinate, will insist on receiving copies of End Stage Reports and will want to be part of the decision on whether to approve a Stage Plan – or will try to make that decision personally. This happens in

TABLE 11.4

Management information	Usage	Explanation
Lessons Log	Input	Any lessons to be learned about communication.
Risk Register	Input	Any existing risks that might affect project communication.
Issue Register	Input	Any existing issues that might affect project communication.
Corporate or programme strategies	Input	If available, decide on their use in the project.
Quality Management Strategy	Input	Any communication needs defined or inherent in the strategy that need to be recorded.
Risk Management Strategy	Input	Any communication needs defined or inherent in the strategy that need to be recorded.
Configuration Management Strategy	Input	Any communication needs defined or inherent in the strategy that need to be recorded.
Communication Management Strategy	Output	The procedures to be used for communication, plus identification of all who are to receive and provide communication.
Risk Register	Update	Does the strategy affect existing risks or raise new ones?
Issue Register	Update	Does the strategy affect existing issues or raise new ones?

the armed forces in particular, and can delay decisions for days, weeks or even months.

11.4.6 For small projects

The list of stakeholders may be very small, in which case you can probably keep a list in the Daily Log. It is easiest if you can agree that any stakeholder other than the Project Board will just get a copy of reports that you send to the Project Board.

11.5 CREATE THE PROJECT PLAN

11.5.1 What does the activity do?

- Produces the Project Plan.

11.5.2 Why?

As part of its decision on whether to proceed with the project, the Project Board needs to know how much the project is likely to cost and how long it will take. Details of the Project Plan also feed into the Business Case to indicate the viability of the project.

11.5.3 How?

- Understand from the Project Brief what the project has to deliver.
- Identify any corporate or programme standards, or tools that have to be used.
- Discuss with the Project Board the format in which it wants the Project Plan to be produced.
- Understand the project approach to be taken.
- Check for any lessons in the Lessons Log that relate to planning.
- Create the Project Plan (ideally using the PRINCE2 Product-based Planning technique).
- Review the plan against any project (and particularly resource) constraints.
- Modify the plan accordingly.
- Check that the plan meets the requirements of the Quality, Risk and Configuration Management Strategies.
- Check the plan informally with Project Assurance.

11.5.4 Information needs

See Table 11.5.

TABLE 11.5

Management information	Usage	Explanation
Lessons Log	Input	Are there any lessons to be learned about the preparation of a Project Plan?
Risk Register	Input	Are there any existing risks that might affect the Project Plan?
Issue Register	Input	Are there any existing issues that might affect the Project Plan?
Corporate or programme strategies	Input	If available, decide on their use in planning the project.
Project Brief	Input	Details of what the project has to provide, the resources needed and target dates. The project approach gives details of how the solution is to be provided.
Quality Management Strategy	Input	Does the plan meet the needs of the strategy?
Risk Management Strategy	Input	Does the plan meet the needs of the strategy?
Configuration Management Strategy	Input	Does the plan meet the needs of the strategy?
Communication Management Strategy	Input	Does the plan meet the needs of the strategy?
Project Plan	Output	An overview plan of the whole project, showing time frame, resource use and AA.

11.5.5 In practice

A Project Plan is always needed. The breakdown into stages may be encouraged by other considerations than just the project size; e.g. risk assessment, major cash-flow moments (invoice payment or invoice submission) and Project Board membership changes.

11.5.6 For small projects

It may not be necessary to produce Stage Plans if the Project Plan can hold sufficient detail to allow day-to-day control. The Project Manager should decide at what point the inclusion of sufficient details makes the Project Plan too large to be effective.

11.6 SET UP THE PROJECT CONTROLS

11.6.1 What does the activity do?

- Establishes control points for the project based on the project's size, criticality, risk situation, the customer's and supplier's control standards, and the diversity of stakeholders.

11.6.2 Why?

In order to keep the project under control it is important to ensure that:

- The right decisions are made by the right people at the right time;
- The right information is given to the right people at the right frequency and timing.

11.6.3 How?

- Check the Project Brief for corporate or programme standards for project control.
- Check for any lessons in the Lessons Log on project control.
- Check the Risk and Issue Registers for anything that might affect project control.
- Ensure that role descriptions define all decision-making authorities and responsibilities.
- Agree a suitable breakdown of the project into stages with the Project Board.
- Agree the format of reports to the Project Board and stakeholders.
- Agree the frequency of Project Board and stakeholder reports.
- Establish reporting requirements from the team(s) to Project Manager.

TABLE 11.6

Management information	Usage	Explanation
Lessons Log	Input	Are there any lessons to be learned about the controls that should be applied to the project?
Risk Register	Input	Are there any existing risks that might affect controls?
Issue Register	Input	Are there any existing issues that might affect controls?
Project Brief	Input	Identify any corporate or programme strategies or standards that have to be applied.
Quality Management Strategy	Input	What controls are needed to ensure that the required quality is being met?
Risk Management Strategy	Input	What controls are needed to identify and monitor risks?
Configuration Management Strategy	Input	What controls are needed to ensure that issues are captured and managed in a timely fashion? What controls are needed to ensure the management, security and control of the project's products?
Communication Management Strategy	Input	What controls are needed in order to meet the requirements of this strategy.
Project Plan	Update	Assess and confirm where Stage Boundaries need to be set for the level of control required.
Role descriptions	Update	Review against control requirements to ensure there are no gaps or ambiguities in responsibilities.
Project management team	Update	Appoint any extra roles if the controls show a gap in the current allocation of responsibilities.
Project Initiation Documentation	Update	Document the project control requirements.

- Check that there are sufficient risk and Business Case monitoring activities in the plans.

11.6.4 Information needs

See Table 11.6.

11.6.5 In practice

If there are comprehensive control standards in existence, it may be sufficient to indicate the manual containing them and mention any that will not apply, or detail any extra ones. This may require some tailoring of PRINCE2 reports and procedures. The frequency of reports and controls should still be agreed for the project.

11.6.6 For small projects

It may be acceptable to the Project Board for many of the reports to be given orally, but there should always be a formal initiation and a formal close.

11.7 REFINE THE BUSINESS CASE (AND RISKS)

11.7.1 What does the activity do?

- Takes whatever outline Business Case exists for the project, plus the Project Plan, and creates a full Business Case for inclusion in the Project Initiation Documentation.
- Carries out a further risk analysis and management for the project based on the new information created.
- Creates the Benefits Review Plan.

11.7.2 Why?

Before commitment to the project it is important to ensure that there is sufficient justification for the resource expenditure and that there is a sound balance between business justification and the risks.

Initiating a Project (IP)

11.7.3 How?

- If a Business Case was included in the project mandate, check if its circumstances and assumptions have changed.
- Investigate the work reasons for the project with the customer.
- Investigate the business reasons for the project with the Executive.
- Quantify the benefits wherever possible.
- Incorporate the costs from the Project Plan.
- Identify how achievement of each benefit is to be measured.
- Take baseline measures of the current situation of each benefit area against which achievement can be measured.
- Identify when benefits should have been achieved so that benefit reviews can be planned.
- Update the Risk Register with any new or changed risks.
- Modify the Project Plan to reflect any changes caused by risk analysis.

11.7.4 Information needs

TABLE 11.7

Management information	Usage	Explanation
Lessons Log	Input	Are there any lessons to be learned relating to the Business Case?
Project Brief	Input	The outline Business Case is extracted for expansion.
Project Plan	Input	Provides costs and timescale to the Business Case.
Risk Register	Input	Are there any risks that might affect the Business Case?
Benefits Review Plan	Output	A plan for the timing and measurement of expected benefits.
(Detailed) Business Case	Output	Updated with costs and timescale of the project, major risks, expected benefits and benefit tolerances.

11.7.5 In practice

The Project Manager will normally have the work of collating the various inputs to the Business Case.

If the project is part of a programme, the programme will provide the overall Business Case. In such cases it may be sufficient to refer to the programme's Business Case in the Project Initiation Documentation.

11.7.6 For small projects

This should still be done for small projects, but it will be a much simpler task.

11.8 ASSEMBLE THE PROJECT INITIATION DOCUMENTATION

11.8.1 What does the activity do?

- Gathers together the information from the other *Initiating a Project* activities and assembles the Project Initiation Documentation.
- Prepares a plan for the next stage (See Chapter 15 *Managing a Stage Boundary*).

11.8.2 Why?

The Project Initiation Documentation encapsulates all the information needed for the Project Board to make the decision on whether to go ahead with the project or not. It also forms a formal record of the information on which the decision was based, and can be used after the project finishes in order to judge how successful the project was.

If the Project Board makes a general decision to proceed with the project, it needs to have more detailed information about the costs and time of the next Stage Plan before committing the required resources.

Initiating a Project (IP)

11.8.3 How?

- Assemble the required information.
- Decide how best to present the information.
- Create the Project Initiation Documentation.
- Invoke the *Managing a Stage Boundary* process to produce the next Stage Plan.
- Check that the plan meets the requirements of the Quality Management Strategy.
- Distribute the two documents to the Project Board, anyone with Project Assurance roles and any other stakeholders.

11.8.4 Information needs

TABLE 11.8

Management information	Usage	Explanation
Project Brief	Input	Extract the project definition and project approach with any necessary revisions.
(Detailed) Business Case	Input	Include or refer to.
Quality Management Strategy	Input	Include or refer to.
Risk Management Strategy	Input	Include or refer to.
Configuration Management Strategy	Input	Include or refer to.
Communication Management Strategy	Input	Include or refer to.
Project Plan	Input	Include or refer to.
Project Initiation Documentation	Update	All the sections assembled.

11.8.5 In practice

Discuss with the Project Board whether it wants the Project Initiation Documentation to present all the information in full or whether certain sections, such as Product Descriptions and job descriptions, are to be referred to but not included.

11.8.6 For small projects

The Project Initiation Documentation should be a small document. It needs only to include the major points, and refer to the other material that is located in other documentation.

Chapter 12

Directing a Project (DP)

All activities are the responsibility of the Project Board (Figure 12.1).

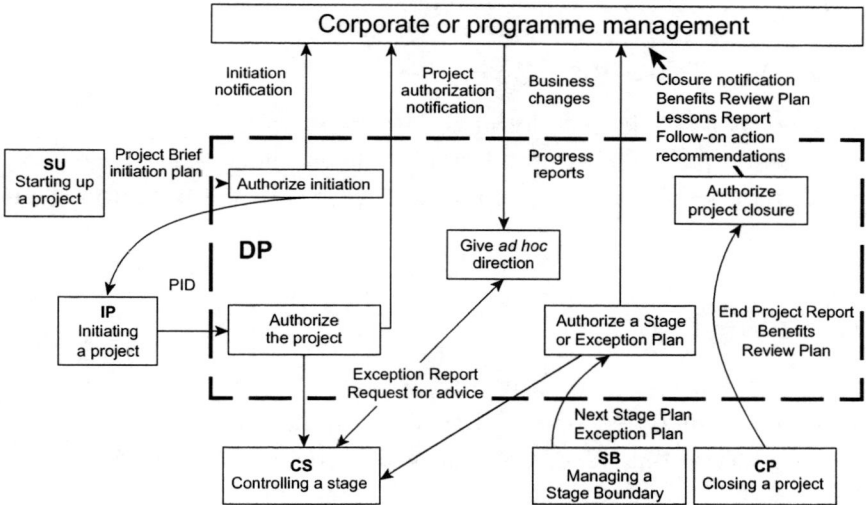

FIGURE 12.1 Directing a Project

12.0.1 What does the process do?

- Authorizes project initiation.
- Authorizes the project.
- Provides liaison with corporate or programme management.
- Advises the Project Manager of any external business events which might impact the project.
- Approves Stage Plans.

- Approves stage closure.
- Decides on any changes to approved products.
- Approves any Exception Plans.
- Gives *ad hoc* advice and direction throughout the project.
- Safeguards the interests of the customer and supplier.
- Approves project closure.

12.0.2 Why?

Day-to-day management is left to the Project Manager, but the Project Board must exercise overall control and make the key decisions.

12.1 AUTHORIZE INITIATION

12.1.1 What does the activity do?

- Checks that adequate terms of reference exist.
- Checks and approves the initiation Stage Plan.
- Commits the resources required to carry out the initiation stage work.

12.1.2 Why?

The initiation stage confirms that a viable project exists and that everybody concerned agrees what is to be done. Like all project work, the effort to do this needs the approval of the Project Board.

12.1.3 How?

- Confirm the terms of reference in the Project Brief; checking, if necessary, with corporate or programme management.
- Review and approve the Project Product Description.
- Confirm the customer's quality expectations and acceptance criteria.
- Check that the outline Business Case shows that there are valid reasons to at least authorize initiation.
- Confirm that the recommended project approach is suitable.

Directing a Project (DP)

- Formally approve appointments to the project management team and confirm that everyone has an agreed role description.
- Check the initiation Stage Plan and approve it, if satisfied.
- Agree tolerance margins for the initiation stage.
- Agree control and reporting arrangements for the initiation stage.
- Inform all stakeholders that initiation has been authorized, and request any support required from them for initiation.
- Commit the resources required by the plan.

12.1.4 Information needs

TABLE 12.1

Management information	Usage	Explanation
Project Brief	Input	Confirm the project definition and project approach.
		Formally confirm project management team appointments.
		Review and approve the Project Product Description.
		Verify the outline Business Case demonstrates a viable project.
Initiation Stage Plan	Input	Commit resources to achieve the plan's products.
Authority to initiate a project	Output	Authority for the Project Manager to proceed into the initiation stage.
Initiation notification	Output	Advise stakeholders and request any necessary support and equipment.

12.1.5 In practice

The Project Board should expect to be heavily involved in the work of the initiation stage and therefore should check and advise the Project Manager of its availability during this stage.

12.1.6 For small projects

This activity can be done informally if the Project Board feels that it is suitable. The stage may be so short that no reporting during the stage is required.

12.2 AUTHORIZE THE PROJECT

12.2.1 What does the activity do?

- Decides whether to proceed with the rest of the project or not.
- Approves the next Stage Plan.

12.2.2 Why?

The activity gives the Project Board a decision point before major resource commitment to the project.

12.2.3 How?

- Confirm that the project's objectives and scope are clearly defined and understood by all.
- Confirm that the objectives are in line with corporate or programme objectives.
- Confirm that all authorities and responsibilities are agreed.
- Confirm that the Business Case is adequate, clear and, wherever possible, measurable.
- Confirm that any useful lessons from previous projects have been incorporated.
- Confirm the existence of a credible Project Plan that is within the project constraints.
- Check that the proposed project controls are prepared and are suitable for the type and size of the project.
- Confirm that the Quality, Risk, Configuration and Communication Management Strategies are prepared and should provide adequate management and control over their areas.
- Confirm tolerance levels for the project have been set by corporate or programme management and are realistic.

Directing a Project (DP)

- Check that the Benefits Review Plan is established, covers all the expected benefits, and provides details of how and when each benefit will be measured.
- Have any desired changes made to the draft Project Initiation Documentation.
- Check that the next Stage Plan is reasonable and matches that portion of the Project Plan.
- Establish the tolerances for the next stage.
- Give written approval for the next Stage Plan (or not, if unhappy with any of the details).
- Arrange a date for the next stage's end stage assessment.
- Notify all stakeholders that the project has been authorized.

12.2.4 Information needs

TABLE 12.2

Management information	Usage	Explanation
Lessons Log	Input	Confirm that any lessons from previous projects have been reviewed and incorporated.
Project Initiation Documentation	Input	For review and approval.
Benefits Review Plan	Input	For review and approval.
Project authorization notification	Output	Notify corporate or programme management that the project has been authorized.
Premature close instruction	Output	If it is decided not to proceed with the project.

12.2.5 In practice

The Project Manager should have been in regular informal contact with the Project Board to ensure that there will be no surprises when the Project Initiation Documentation is presented. If this contact has been maintained, the above list should be a quick confirmation.

If some minor item in the Project Initiation Documentation needs further work but in general the Project Board is satisfied, then approval to proceed can be given with the proviso that the corrective work be done – usually with a target date.

Very often the Project Board members are so busy with day-to-day duties that it is not easy to arrange an end stage assessment at short notice. It is better to plan the next end stage assessment date at the end of the previous stage.

12.2.6 For small projects

The Project Initiation Documentation details may have been discussed and agreed informally over a (short) period of time. It may be sufficient for the Project Board to give the go-ahead when the last piece of information is presented without a formal full presentation. Approval to proceed should still be confirmed in writing as an important management document.

12.3 AUTHORIZE A STAGE OR EXCEPTION PLAN

12.3.1 What does the activity do?

- The activity authorizes each stage (except initiation) and any Exception Plans that are needed.

12.3.2 Why?

An important control for the Project Board is to approve only one stage at a time. At the end of one stage the Project Manager has to justify both progress so far and the next Stage Plan before being allowed to continue.

12.3.3 How?

- Compare the results of the current stage against the approved Stage Plan.
- Assess progress against the Project Plan.

Directing a Project (DP)

- Assess the acceptability of the next Stage Plan against the Project Plan.
- Review the prospects of achieving the Business Case.
- Review the risks facing the project.
- Get direction from corporate or programme management if the project is forecast to exceed tolerances, or there is a significant change to the Business Case.
- Review tolerances for the next stage.
- Review reporting arrangements for the next stage.
- Give approval to move into the next stage (if satisfied).

12.3.4 Information needs

TABLE 12.3

Management information	Usage	Explanation
End Stage Report	Input	How the current stage performed.
Next Stage Plan (or Exception Plan)	Input	Review and approve any new Product Descriptions and confirm the achievability of the plan. Set tolerances.
Risk Register	Input	Check that the risk exposure is still acceptable.
Benefits Review Plan	Input	Review and approve any updates.
Project Initiation Documentation	Input	Confirm that the Project Plan is still achievable and that a viable Business Case is still demonstrated.
Stage authorization	Output	Authorize the Project Manager to proceed with the next stage.

12.3.5 In practice

The Project Board can stop the project for any reason; e.g. if the Business Case becomes invalid, project tolerances are going to be exceeded, product quality is unacceptable or the risks become unacceptably high.

If the end stage assessment date was arranged some time ago and occurs before the actual end of the stage, the Project Board can give provisional approval to proceed based on one or more target dates being met to complete the current stage.

If the stage finishes before the planned assessment date, interim approval can be given to do some of the next stage work before formal approval is given. In such a case, the Project Board would clarify what work was to be done before the assessment, rather than give carte blanche to the Project Manager.

12.3.6 For small projects

The decisions can be made informally, but the Project Board should still carry out the above activities and a record should be kept of the decisions.

12.4 GIVE *AD HOC* DIRECTION

12.4.1 What does the activity do?

- Advises the Project Manager about any external events which impact the project.
- Gives direction to the Project Manager when asked for advice or a decision about an issue.
- Advises on, or approves, any changes to the project management team.
- Makes decisions on the actions to take on receipt of any Exception Reports.

12.4.2 Why?

There may be a need for occasional and immediate Project Board direction outside end stage assessments.

12.4.3 How?

- Check for external events, such as business changes, which might affect the project's Business Case or risk exposure, and keep the Project Manager aware of this information.

Directing a Project (DP)

- Respond to any requests for advice and guidance from the Project Manager.
- Monitor any allocated risk situations.
- Keep a check on the status of the stage by reviewing Highlight Reports.
- Make decisions on any Exception Reports.
- Make decisions on any requests for concessions where a product is not fully meeting its specification.
- Ensure that the project remains focused on its objectives and the achievement of its Business Case.
- Keep corporate or programme management and stakeholders advised of project progress.
- Ask for any required advice or direction from corporate or programme management.
- Make decisions about any necessary changes to the project management team.
- Make decisions on Issue Reports brought to the attention of the Project Board.

12.4.4 Information needs

TABLE 12.4

Management information	Usage	Explanation
Highlight Report	Input	Review to understand the stage and project status.
Exception Report	Input	Review in order to decide on a response.
Issue Report	Input	Review in order to decide on a response.
Informal requests for advice	Input	Review in order to decide on a response.
External influences	Input	Advise the Project Manager of any changes in the project environment.
Project Board composition	Update	Revise if there is any change to the composition.
Instructions or advice	Output	Response to requests.

12.4.5 In practice

The key activity in this process is deciding what action, if any, should be taken in response to any issues, including requests for change and off-specifications. The procedure to be followed should have been agreed and documented in the Project Initiation Documentation.

This process does not encourage general interference with the work of the Project Manager. The need for Project Board direction will be triggered by either a problem reported in a Highlight Report or an Exception Report, or an external event that the Project Board is monitoring on behalf of the project.

12.4.6 For small projects

It may be sufficient for the Project Board and Project Manager to agree informally on what action, if any, should be taken in response to an issue as soon as it is documented.

There may be agreement that any Highlight or Exception Reports can be delivered orally to the Project Board.

12.5 AUTHORIZE PROJECT CLOSURE

12.5.1 What does the activity do?

- Checks that the objectives of the project have been met.
- Checks that there are no loose ends.
- Advises senior management of the project's termination.
- Recommends a plan for checking on the achievement of the expected benefits.

12.5.2 Why?

There must be a defined end to a project in order to judge its success. The Project Board must assure itself that the project's products have been handed over and are acceptable. Where contracts (and money) are involved, there must be agreement between customer and supplier that the work contracted has been completed.

Directing a Project (DP)

12.5.3 How?

- The Senior Supplier gains acceptance from the Senior User(s) and Executive that all the required products have been delivered and the acceptance criteria have been met.
- Check that there has been a satisfactory handover of the finished product to those responsible for its use and support.
- Check that there are no outstanding issues.
- Review the performance of the project against the original and current versions of the Project Initiation Documentation.
- Review and approve the End Project Report.
- Approve the follow-on action recommendations contained in the End Project Report and pass them to the appropriate group.
- Approve the Lessons Report and pass it to the appropriate body.
- Release the resources allocated to the project.
- Confirm that the Benefits Review Plan addresses all the benefits whose achievement cannot yet be measured, and transfer responsibility for carrying out this plan to corporate or programme management.
- Advise corporate or programme management of the project's closure.
- The Project Board should issue a project closure notification to disband the project management team and advise suppliers of the closing date for costs to be charged to the project.

12.5.4 Information needs

See Table 12.5.

12.5.5 In practice

It is sensible for the Project Manager to obtain written confirmation from the users and those who will support the final product that they have accepted the outcome of the project, and present this confirmation to the Project Board.

12.5.6 For small projects

Not all the reports may be needed, but there should still be a formal sign-off by the Project Board to close the project.

TABLE 12.5

Management information	Usage	Explanation
User acceptance	Input	Confirm that the product has user acceptance.
Operations and maintenance acceptance	Input	Confirm that the product is accepted by those who will support and operate the final product.
Project Initiation Documentation	Input	For comparison against actual results.
End Project Report	Input	Review project performance.
Lessons Report	Distribute	Review and agree who should receive it.
Benefits Review Plan	Distribute	Confirm that all expected benefits are covered.
Follow-on action recommendations	Distribute	Review and agree who should receive them.

Chapter 13

Controlling a Stage (CS)

All activities are the responsibility of the Project Manager (Figure 13.1).

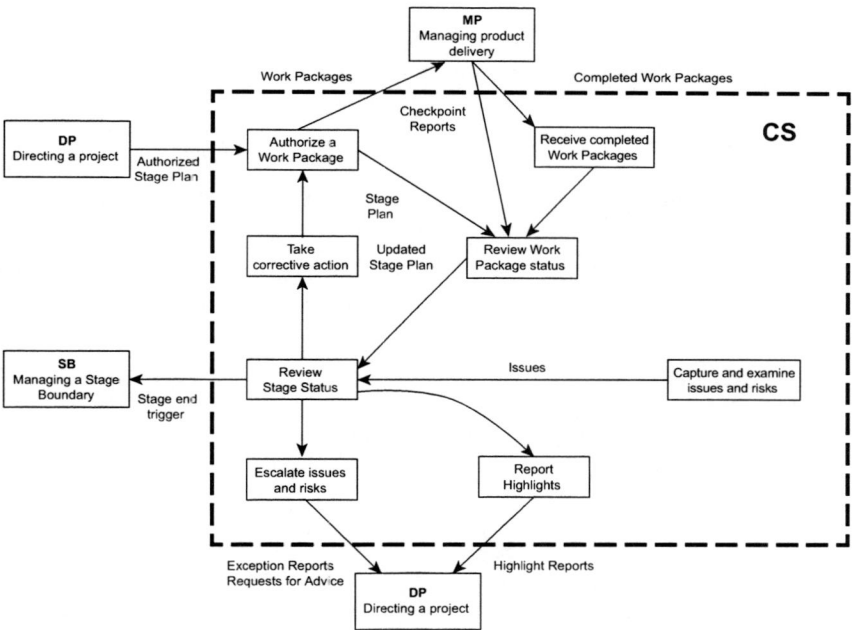

FIGURE 13.1 Controlling a Stage

13.0.1 What does the process do?

- Manages the stage from stage approval to completion.

13.0.2 Why?

The production of the stage's product within budget and schedule, and to the required quality, must be driven by the Project Manager and requires careful monitoring and control.

13.1 AUTHORIZE A WORK PACKAGE

13.1.1 What does the activity do?

- Allocates work to be done to a team or individual, based on the needs of the current Stage Plan.
- Ensures that any work handed out is accompanied by measurements such as target dates, the customer's quality expectations, delivery and reporting dates.
- Ensures that agreement has been reached with the recipient on the reasonableness of the work demands.

13.1.2 Why?

The Project Manager must control the sequence of at least the major activities of a stage and when they begin. This ensures that the Project Manager knows what those working on the project are doing, and that the Stage Plan correctly reflects the work and progress.

13.1.3 How?

- Ensure that there are Product Descriptions for the work to be done and that these are complete.
- Make up the Work Package (see the Work Package Product Description – Appendix A.29 – for the information required).
- Discuss the Work Package with the Team Manager.
- Jointly assess any risks or problems and modify the Work Package and Risk Register as necessary.
- Review and agree the Team Plan to ensure that sufficient resources and time have been allocated for the work.
- Agree sensible tolerances for the Work Package. These must be within the stage tolerances given to the Project Manager. Quality tolerances are in the Product Descriptions, but time, cost and scope tolerances should be defined.

Controlling a Stage (CS)

- Record the agreement of the Team Manager in the Work Package.
- Update the Stage Plan with any adjustments made as part of the agreement.
- Update the relevant Configuration Item Records to reflect their allocation.
- Update the Quality Register with details of agreed additional quality checking activities and resources.
- Update the Risk Register with any new or changed risks.

13.1.4 Information needs

TABLE 13.1

Management information	Usage	Explanation
Stage Plan	Input	Provides products to be developed and available tolerances.
Product Description	Input	Describes the products to be developed.
Quality Management Strategy	Input	Details of quality standards and procedures.
Configuration Management Strategy	Input	Details of product identification, submission, status options.
Project controls	Input	Progress reporting requirements.
Work Package	Output	
Team Plan	Input	Confirm that it meets the requirements of the Work Package.
Stage Plan	Update	Reflect the timings and effort in the Team Plan.
Configuration Item Records	Update	Reflect the status that the products have been allocated.
Quality Register	Update	Add the planned quality checks and personnel.
Risk Register	Update	Does the work authorized change any risks or bring up new ones?

13.1.5 In practice

If the Team Manager represents a different company, then this activity should be used formally with appropriate documentation of both the Work Package and the Team Manager's agreement to its targets. In such cases it is sensible to specifically refer to the manner of work allocation in the contract.

If the Stage Plan were to be merely a summary of the start and finish times of major deliverables from a number of teams, there would be a Work Package for each of these major deliverables. There should be definitions in the section of the relevant Product Description on the quality methods and quality skills required of those who will check the product on behalf of the Project Manager (and/or Project Board), and at which points in the product's development.

If a Team Manager uses contractors to deliver any parts of a Work Package, it is recommended that this is also handled in the same way, i.e. as a Work Package between the Team Manager and the third party.

13.1.6 For small projects

The same process can be used if the work is being allocated to an individual, rather than to a team, but it can be done less formally. The Project Manager should, however, consider if a record is needed for any later appraisal of an individual's performance. Where the Project Manager is also personally performing the work, the process should not be needed.

13.2 REVIEW WORK PACKAGE STATUS

13.2.1 What does the activity do?

- Gathers information to update the Stage Plan to reflect actual progress, effort expended and quality work carried out.

13.2.2 Why?

In order to control the stage and make sensible decisions on what, if any, adjustments need to be made, it is necessary to gather information

Controlling a Stage (CS)

on what has actually happened and be able to compare this against what was planned.

13.2.3 How?

- Collect Checkpoint Reports.
- Collect Team Plan progress information.
- Obtain estimates on time, cost and effort needed to complete work which is in progress.
- Check whether sufficient resources are available to complete the work as now estimated.
- Check the Quality Register for feedback on quality activities.
- Check that the Configuration Item Records reflect changes in the status of the Work Package products.
- Note any potential or real problems.
- Update the Risk and Issue Registers if required.
- Update the Stage Plan with the information.

13.2.4 Information needs

TABLE 13.2

Management information	Usage	Explanation
Checkpoint Reports	Input	Work Package progress.
Team Plan	Input	Details of effort and cost expended.
Work Package	Input	Reminder of interfaces.
Quality Register	Input	Current status of quality inspections.
Risk Register	Update	Any changes or new risks.
Issue Register	Update	Any changes or new issues.
Stage Plan	Update	Update with details of the work done.

13.2.5 In practice

According to the size and environment of the project, the Checkpoint Reports may be written or verbal.

In fixed-price contracts the Project Manager may not be interested in the gathering of costs or the remaining effort of team work, just any changes to estimated completion dates and any risks and/or issues.

13.2.6 For small projects

The Checkpoint Reports may be verbal.

13.3 RECEIVE COMPLETED WORK PACKAGES

13.3.1 What does the activity do?

- Records the completion and return of approved Work Packages.

13.3.2 Why?

Where work has been recorded as approved to a team or individual, there should be a matching activity to record the return of the completed product and its acceptance (or otherwise).

13.3.3 How?

- Check the delivery against the requirements of the Work Package.
- Check that any quality activities have been completed satisfactorily.
- Check that the recipients have accepted the products.
- Ensure that the delivered products have been baselined.
- Document any relevant team member appraisal information.
- Pass information about completion to update the Stage Plan.

13.3.4 Information needs

See Table 13.3.

13.3.5 In practice

This activity is ongoing throughout the stage.

TABLE 13.3

Management information	Usage	Explanation
Completed Work Package	Input	Check delivery.
Quality Register	Input	Check for satisfactory quality results.
Stage Plan	Update	Work Package completion.
Configuration Item Records	Update	Status.

13.3.6 For small projects

The formality of this activity will relate to the formality of the activity *Authorize a Work Package*. Both will often be informal and brief.

13.4 CAPTURE AND EXAMINE ISSUES AND RISKS

For issues:

13.4.1 What does the activity do?

- Makes a note in the Daily Log of any issues that can be dealt with by the Project Manager informally.
- Captures, log and categorizes new Issue Reports.
- Analyses each new Issue Report and recommends a course of action.
- Reviews each open Issue Report for any changes to its circumstances or impact and potentially makes a new recommendation.
- Reviews all open Issue Reports for any impact on the project risks or the Business Case.

13.4.2 Why?

At any time during the project a problem may occur, a change may be requested or the answer to a question may be sought. If these are missed, it may mean that the project fails to deliver what is required. Alternatively the project may run into some other trouble that could have been foreseen had the issue been noted at the time it arose. There must be a process to capture these so that they can be presented for the appropriate decision and response.

Having captured all issues, these should be examined for impact.

13.4.3 How?

- Ensure that all possible sources of issues are being monitored.
- Enter new issues on the Issue Register.
- Assemble all pertinent information about the issue.
- Carry out impact analysis on the technical effort required to resolve the issue.
- Update the Risk Register if the issue reveals a new risk or a change to a known risk.
- Assess whether the issue or its resolution would impact the Business Case.
- Prepare a recommended course of action.
- Update the Issue Register with the impact analysis result.

For risks:

13.4.4 What does the activity do?

- Enters the risk in the Risk Register.
- Assesses the risk.

13.4.5 Why?

Like an issue, a risk may arise at any time. The situation should be monitored constantly for new risks and for changes in existing risks.

13.4.6 How?

- Ensure that all possible sources of risk are being monitored.
- Enter new risks on the Risk Register.
- Perform risk analysis on the risk.
- Assess whether a new risk or its resolution would impact the Stage Plan, Project Plan and/or Business Case.

Controlling a Stage (CS)

- Review existing risks for any change.
- Plan selected responses.
- Check the Risk Management Strategy and Communication Management Strategy for any reporting needs.

13.4.7 Information needs

TABLE 13.4

Management information	Usage	Explanation
Stage Plan	Input	Assess the impact of new issues or risks.
Project Plan	Input	Assess the impact of new issues or risks.
Business Case	Input	Assess the impact of new issues or risks.
Configuration Management Strategy	Input	Details of the change control procedure and reporting.
Communication Management Strategy	Input	Reporting needs.
Daily Log	Update	Add any issues which can be handled informally.
Issue Report	Create	Issue that needs to be handled formally.
Issue Register	Update	New formal issues.
Risk Register	Update	New risks.

13.4.8 In practice

The Project Manager may ask a Team Manager or team member to carry out the analysis, depending on the expertise required. It will be necessary to analyse the financial impact as well as the technical impact. It is part of the Project Assurance role of the Executive to review this. Thought should be given to the time required to do this analysis when designing the project management team, or at least the Executive's Project Assurance role. When producing Stage or Team Plans, an allowance should always be made for the time that the senior specialist people are likely to spend in performing impact analysis on project issues. Thought should be given to the likely volume of issues.

Possible responses to issues or risks are to *Take corrective action*, seek advice from the Project Board or raise an Exception Report in the activity *Escalate issues and risks* (see section 13.8), part of the *Controlling a Stage* process. Before taking any of these actions, the Project Manager should run through the *Review stage status* activity (see section 13.5) in the *Controlling a Stage* process in order to understand the full situation.

A check should be made to ensure that the procedure covers not only requests to change the specification but also potential failure to meet the specification; potential deviations from objectives or plans; and questions about aspects of the project which require answers.

13.4.9 For small projects

Requests for change or failures on the part of the supplier still need to be documented as part of the audit trail of the project.

The Project Manager may be able to carry out impact analysis as soon as the Issue Report or risk is presented and get a decision on the action to take. Thus, in practice, it may be possible to combine the capture and examination processes with the taking of corrective action or the escalation of the Issue Report to the Project Board for a decision.

13.5 REVIEW STAGE STATUS

13.5.1 What does the activity do?

- Provides a regular reassessment of the status of the stage.
- Triggers new work.
- Triggers corrective action for any problems.
- Provides the information for progress reporting.

13.5.2 Why?

It is better to check the status of a stage on a regular basis and take action to avoid potential problems than have problems come as a surprise and then have to react to them.

Controlling a Stage (CS)

13.5.3 How?

- Review Checkpoint Reports.
- Check the status of quality checks.
- Review progress against the Stage Plan.
- Where useful, request a Product Status Account to verify that records and actual progress match.
- Review resource and money expenditure.
- Review the impact of any implemented issues on Stage and Project Plans.
- Assess if the stage and project will remain within tolerances.
- Check the continuing validity of the Business Case.
- Check for changes in the status of any risks.
- Check for any changes that are external to the project but that may impact on it.

13.5.4 Information needs

TABLE 13.5

Management information	Usage	Explanation
Quality Register	Input	Status of quality work.
Product Status Account	Input	Any variation between planned and actual progress.
Issue Register	Input	Status.
Risk Register	Input	Status.
Checkpoint Reports	Input	Status of Work Packages.
Business Case	Input	Impact of any issues and risks.
Project Plan	Input	Impact of any issues and risks.
Benefits Review Plan	Input	Any benefits due?
Stage Plan	Update	Review status and update from forecast.
Lessons Log	Update	New lessons.
Issue Register	Update	New or modified issues.
Risk Register	Update	New or modified risks.

13.5.5 In practice

The activity should be viewed as one that is happening continuously throughout a stage, rather than one that is done, for example, every two weeks. Each activity may not need to be daily, but the Project Manager should ensure that there are sufficient monitoring points (and people allocated to do them) to keep a continuous check. This does not mean that there should always be an instant change of plan in reaction to each slight deviation, but rather an extra monitoring point that would produce a forecast of the potential impact if the situation were to get worse, and a tolerance setting at which to trigger remedial work.

A change that affects the Business Case or the risk situation may come at any time. As well as trying to identify such a change as it occurs, it is useful to review the assumptions on which the Business Case and risks are based on a formal and regular basis.

The Project Manager may seek guidance on any issue from the Project Board, and should always do so if there is a threat to the stage or project tolerances.

13.5.6 For small projects

These activities are still required. The Project Manager should make a decision about their frequency according to the project situation and environment.

13.6 REPORT HIGHLIGHTS

13.6.1 What does the activity do?

- Produces Highlight Reports for the Project Board.

13.6.2 Why?

The Project Board and stakeholders need to be kept informed of project progress if they are to exercise proper control over the project. Rather than have regular progress meetings, reports at regular intervals are recommended between the assessments at the end of each stage.

Controlling a Stage (CS)

The Project Board decides the frequency of the reports during project initiation.

13.6.3 How?

- Collate the information from any Checkpoint Reports made since the last Highlight Report.
- Identify any significant Stage Plan revisions made since the last report.
- Identify any current or potential risks to the Business Case.
- Identify any change to other risks.
- Assess the Issue Register for any potential problems that require Project Board attention.
- Review the previous Highlight Report for what was forecast to be done in this period.
- Prepare a Highlight Report for the Project Board, including a review of the progress forecast in the previous Highlight Report.
- Check the Communication Management Strategy for stakeholders who should receive a copy of this Highlight Report.

13.6.4 Information needs

TABLE 13.6

Management information	Usage	Explanation
Checkpoint Reports	Input	Basis for Highlight Report.
Previous Highlight Report	Input	What actions and products were promised?
Risk Register	Input	Status.
Issue Register	Input	Status.
Quality Register	Input	Status.
Stage Plan	Input	Status.
Daily Log	Input	Status.
Communication Management Strategy	Input	Who should receive copies?
Highlight Report	Output	Progress report for the Project Board.

13.6.5 In practice

Input should come from the activity *Review the Work Package status* in the *Controlling a Stage* process.

The Highlight Report is a formal means of giving a progress update from the Project Manager to the Project Board. It can be used to bring to Project Board attention any failing in resources not under the direct control of the Project Manager, and to give early warning of any potential problems that could be avoided with Project Board attention.

The report should be kept brief in order to hold the attention of busy senior management.

It does not prevent informal contact between Project Manager and the Project Board if there is an urgent need for information to be passed, or advice sought.

13.6.6 For small projects

The Highlight Report need not be in writing if the Project Board agrees to a verbal one.

13.7 TAKE CORRECTIVE ACTION

13.7.1 What does the activity do?

- Within the limits of the tolerance margins established by the Project Board, the Project Manager takes action to remedy any problems that arise.

13.7.2 Why?

Failing to take action when the project is drifting away from the Stage Plan risks loss of control.

13.7.3 How?

- Assemble information about any plan deviation.
- Identify possible solutions.

Controlling a Stage (CS)

- Obtain any necessary advice from the Project Board on the proposed corrective actions.
- Create new Work Packages or amend existing ones to reflect the corrective actions.
- Update, where necessary, the Stage Plan, Configuration Item Records, Issue Reports, Issue and Risk Registers with the action taken.

13.7.4 Information needs

TABLE 13.7

Management information	Usage	Explanation
Daily Log	Input	Information on any plan deviation.
Issue Register	Update	Relevant information and updated with corrective actions.
Risk Register	Update	Relevant information and updated with corrective actions.
Issue Report	Update	Relevant information and updated with corrective actions.
New Work Package	Create	To take corrective action.
Stage Plan	Update	Any corrective actions.
Configuration Item Records	Update	Update the information on any affected products.

13.7.5 In practice

This activity is normally triggered by the activity *Review stage status* (section 13.5) and typically deals with seeking advice from the Project Board and acting on that advice. The situation leading to the need to take corrective action should be formally recorded as part of the project audit trail, and the Issue Register is the easiest and most available means of doing this. Many of the reasons for corrective action will be issues raised by other people.

13.7.6 For small projects

It is still important to put in the Daily Log why plans were changed. Much of the corrective action can be taken without changing plans, such as by having a word with the Team Manager or team member who is causing the problem.

13.8 ESCALATE ISSUES AND RISKS

13.8.1 What does the activity do?

- Where an issue threatens to go beyond tolerances and the Project Manager feels that they cannot take corrective action within the authority limits imposed by the Project Board, the situation is brought to the attention of the Project Board for advice.

13.8.2 Why?

Part of the concept of *management by exception* is that the Project Manager will bring to the immediate attention of the Project Board anything that can be forecast to drive the plan outside the tolerance limits agreed with the Project Board. This is part of the method by which the Project Board stays in overall control.

13.8.3 How?

- Review the impact analysis of the deviation.
- Identify and evaluate options for recovery.
- Select a recommendation.
- Make out an Exception Report to the Project Board, detailing the problem.

13.8.4 Information needs

See Table 13.8.

13.8.5 In practice

If it is likely to take some time to gather all the information required for an Exception Report, it is sensible to alert the Project Board to the

Controlling a Stage (CS)

TABLE 13.8

Management information	Usage	Explanation
Project Plan	Input	Project status and impact of the deviation.
Stage Plan	Input	Extent of the deviation.
Business Case	Input	Impact of options.
Issue Report	Update	Details of the deviation updated with Project Board response.
Issue Register	Update	Details of the deviation updated with Project Board response.
Risk Register	Update	Details of the deviation updated with Project Board response.
Exception Report	Output	Situation report with options and recommendation.

situation immediately and follow up with the Exception Report when all data has been gathered.

There are many reasons why the tolerances set for a plan might come under threat: the plan could have been too optimistic; resources may not be performing at expected levels; unexpected activities or events, such as illness, may have arisen. The opposite may also be true: the work may finish earlier than the plan's time tolerance or cost less than the budget tolerance.

The most likely cause of a deviation beyond tolerance margins is the work involved in implementing one or more Issue Reports. Let's be clear about where a Project Manager stands here. Tolerances are not there to allow the Project Manager (or Team Manager) to 'fit in' change requests. They are there because planning is not an exact science. If the customer wants to add new facilities or change those that were specified, this should lead to the provision of more cash and time from the Project Board. So the Exception Report would say, "You've changed your mind. This is what it will cost you. Do you want to provide the extra cash and time?"

Another reason for a forecast deviation may be an off-specification; i.e. some failing of the current solution to meet part of the specification. The onus here is on the Project Manager to find a remedy within the current tolerances. Only if this cannot be done should the Project Manager resort to an Exception Report.

A Team Manager should act in the same way as the Project Manager when dealing with issues; i.e. the tolerances for the Work Package are not there to pay for any extra work that the Project Manager may request, and the Team Manager should try to find a remedy for any off-specifications in the team's work within the Work Package tolerances before reporting the problem to the Project Manager.

13.8.6 For small projects

The formality of this process will relate to the formality of the activity *Report Highlights* (section 13.6). Both will often be informal and brief.

Any event that gives the possibility of exceeding stage or project tolerances should be escalated to the Project Board as soon as possible. There may be an agreement with the Project Board to do this verbally, rather than in a document, but the Project Manager should consider whether it is better to document the matter for possible later reference.

Chapter 14

Managing Product Delivery (MP)

All activities are the responsibility of the Team Manager (Figure 14.1).

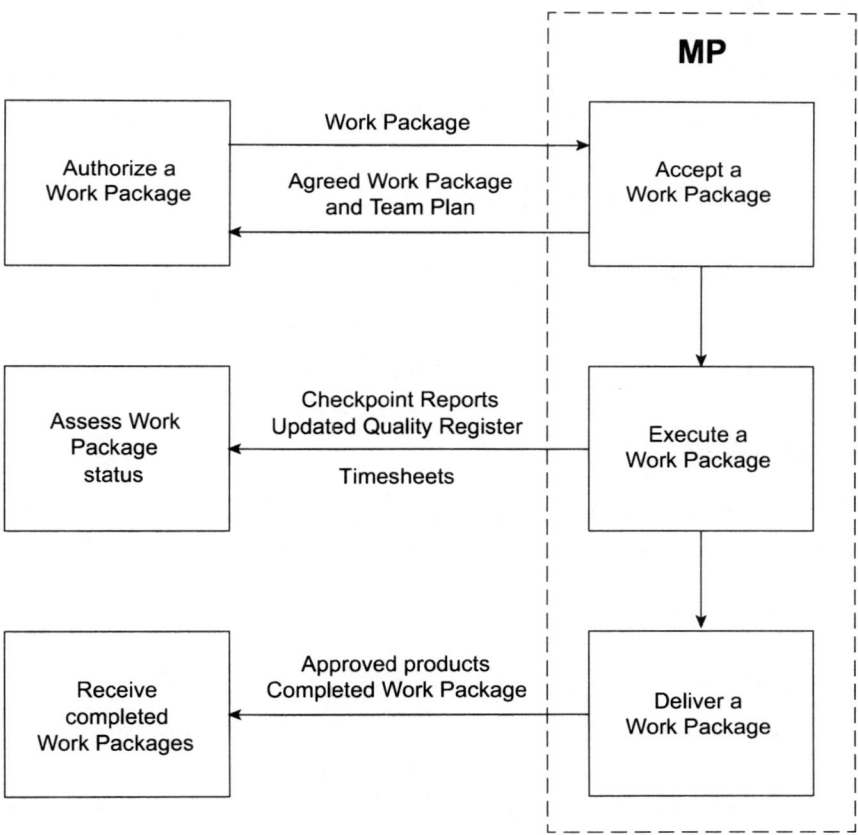

FIGURE 14.1 Managing Product Delivery

14.0.1 What does the process do?

- Agrees work requirements with the Project Manager.
- Completes the work.
- Keeps the Project Manager informed on progress, quality and any problems.
- Gets approval for the finished work.
- Notifies the Project Manager that the work is finished.

14.0.2 Why?

Where the Project Manager delegates work, there must be appropriate steps by the team or person to whom the work is delegated to indicate understanding and acceptance of the work. While the work is being done, there may be a need to report progress and confirm quality checking. When the work is complete there should be an agreed way of confirming the satisfactory completion.

14.1 ACCEPT A WORK PACKAGE

14.1.1 What does the activity do?

- Agrees the details of a Work Package with the Project Manager.
- Plans the work necessary to complete the Work Package.

14.1.2 Why?

There must be understanding and agreement between a Team Manager (or an individual) and the Project Manager on any delegated work.

14.1.3 How?

- Agree with the Project Manager on what is to be delivered.
- Ensure that the quality requirements are clear.
- Identify any independent people who must be involved in quality checking.
- Identify any target dates and/or constraints for the work.

Managing Product Delivery (MP)

- Identify any reporting requirements.
- Understand how the products of the Work Package are to be handed over when complete.
- Make a Team Plan to do the work.
- Assess the Team Plan for risks.
- Adjust the plan or negotiate a change to the Work Package so that it is achievable within the agreed constraints.
- Agree suitable tolerance margins for the Work Package.

14.1.4 Information needs

TABLE 14.1

Management information	Usage	Explanation
Work Package	Approve	
Team Plan	Output	Plan to complete Work Package tasks.
Quality Register	Update	Additional information.
Risk Register	Update	Any new or changed risks.

14.1.5 In practice

Where the Team Manager works for an external contractor, care should be taken to ensure that all the work requirements, as defined above, are understood. A Team Plan for the work will have to be created before the Team Manager can confirm the ability to meet target dates. A Team Manager should avoid pressure from the Project Manager or management within their own company to agree to a commitment before checking that the targets can be achieved. This may include confirmation with the Senior Supplier that the necessary resources will be made available.

14.1.6 For small projects

If it is just a single team working directly under the Project Manager, then the activities in the processes *Controlling a Stage* (see chapter

13) and *Managing Product Delivery* (see chapter 14) of agreeing work that the Project Manager wants to have done will simply be an agreement between the Project Manager and the individual team member. This can either be done formally or informally. The same points need to be covered, but common sense will indicate how much should be documented. The Project Manager should consider whether a record of the work needs to be kept for any future performance appraisal of the individual. It is easy to think that a formal Work Package is not required and, for simple tasks, this may be so, but following the structure and information requirements of the Work Package, even if it is given out verbally, can often avoid the omission of vital information.

14.2 EXECUTE A WORK PACKAGE

14.2.1 What does the activity do?

- Manages the development or supply of the products or services defined in the Work Package.

14.2.2 Why?

Having agreed and committed to work, this activity covers the management of that work until its completion.

14.2.3 How?

- Allocate work to team members.
- Capture and record the effort expended.
- Ensure that work is done according to the techniques, processes and procedures specified in the Work Package.
- Monitor progress against the tolerances agreed for the work.
- Monitor and control the risks.
- Evaluate progress and the amount of effort still required to complete the product(s) of the Work Package.
- Feed progress reports back to the Project Manager at the frequency agreed in the Work Package.

Managing Product Delivery (MP)

- Ensure that the required quality checks are carried out.
- Ensure that any personnel identified in the Quality Register are involved in the quality checking.
- Update the Quality Register with results of all quality checks.
- Raise issues and/or risks to advise the Project Manager of any problems.

14.2.4 Information needs

TABLE 14.2

Management information	Usage	Explanation
Work Package	Input	Details of products required, interfaces, procedures and reporting.
Team Plan	Update	Update with actual progress.
Quality Register	Update	Details of quality work done.
Configuration Item Records	Update	Status change for completed products.
Checkpoint Reports	Output	Progress reports to the Project Manager.
Issue	Output	Any forecast that Work Package tolerances are in danger.
New risk	Output	Any new risk.

14.2.5 In practice

Depending on the size of the Work Package, this is a continuous, cyclic process. The emphasis is on being aware of the status of team members' work and keeping the Project Manager up to date on that status.

As long as the work is forecast to stay within the tolerance limits defined in the Work Package, the Team Manager manages the activity, including taking any necessary corrective action. If it is forecast to exceed a tolerance, the Team Manager must send an issue to the Project Manager detailing the forecast deviation.

14.2.6 For small projects

Where the project is too small to have Team Managers, the Project Manager or a member of his team will carry out this activity.

14.3 DELIVER A WORK PACKAGE

14.3.1 What does the activity do?

- Obtains approval of the products developed or supplied.
- Hands over the products to whoever is responsible for configuration management.
- Advises the Project Manager of the completion of the work.

14.3.2 Why?

There has to be an activity to deliver the requested product(s) and document the agreement that the work has been done satisfactorily.

14.3.3 How?

- Confirm that the Quality Register has been updated with details of a successful check on the quality of the products.
- Confirm that the Configuration Item Record for the Work Package products reflect the completed status.
- Obtain approval from whoever is defined in the Work Package that the package is complete.
- Transfer the products and control their release to the project's Configuration Librarian.
- Advise the Project Manager that the Work Package is complete.

14.3.4 Information needs

See Table 14.3.

14.3.5 In practice

This can be done formally or informally – the formality usually depends on the criticality of the product and the state of the

Managing Product Delivery (MP)

TABLE 14.3

Management information	Usage	Explanation
Quality Register	Input	Verify all quality work completed.
Configuration Item Records	Input	Check the status is correct.
Work Package	Update	Confirm completion.
Team Plan	Update	Show work has been completed.

relationships between the customer and the supplier. The original Work Package should say how it is to be done.

14.3.6 For small projects

This is usually a very simple, informal process of passing the work back to the correct recipient and informing the Project Manager that the work is complete. If you expect the work to form part of a later appraisal of your work, you should ensure that the Project Manager documents how well you did. You should be shown or given a copy of the appraisal.

Chapter 15

Managing a Stage Boundary (SB)

All activities are the responsibility of the Project Manager (Figure 15.1).

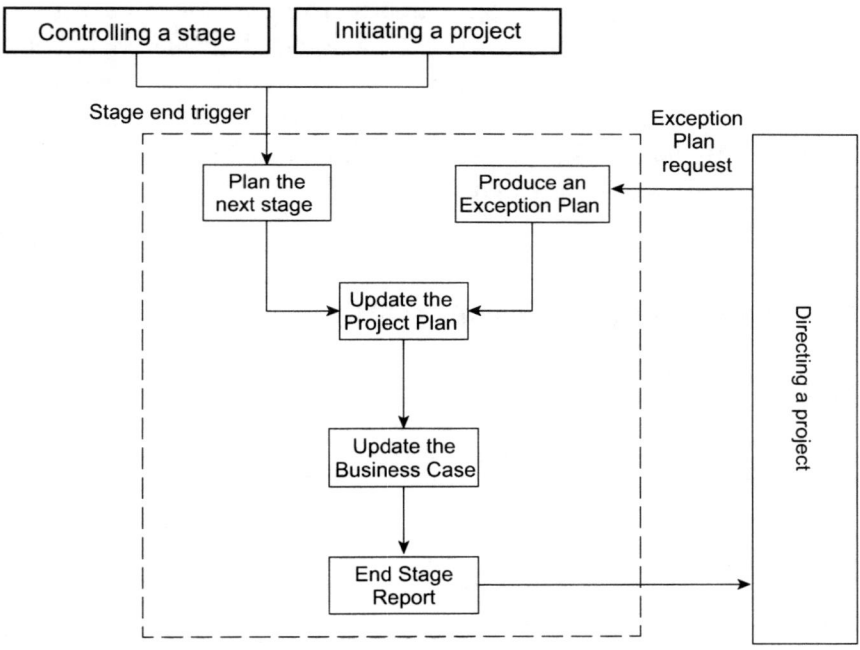

FIGURE 15.1 Managing a Stage Boundary

15.0.1 What does the process do?

- Confirms to the Project Board that products planned to be produced in the current Stage Plan have been delivered.

- Gives reasons for the non-delivery of any products which were planned (in the case of deviation forecasts).
- Verifies that any useful lessons learned during the current stage have been recorded in the Lessons Log.
- Provides information to the Project Board to allow it to assess the continued viability of the project.
- Obtains approval for the next Stage Plan or the Exception Plan.
- Ascertains the tolerance margins to be applied to the new Stage Plan.

15.0.2 Why?

The ability to authorize a project to move forward a stage at a time is a major control for the Project Board. There is also a need for a process to create a plan to react to a forecast deviation beyond tolerances. This process aims to provide the information needed by the Project Board about the current statuses of the Project Plan, Business Case and risks to judge the continuing viability of the project and commitment to a new plan.

15.1 PLAN THE NEXT STAGE

15.1.1 What does the activity do?

- Prepares the next Stage Plan.

15.1.2 Why?

In order to adequately control a stage, the Project Manager needs a plan in which the detailed activities are planned down to the level of a handful of days.

15.1.3 How?

- Check the Project Initiation Documentation for any changes to acceptance criteria.

Managing a Stage Boundary (SB) 199

- Check the project approach for any changes and guidance on how the products of the next stage are to be produced.
- Check the Issue Register for any issues which may affect the next Stage Plan.
- Check the Risk Register for any risks which may affect the next Stage Plan.
- Check the Quality Management Strategy for the quality standards to be used.
- Create the next Stage Plan.
- Create or update any Configuration Item Records required for the next stage.
- Document any changes to the personnel of the project management team.
- Discuss the draft plan with those who have Project Assurance responsibilities.
- Add any formal quality reviews and any other quality checks required for Project Assurance purposes to the Quality Register.
- Identify (as a minimum) the chairperson of each formal quality review.
- Identify those with Project Assurance responsibilities, the required reviewer skills and authority for each formal quality review.
- Ensure that the next Stage Plan includes all required management products.
- Check the next Stage Plan for any new or changed risks and update the Risk Register.
- Modify the next Stage Plan, if necessary, in the light of the risk analysis.
- Create contingency plans for any serious risks which cannot be avoided or reduced to manageable proportions.

15.1.4 Information needs

See Table 15.1.

15.1.5 In practice

Although Team Plans are described as being created in the *Managing Product Delivery* process, it may be necessary to have them produced

TABLE 15.1

Management information	Usage	Explanation
Project Initiation Documentation	Input	Any changes. Details of quality standards required in the next Stage Plan.
Lessons Log	Input	
Project Plan	Input	Details of the products to be created in the next Stage Plan.
Stage Plan	Output	Plan for the next stage.
Product Descriptions	Output	Any new products to be created in the next Stage Plan.
Configuration Item Records	Update	Any new products to be created in the next Stage Plan.
Issue Register	Update	Any issues that may affect the next Stage Plan.
Risk Register	Update	Any risks that may affect the next Stage Plan. Update with any new or changed risks found during planning.
Quality Register	Update	Details of planned quality checks

in parallel with the Stage Plan to get an accurate picture of target dates and resource requirements. If the company has a centre of expertise, this may include expertise in use of the standard planning tools, and this may be available through the role of Project Support.

15.1.6 For small projects

It is dangerous to believe that a project is so small that it doesn't need to be planned. It doesn't need to be a big effort and a planning tool may not be needed, but you should think through what products are needed and in what sequence. This often shows up products or steps that you had overlooked.

Managing a Stage Boundary (SB)

15.2 UPDATE THE PROJECT PLAN

15.2.1 What does the activity do?

- Updates the Project Plan with the actual costs and schedule from the stage that has just finished, plus the estimated cost and schedule of the next Stage Plan.

15.2.2 Why?

As one stage is completed and the next one planned, the Project Plan must be updated so that the Project Board has the most up-to-date information on likely project costs and schedule on which to partially base its decision on whether the project is still a viable business proposition.

15.2.3 How?

- Ensure that the current Stage Plan has been updated with final costs and dates.
- Create a new version of the Project Plan ready to be updated.
- Update the new version of the Project Plan with the actual costs and dates of the current stage.
- Update the new version of the Project Plan with the estimated costs, resource requirements and dates of the next Stage Plan or Exception Plan.
- Update any later stages of the Project Plan on the basis of any relevant information made available since the last update.
- Check to see if events mean that the Project Initiation Documentation has to be modified.

15.2.4 Information needs

See Table 15.2.

15.2.5 In practice

Text should be added to the new version explaining why any changes have occurred. This is an important part of the Project Manager's audit trail of documents covering the management of the project.

TABLE 15.2

Management information	Usage	Explanation
Current Stage Plan	Input	Provides actuals to update the Project Plan.
Project Initiation Documentation	Input	Any changes.
Issue Register	Update	Any new issues.
Risk Register	Update	Any new or changed risks.
Project Plan	Update	Actuals from current stage and details from next stage.

15.2.6 For small projects

All the activity detail may be in the Project Plan with no separate Stage Plans. The Project Plan should be updated with the information described above.

15.3 UPDATE THE BUSINESS CASE

15.3.1 What does the activity do?

- Modifies the Business Case, where appropriate, on the basis of information from the current stage and the plan for the next stage.
- Checks the known risks to project success for any change to their circumstances and looks for any new risks.

15.3.2 Why?

The whole project should be business driven so the Project Board should review a revised Business Case as a major part of the check on the continued viability of the project. Part of the assessment of the project's viability is an examination of the likelihood and impact of potential risks.

Managing a Stage Boundary (SB)

15.3.3 How?

- Create a new version of the Business Case ready to be updated.
- Review the expected costs in the investment appraisal against the revised forecast in the updated Project Plan.
- Review the financial benefits in the investment appraisal against any modified benefit forecasts.
- Review the reasons in the Business Case and check that there has been no change and no new reasons have come to light.
- Check if any benefits were achieved during the current stage.
- Ensure that the Risk Register is up to date with the latest information on the identified risks.
- Modify the new version of the Business Case in the light of any changes to the forecast.

15.3.4 Information needs

TABLE 15.3

Management information	Usage	Explanation
Project Plan	Input	Revised costs.
Issue Register	Input	Any changes that might affect the Business Case.
Risk Register	Input	Check aggregate risk exposure.
Business Case	Update	New version for Project Board approval.
Benefits Review Plan	Update	Any benefits achieved in the current stage.

15.3.5 In practice

The Business Case should be reviewed *minimally* at each stage end, but more frequently if the stages are long or the Business Case is at all at risk. (It would be much better to have two shorter stages than one long one.)

An assessment of the risks should be part of the End Stage Report. In practice, the Project Manager should informally discuss any serious risks with the Project Board so that the risk situation and any extra costs incurred in reacting to those risks do not come as a surprise at the end stage assessment.

15.3.6 For small projects

It should not be assumed that the Business Case is unimportant for a small project. Many of the above actions (detailed in section 15.3.3) will only take minutes to do.

Continuous risk assessment and management are important to all levels of project.

15.4 REPORT STAGE END

15.4.1 What does the activity do?

- Reports on the results of the current stage or the situation that caused the creation of a Exception Plan.
- Forecasts the time and resource requirements of the next stage, if applicable.
- Looks for a Project Board decision on the future of the project.

15.4.2 Why?

Usually, the Project Board manages by exception and therefore only needs to meet if projects are forecast to deviate beyond tolerance levels. As part of its control the Project Board only gives approval to the Project Manager to undertake one stage at a time, at the end of which the Project Board reviews the anticipated benefits, costs, timescale and risks, and makes a decision whether to continue with the project or not. The same review of benefits, time cost and risks is done if the Project Board asks for an Exception Report.

15.4.3 How?

- Report on the actual costs and time of the current stage and measure these against the Stage Plan that was approved by the Project Board.

Managing a Stage Boundary (SB)

- Report on the impact of the current stage's costs and time taken on the Project Plan.
- Report on any impact from the current stage's results on the Business Case, including any benefits realized during the stage.
- Consider (in long projects) whether the production of a Lessons Report at this point would be of value to corporate or programme management.
- Report on the status of the Issue Register.
- Report on the extent and results of the quality work done in the current stage.
- Provide details of the next Stage Plan (if applicable) or Exception Plan.
- Identify any necessary revisions to the Project Plan caused by the next Stage Plan.
- Identify any changes to the Business Case caused by the next Stage Plan.
- Report on the risk situation.
- Recommend the next action; for example, approval of the next Stage Plan.

15.4.4 Information needs

TABLE 15.4

Management information	Usage	Explanation
Current Stage Plan	Input	Measurement of actual performance against what was planned.
Next Stage Plan	Input	Plan for which approval is sought.
Business Case	Input	Status.
Lessons Report (optional)	Output	Is there value in producing a report at this point?
End Stage Report	Output	Review of the performance of the current stage, Business Case and Project Plan status.

15.4.5 In practice

The activity should take place as close to the end of a stage as possible without causing delay to the Project Board decision.

The Project Board should be aware of what will be in the End Stage Report before it formally receives it. They are kept informed of progress and any problems discussed and advice sought via the activity *Give ad hoc direction* (part of the *Directing a Project* process – see chapter 12) before presentation of the Stage Plan.

It is usually sensible to create an End Stage Report even if the current stage is to be replaced by an Exception Plan.

15.4.6 For small projects

In a very small project, there may be only one specialist stage, so this activity may not be needed. The project may be small enough that the Project Plan contains sufficient detail to manage the two stages (initiation and the one specialist stage), thus separate Stage Plans are not needed. The report may be verbal, if this has the agreement of the Project Board.

It is unlikely, although not impossible, that benefits reviews will be carried out within the stage.

15.5 PRODUCE AN EXCEPTION PLAN

15.5.1 What does the activity do?

- In response to an Exception Report, the Project Board may request the Project Manager to prepare a new plan to replace the remainder of the current plan.

15.5.2 Why?

The Project Board approves a Stage Plan on the understanding that it stays within its defined tolerance margins. When an Exception Report indicates that the current tolerances are likely to be exceeded, the Project Board may ask for a new plan to reflect the changed situation

Managing a Stage Boundary (SB)

and that can be controlled within newly specified tolerance margins. The Project Board may take other measures, such as premature closure of the project or removal of the problem causing the deviation.

An Exception Plan has exactly the same format as a Stage Plan and covers the time from the present moment to the end of the plan that is to be replaced.

15.5.3 How?

- Update the Issue Register with the Project Board's decision to request an Exception Plan.
- Review the Project Initiation Documentation for any items that require changes, such as:
  o Customer's quality expectations;
  o Continued suitability of the project approach;
  o Project controls;
  o Project management team.
- Examine the current Stage Plan in order to extract the products that still need to be created.
- Examine the Exception Report for new products and actions that will be required.
- Review the Quality Management Strategy for the standards and procedures required for any new product creation.
- Produce an Exception Plan.
- Update the Risk Register with any changed or new risks.

15.5.4 Information needs

See Table 15.5.

15.5.5 In practice

Although not a planned Stage Boundary, the production of an Exception Plan for a stage is treated in the same way as a normal stage end.

In extreme cases the Exception Plan may be for the Project Plan. In such cases the Stage Plan will need to be replaced as well. The Project

TABLE 15.5

Management information	Usage	Explanation
Current Stage Plan	Input	Incomplete work.
Exception Report	Input	New products and actions required.
Quality Management Strategy	Input	Standards and procedures for any new products.
Project Initiation Documentation	Update	Any changes to project approach, customer's quality expectations, project management team, controls.
Risk Register	Update	New or changed risks.
Issue Register	Update	Record the Project Board decision.
Exception Plan	Output	Plan for which approval is sought.

Board must consider whether this can be done within the project tolerances, or whether the project should be stopped and restarted with revised constraints and tolerances from corporate or programme management.

There can be many reasons for the deviation in forecast, such as:

- Work on approved requests for change cannot be done within current tolerances;
- The supplier has discovered that it cannot supply part of the solution;
- The stage cannot deliver all its products within the current tolerances.

Remember that a request for an Exception Plan is not the only possible outcome from the activity *Give ad hoc direction* (part of the *Directing a Project* process – see chapter 12) when an Exception Report is presented. Other possible results are premature closure of the project, a concession from the Project Board to accept whatever the current lack or fault may be or a decision to delay the requested change until after the current project finishes.

15.5.6 For small projects

There is the temptation not to replan, but only to 'remember' that changes have occurred. It is, however, important to advise the Project Board of any potential deviation beyond tolerances and to have a record that the Stage Plan was changed to accommodate the change *and that the Project Board approved* the new targets.

The same concept can be applied by the Project Manager to the Team Plans if they are forecast to deviate beyond tolerances.

Chapter 16

Closing a Project (CP)

All activities are the responsibility of the Project Manager (Figure 15.1).

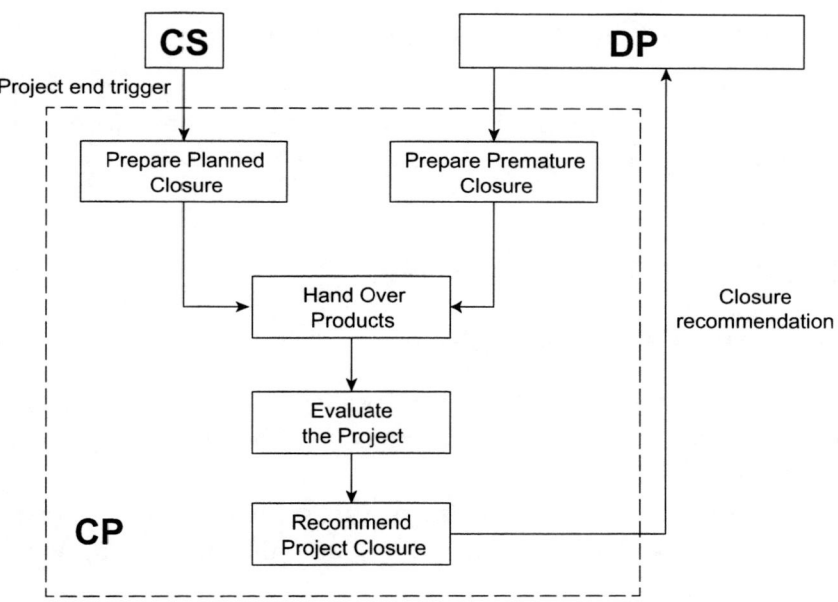

FIGURE 16.1 Closing a Project

16.0.1 What does the process do?

- Checks that all required products have been delivered and accepted.
- Checks that the products can be maintained and supported after the project disbands.

- Checks that all issues have been dealt with.
- Records any recommendations for subsequent work on the product.
- Recognizes that the project has nothing more to contribute (possibly a premature close).
- Reviews project performance against what it set out to do.
- Passes on any lessons learned from the project.
- Recommends closure of the project to the Project Board.
- Updates plans to measure the achievement of the project's benefits.

16.0.2 Why?

Every project should come to a controlled completion.

To measure the success of a project, it must be brought to a close when the Project Manager believes that it has met the objectives set out in the project contract.

16.1 PREPARE PLANNED CLOSURE

16.1.1 What does the activity do?

- Produces the final picture of the project costs and duration.
- Gets agreement from the customer that the acceptance criteria have been met.
- Confirms acceptance of the project's final product from the customer and those who will support the product during its operational life.
- Prepares notification of project closure for the Project Board to send to corporate or programme management.

16.1.2 Why?

The customer and supplier must agree that a project has met its objectives before it can close, and the Project Board will need to know the results and final costs of the project.

Closing a Project (CP)

16.1.3 How?

- Update the Project Plan with figures from the final Stage Plan.
- Review the Project Product Description with the customer and get the customer's agreement that the acceptance criteria have been met.
- Obtain a Product Status Account to confirm that all products have been completed and accepted by the customer.
- Ensure that, where applicable, those who will be responsible for maintenance and support of the products are ready to accept the product.

16.1.4 Information needs

TABLE 16.1

Management information	Usage	Explanation
Product Status Account	Input	Check for acceptance status.
Project Plan	Update	Actuals from final stage.
Project Product Description	Input	Confirm that acceptance criteria have been met.

16.1.5 In practice

There will need to be a carefully managed handover of the products between the project and operational and/or support staff unless one central group had handled configuration management methods for both parts of the product's life cycle.

If any acceptance criteria have not been fully met, the customer and supplier may agree to record this as an issue (off-specification) to be dealt with in a later project.

The final product may be handed over to a new third party to operate and maintain, and there may be contractual arrangements involved in the acceptance of the product.

16.1.6 For small projects

Notification of the release of resources may be very informal, if required at all.

16.2 PREPARE PREMATURE CLOSURE

16.2.1 What does the activity do?

- Ensures that any completed products created so far have been handed over to the customer.
- Reviews the state of any unfinished products for risk situations that they may cause or maintenance work that will be required after the project has closed.

16.2.2 Why?

For a number of reasons the Project Board may instruct the Project Manager to bring a project to a premature close. In such circumstances, the work done so far should not be thrown away. An effort should be made to salvage any products created so far, and any risks or gaps left by the uncompleted project should be brought to the attention of the Project Board for it to pass on.

16.2.3 How?

- Update the Project Plan with figures from the final Stage Plan.
- Obtain a Product Status Account and determine which products:
    o   Have already been accepted;
    o   May be useful to other projects;
    o   Have been started and need to be finished;
    o   Are covered by concessions;
    o   Need to be made safe and secure.
- From the above list, discuss with the Project Board any completion work that is needed and, if necessary, create a suitable Exception Plan.
- Identify if measurement could be made of any of the original planned benefits and, if so, prepare a plan to carry out that measurement.
- Perform a reduced version of the other closure activities.

Closing a Project (CP)

16.2.4 Information needs

TABLE 16.2

Management information	Usage	Explanation
Product status	Input	Confirm completed products, completion account work needed, products not started.
Project Plan	Update	Final stage actuals.

16.2.5 In practice

How much work is entailed will depend on where in the project life cycle the project is terminated. Where the project is part of a programme, any recommendations for follow-on actions should be passed to the programme via the Project Board.

16.2.6 For small projects

There may be so few products in the project that a Product Status Account may not be needed or may be dealt with by a discussion with the team members.

16.3 HAND OVER PRODUCTS

16.3.1 What does the activity do?

- Identifies any work which should be done following the project.
- Prepares a plan for when the realization of the project's expected benefits should be checked.
- Checks that all issues are closed.
- Arranges archiving of the project files.

16.3.2 Why?

Any knowledge of unfinished business at the end of a project should be documented, checked with the Project Board and passed to the appropriate body for action. There must be a check that there are no outstanding problems or requests.

The project documentation, particularly agreements and approvals, should be preserved for any later audits.

16.3.3 How?

- Check that all issues have been closed or transferred to the follow-on action recommendations.
- Check for any omissions in the product or suggestions on how to improve the product and put these on the follow-on action recommendations.
- Ensure that the omissions and suggestions are recorded as follow-on action recommendations.
- Check the Issue Register for any issues which were not completed or rejected and transfer them to the follow-on action recommendations.
- Check the Risk Register for any risks that may affect the product in its operational life and add these to the follow-on action recommendations.
- Check the Configuration Management Strategy for details of how products are to be handed over.
- Check that the Benefits Review Plan is up to date and show how and when the materialization of all benefits that will be achieved during the final product's operational life will be achieved.

16.3.4 Information needs

See Table 16.3.

16.3.5 In practice

If the project is part of a programme, any post-project benefits reviews will be planned and done by the programme.

It may be sensible to set a number of phases for the measurement of benefits to reflect, for example, the learning curve in using the new products and the spread of their use. For example, with an Information Technology product, there may be a period of tuning the computer

TABLE 16.3

Management information	Usage	Explanation
Issue Register	Input	Confirm all issues are closed.
Risk Register	Input	Confirm all risks are closed.
Configuration Management Strategy	Input	How products are to be handed over.
Benefits Review Plan	Update	Confirm that all actions to measure future benefits are in place.
Follow-on action recommendations	Output	Any issues, risks or uncompleted work that still require attention.

environment to best suit the new system; alternatively, spreading training across a multi-location company may take a long time, with benefits measured as each new area comes on board. The speed of a Channel Tunnel rail journey may have had one measurement when it first opened, but may need measuring again since High Speed 1, the fast link between St Pancras and the Channel Tunnel, has become operational.

If the project was an internal one, the Configuration Item Records may not physically move.

16.3.6 For small projects

There may not be any need to move the configuration library, but it should be kept and archived with the rest of the project documentation.

16.4 EVALUATE THE PROJECT

16.4.1 What does the activity do?

- Assesses the project's results against its objectives.
- Provides statistics on the performance of the project.
- Records useful lessons learned.

16.4.2 Why?

One way in which to improve the quality of project management is to learn from the lessons of past projects.

As part of the *Closing a Project* process, the Project Board needs to assess the performance of the project and the Project Manager. This may also form part of the customer's appraisal of a supplier, to see if the contract has been completed, or to see if that supplier should be used again.

16.4.3 How?

- Compare the project's achievements and performance against the original Project Initiation Documentation and the latest version of it.
- Write the End Project Report, evaluating the management, quality and technical methods, tools and processes used.
- Add to the End Project Report any follow-on action recommendations (See the *Hand over products* activity).
- Complete the Lessons Report from the following:
  o Examine the Risk Register for any actions taken, if any, and record any useful comments;
  o Examine the Issue Register for any actions taken, if any, and record any useful comments;
  o Examine the Quality Register and record any useful comments.

16.4.4 Information needs

See Table 16.4.

16.4.5 In practice

The Lessons Log should have been updated throughout the project.

If there are suggestions that the Quality Management Strategy used by the project needed modification, then this should be made clear and such comments directed to the appropriate quality assurance or centre of expertise function.

Closing a Project (CP)

TABLE 16.4

Management information	Usage	Explanation
Project Initiation Documentation	Input	The project's original intent.
Issue Register	Input	Any lessons learned?
Risk Register	Input	Any lessons learned?
Quality Register	Input	Any lessons learned?
Lessons Report	Output	Useful lessons learned for future projects.
End Project Report	Output	Review of project performance.

16.4.6 For small projects

The Project Board may not require an extensive End Project Report.

16.5 RECOMMEND PROJECT CLOSURE

16.5.1 What does the activity do?

- Once the Project Manager can confirm that the project can be closed, a closure recommendation should be sent to the Project Board.

16.5.2 Why?

The Project Board should receive confirmation from the Project manager that everything has been finished before it informs corporate or programme management. It is the Project Board's responsibility to release project resources and advise suppliers of the need to submit final invoices.

16.5.3 How?

- Ensure that the Issue, Quality and Risk Registers and the Daily and Lessons Logs have been closed.

- Complete and archive the project files.
- Provide the Project Board with a project closure notification for it to forward to corporate or programme management.

16.5.4 Information needs

TABLE 16.5

Management information	Usage	Explanation
Communication Management Strategy	Input	Who needs to know that the project is closing?
Issue Register	Close	
Risk Register	Close	
Quality Register	Close	
Lessons Log	Close	
Daily Log	Close	
Project closure notification	Output	For Project Board review.
All project files	Archive	Save for audit or future use.

16.5.5 In practice

Although the Project Manager officially only sends a recommendation for closure, the Project Board will expect all of the copies for relevant stakeholders to have been prepared when it endorses the closure to corporate or programme management.

16.5.6 For small projects

There may be no Communication Management Strategy, because the circle of those who need to know is small and they are well known to the Project Manager and Project Board.

The Project Manager may have kept all the registers in the Daily Log.

Chapter 17

Tailoring PRINCE2 to the Project Environment

There are two terms that can be confused: 'tailoring PRINCE2' and 'embedding PRINCE2'. Tailoring refers to any adjustment made to the PRINCE2 method for a specific project in terms of the project's:

- Scale;
- Complexity;
- Geography;
- Culture.

and whether the project is part of a programme or not.

Embedding refers to the adoption of PRINCE2 across a business.

17.1 TAILORING IS NOT . . .

Tailoring is not dropping parts of the method. The processes and themes are interlinked throughout the method. Any isolated decision to drop a process or a theme will result in a flawed use of the system and may cause project failure.

17.2 TAILORING IS . . .

Tailoring is adopting the method to allow for factors such as existing business standards, documentation and procedures. For example, the business may already have a change control procedure and set of documents to support it that the business wants to use. A project may be so small that it is sensible to combine Team Plans into the Stage

Plan. Also, it may make sense to combine two or more of the PRINCE2 roles for a given project.

17.3 ADAPTATION

Most adaptation questions come from those who wish to use the method on small projects, but view the full method as too bureaucratic. The key question is "How much of this theme, process or technique do we need to use for this project?"

17.3.1 Principles

The first point to recognize is that the basic principles of PRINCE2 must be preserved and form part of the tailored method. As a reminder, the seven PRINCE2 principles are:

- Continued business justification;
- Learn from experience;
- Defined roles and responsibilities;
- Manage by stages;
- Manage by exception;
- Focus on products;
- Tailor to suit the project environment.

By keeping these in mind, the method can be tailored without losing value.

17.3.2 Themes

It may be that the business has standards in certain areas of project work that it wishes to retain: contractual, organizational, change control, quality, risk management, configuration management, and so on. It may be that a project is too small to need to use the full PRINCE2 method. The Project Manager must understand the PRINCE2 method and be able to judge at what level each theme needs to be used.

Business Case

There should always be justification for a project, however small. It may only be the reasons for doing the project, but there should always be understanding that the benefits from a project outweigh the cost. Typically, small maintenance jobs are covered by an annual budget and would not require a full Business Case. It may be sufficient to note the reasons for the job and how much of the annual budget is to be used on it.

Organization

This theme may be the most affected when tailoring, especially for simple projects. All the responsibilities are needed whatever the size of project. It's just a question of who should take which role or roles. In simple projects it may be sensible to combine roles, such as the Executive and Senior User. The Project Board members may do their own Project Assurance. The Project Manager may also pick up the Project Support role. A team member may also act as Configuration Librarian. In a large project, several people may need to share the role of Senior User or Senior Supplier. A team of people may be required to perform the Project Assurance role for the Senior User.

PRINCE2 does not recommend sharing the role of Project Manager, nor that of the Executive, but if the project is partly or wholly funded by someone other than the customer, even the role of Executive may be shared. For example, in the United Kingdom, this could be a privately financed initiative where the supplier provides the funding and takes profits from the use of the outcome.

The most common example of sharing project roles is where the project is part of a programme and someone from the programme management team also takes a place on the project's Project Board.

More about project–programme organization tailoring

The Executives of the projects within a programme could sit on the programme board to improve communications and decision-making. The business change manager of a programme, responsible for benefits definition, may take a role as Senior User in one or more of the programme's projects. Project Support may be handled by the programme for all its projects. A programme's design authority may have a role in the Change Authority or Project Assurance of one or more of its projects.

Plans

In a small project there are a number of possibilities. The Project Plan, Stage Plans and Team Plans may be combined into one plan if this gives enough detail to provide control on a day-to-day basis. It may be acceptable to use a single Product Checklist instead of drawing a Product Breakdown Structure, Product Flow Diagram, network plan and Gantt chart. (See *Quality*, discussed in the next section, for how to deal with Product Descriptions.)

Quality

Great care is needed when thinking of scaling down the quality work described in PRINCE2. It is strongly recommended that Product Descriptions for the key products are written, whatever the size of project. It may be enough to keep a record of the quality checks in the Daily Log.

Risk

Risk is present in every project, large or small. The risk activities defined in the *Risk* theme can be done far more informally for small projects than for medium or large ones, but they should always be done.

Configuration management

There should always be an identification scheme and a simple form of version control.

Change control

Even in the smallest of projects changes will occur and should be recorded. The procedure can be simplified, but must be done.

Progress

Some form of progress control and reporting is required, however simple. Full Checkpoint and Highlight Reports, even End Stage Reports, may not be required and reports can be oral, rather than written.

17.3.3 Processes

All the activities described in the processes have to be done or at least have to be reviewed deliberately to see if they are needed. This avoids the danger of omitting some activities that you later regret, such as checking on risks, performing change control thoroughly, not updating the plans regularly or missing out the odd quality check. In small projects, some of the processes may take less than an hour, but they should still be done.

An easy mistake to make is to omit the start-up and initiation work because of management pressure to 'just get on with it'. Later when there are arguments about the scope of the project or whether the expenditure can be justified, it's either too late to go back or very expensive to correct – and it will always be the Project Manager's fault!

One company, with whom I worked on tailoring the method, decided to combine start-up and initiation. This was OK, but they had to realize that each project's initiation would have to be authorized by corporate or programme management, as there wouldn't be a Project Board in existence.

Small projects may not need Team Managers, which removes the need for Checkpoint Reports, and the Project Manager can decide whether Work Packages are needed. If there is only one specialist stage, there may be no need for separate Stage Plans. All the necessary detail could be held in the Project Plan.

In small projects the Project Manager may decide to use the Daily Log, instead of separate registers for risks, issues, quality, and incorporate that into the Lessons Log. Capturing issues in the Daily Log may avoid the need for Issue Reports.

Dropping reports and meetings are major ways of reducing the management effort in a small project. The Project Board and Project Manager can decide that a number of reports could be given orally. An end stage assessment, for example, can be done without an actual meeting, by simply exchanging information by telephone or email and communicating the necessary decisions and making a note in the Daily Log.

How much of the Project Initiation Documentation does the Project Board wish to see? The Project Initiation Documentation has a number of sections where the only entry may be "See Folder X for full details". Examples of such sections indicate the locations where the project management team structure, the Project Plan, the Business Case and all the strategy documentation would be found. The 2009 PRINCE2 manual suggests that a small project may run with only four sets of documentation:

- The Project Initiation Documentation;
- Highlight Reports (verbal?);
- Daily Log;
- End Project Report.

Appendix A

Product Descriptions

This appendix contains Product Description outlines for PRINCE2's management products. These are not full Product Descriptions, as defined by the outline of a Product Description given in Appendix A.19, as some elements will vary depending on the project's needs, such as quality method. Format examples are provided, but these are not exhaustive. The contents of these outline Product Descriptions should be tailored to the requirements and environment of each project.

A.1 BENEFITS REVIEW PLAN

A.1.1 Purpose

The purpose of the post-project review is to find out:

- Whether the expected benefits of the product have been realized;
- If the product has caused any problems in use;
- If there are any enhancement opportunities that have been revealed by use of the product.

Each expected benefit is assessed for the level of its achievement so far, and to determine if any additional time is needed for the benefit to materialize.

Unexpected side effects are documented, beneficial or adverse, that use of the product may have brought, with explanations of why these were not foreseen.

Recommendations are made to realize or improve benefits, or counter problems.

A.1.2 Composition

- The benefits that are to be measured.
- Who is accountable for the expected benefits.
- How and when each benefit is to be measured.
- Required resources.
- The baseline measurements of each benefit taken at the start of the project against which the expected improvement is to be gauged.
- Questionnaire to judge the perception of the users.

General comments should be obtained on how the users feel about the product. The type of observation will depend on the type of product produced by the project, but examples could be ease of use, performance, reliability, contribution it makes to their work and suitability for the work environment.

A.2 BUSINESS CASE

A.2.1 Purpose

To document the reasons and justification for undertaking a project based on the estimated cost of development and the anticipated business benefits to be gained. The Project Board will monitor the ongoing viability of the project against the Business Case.

The Business Case may include legal or legislative reasons why the project is needed.

A.2.2 Composition

- Executive summary: a summary of the important points in the Business Case, particularly the main benefits and return on investment.

- Business reasons for undertaking the project: explains how the project will contribute to corporate strategies and objectives.
- Business options considered: the solutions that were considered for the business problem. These should cover doing nothing, doing something and doing the minimal. The section should identify the chosen option.
- Reasons for choosing the selected option.
- Business benefits expected to be gained from development of the product. These should be given in measurable terms compared to the situation that exists before the project.
- Benefits tolerance: tolerances should be set for each benefit and for the aggregated benefit.
- Negative consequences of the project: any bad results of either the project work (for example, disruption of normal production) or the project outcome (for example, loss of some staff if the project relates to a geographical move). These should be evaluated in the investment appraisal.
- Summary of the main risks: what they are, their likely impact and any plans should they occur.
- Development cost and timescale: a summary of the Project Plan.
- Operational costs and benefit realization timescale: the estimated operations and maintenance costs and their funding arrangements.
- Investment appraisal: this takes the development costs, operations and maintenance costs and any negative benefits from the estimated benefits to see if, on balance, the project is worth doing. It is usually shown over a short period of years. Techniques that can be used to carry it out are net present value, internal rate of return, payback period and return on investment.

(These may refer to the programme Business Case if it is part of a programme.)

A.3 CHECKPOINT REPORT

A.3.1 Purpose

To report the progress and status of work for a team at a frequency defined in the Work Package.

A.3.2 Composition

- Date of the checkpoint.
- Period covered by the report.
- Report on any follow-up action from previous reports.
- This reporting period:
    o Products under development during the period;
    o Products completed during the period;
    o Quality work carried out during the period;
    o Lessons identified.
- Next reporting period:
    o Products under development in the next period;
    o Products to be completed during the next period;
    o Planned quality activities in the next period.
- Work Package tolerance status: how much has been used; how much remains; and forecast usage in cost/time/scope.
- Issues and risks: any issues or risks that may affect the Work Package, stage or project.

A.4 COMMUNICATION MANAGEMENT STRATEGY

A.4.1 Purpose

The Communication Management Strategy identifies all parties who require information from the project and those from whom the Project requires information. The plan defines what information is needed and when it should be supplied.

A.4.2 Composition

- Introduction: the person responsible for the strategy, its purpose and scope.
- Communication procedure: reference to the communication methods to be used.
- Tools and techniques: any communication tools and techniques to be used.
- Roles and responsibilities: the person responsible for the various aspects of communication.

Appendix A: Product Descriptions

- For all interested parties, for example, user groups, suppliers, stakeholders, quality assurance, internal audit, determine:
  o Information required by each identified party;
  o Information to be provided to the project by each identified party;
  o Identity of the information provider;
  o Frequency of communication;
  o Method of communication;
  o Format.

A.5 CONFIGURATION ITEM RECORD

A.5.1 Purpose

A record of the information required about a product's status.

A.5.2 Composition

- The project identifier: typically an alphanumeric code unique to the project.
- Item (product) identifier: typically an alphanumeric code unique to the product.
- Latest version number: an alphanumeric sequence, such as V001.1.

The three fields above form a unique identifier for a version of a product.

- Item title and description: this should match the name given to the product in the Product Breakdown Structure.
- Variant (if used): might be used for language variants of instructions, screen displays, user manual.
- Type of product: management, specialist, release.
- Users: the person or group who will use the product.
- Date of last status change.
- Status: the project should have a standard set of values for status, such as 'not yet started', 'in development', 'ready for review', 'approved'.

- Stage(s): during which project stage is the product created or update.
- 'Owner' of the product.
- People who are working on the product.
- Date allocated.
- Library or location where the product is kept.
- Source: e.g. in-house, or purchased from a third-party company.
- Links to related products: products that would be affected if this product were to change or vice versa.
- Copy-holders: who has a copy of this version of the product?
- Cross-references:
  - Issue Report(s) that caused the change to this product;
  - Relevant correspondence or documents: e.g. design, letters from the user;
  - The Product Description.

A.6 CONFIGURATION MANAGEMENT STRATEGY

A.6.1 Purpose

To identify how and by whom the project's products will be stored, controlled and protected.

A.6.2 Composition

This plan consists of:

- Introduction: an explanation of the purpose of configuration management, its objectives in the project and who is responsible for the strategy.
- A description of (or reference to) the configuration management procedure to be used. Any variance from corporate or programme standards should be highlighted together with a justification for the variance.
- Reference to any configuration management systems, tools to be used or with which links will be necessary.
- How and where the products will be stored (for example, project filing structure).
- What filing and retrieval security there will be.

- How the products and the various versions of these will be identified.
- Issue and change control procedure: it should cover capturing and examining issues, recommending responses, decision and implementation. Any variation from corporate or programme procedures should be highlighted and explained.
- Records: a definition of the composition and format of the Issue Register and Configuration Item Records.
- Roles and responsibilities: where responsibility for configuration management and change control lies.
- Priority and severity scales: how requests for change and off-specifications will be prioritized and an indication of which project management level should deal with which severity level.

A.7 DAILY LOG

A.7.1 Purpose

To record required actions or significant events not caught by other PRINCE2 documents. It acts as a diary for the Project Manager or Team Managers. Before creation of the Risk and Issue Registers, it is used to record any early risks or issues.

A.7.2 Composition

(The following are only suggestions.)

- Date of entry.
- Action or comment.
- Person responsible.
- Target date.
- Result.

A.8 END PROJECT REPORT

A.8.1 Purpose

The report is the Project Manager's report to the Project Board (who may pass it on to corporate or programme management) on how the project has performed against the objectives stated in its Project Initiation Document and revised during the project. It should cover comparisons with the original targets, planned cost, schedule and tolerances, the revised Business Case and final version of the Project Plan.

The End Project Report also includes any follow-on action recommendations and the final Lessons Report.

A.8.2 Composition

- Project Manager's report: a summary of the project's performance.
- Assessment of the achievement of the project's objectives.
- Performance against the planned (and revised) target times and costs, tolerances for time, cost, quality, scope, risk and benefits.
- The effects on the original Project Plan and Business Case of any changes which were approved.
- Business Case review:
  o Any benefits achieved within the project life cycle;
  o Assessment of the ability to achieve the post-project benefits;
  o Any revisions to the expected net benefits;
  o Any deviations from the approved Business Case.
- Final statistics on change issues received during the project and the total impact (e.g. on time, money, benefits) of any approved changes, plus any concessions granted.
- Statistics for all quality work carried out.
- Follow-on action recommendations (changes proposed but not carried out and risks that might affect the operational product).
- Product handover: a pointer to the acceptance records from the customer indicating that operations and maintenance are ready to receive the products.
- Lessons Report (See its Product Description in section A.15).

A.9 END STAGE REPORT

A.9.1 Purpose

The purpose of the End Stage Report is to report on a stage that has just completed, the overall project situation and give sufficient

Appendix A: Product Descriptions

information to ask for a Project Board decision on the next step to take with the project.

The Project Board uses the information in the End Stage Report to approve the next Stage Plan, amend the project scope, ask for a revised next Stage Plan or stop the project.

Normally the End Stage Report for the last stage of a project is combined with the End Project Report.

A.9.2 Composition

- Project Manager's report: a summary of the stage performance.
- Review of stage objectives: a review of how well the stage met its planned objectives, targets and tolerances.
- Review of project objectives: a review of how the project is performing in meeting its objectives, plan and tolerances.
- Business Case review:
    o Any benefits achieved during the stage;
    o Assessment of the ability to achieve the post-project benefits;
    o Any revision to the expected net benefits;
    o Any deviations from the approved Business Case.
- Risk review.
- Issue Report situation.
- Quality checking statistics.
- Approval records: a reference to the acceptance records for any products handed over during the stage.
- Phased handover (if applicable): confirmation that operations and maintenance are ready to receive the products of a phased release.
- Follow-on action recommendations (if applicable): if a phased handover has taken place, is there any unfinished work for any of the products in that handover, and are there any issues or risks that relate to any of the products handed over?
- Lessons Report (if required): is there a need to advise other projects at this time of what went well and what went badly?
- Forecast: a forecast produced for the next stage and the remainder of the project against their plans and tolerances.

(Not all of this information would be relevant for the initiation stage.)

A.10 EXCEPTION REPORT

A.10.1 Purpose

An Exception Report is produced when costs and/or timescales for an approved Stage Plan are forecast to exceed the tolerance levels set. It is sent by the Project Manager to warn the Project Board of the adverse situation.

An Exception Report may result in the Project Board asking the Project Manager to produce an Exception Plan.

A.10.2 Composition

- Overview: an overview of the exception being reported.
- A description of the cause of the deviation.
- The consequences of the deviation.
- The available options.
- The effects of each option on the Business Case, risks, project and stage tolerances.
- The Project Manager's recommendations.
- Lessons: whether there are any lessons that can be learned from this exception that will benefit this project in future or other projects.

A.11 HIGHLIGHT REPORT

A.11.1 Purpose

For use by the Project Manager to provide the Project Board with a summary of the stage status at intervals defined by them in the Project Initiation Documentation.

A Highlight Report normally summarizes a series of Checkpoint Reports. The Project Board uses the report to monitor stage and project progress. The Project Manager also uses it to advise the Project Board of any potential problems or areas where the Project Board could help.

A.11.2 Composition

- Date.
- Project.
- Stage.
- Period covered.
- Budget status.
- Schedule status.
- This reporting period:
    o Work Packages not yet allocated, in progress and completed;
    o Products completed during the period;
    o Any early warning indicators: products not started or completed by their planned dates.
- Next reporting period:
    o Work Packages to be authorized, in progress and completed during the next reporting period;
    o Products to be completed during the next period;
    o Any corrective actions to be taken during the next period.
- Project and stage tolerance status: current performance of the project and current stage against their tolerances and forecast performances.
- Issue Report status.
- Actual or potential problems and risks.
- Lessons Report: this is unlikely to be needed, but there may be recommendations that need to be made at this point for corporate or programme management consideration.

A.12 ISSUE REGISTER

A.12.1 Purpose

The purpose of the Issue Register is to:

- Allocate a unique number to each Issue Report;
- Record the type of Issue Report;
- Provide a summary of the Issue Reports, their analysis and status.

A.12.2 Composition

- Issue Report number.
- Issue Report type: request for change, off-specification, or problem/concern.
- Author.
- Issue description: describing the issue's cause, event and effect.
- Priority: should be re-evaluated after impact analysis.
- Severity: an indication of which level of the project management team is required to make the decision.
- Date created.
- Date of last update.
- Status.

A.13 ISSUE REPORT

A.13.1 Purpose

To record any matter that has to be brought to the attention of the project, and requires an answer. An issue may be a:

- Request for change;
- Off-specification;
- Question;
- Statement of concern.

A.13.2 Composition

- Author.
- Date raised.
- Issue identifier.
- Type: request for change, off-specification or problem/concern.
- Description of the issue.
- Impact analysis.
- Recommendation: what action the Project Manager believes should be taken, including the reasons.
- Priority.
- Severity: to indicate which level of the project management team should make the decision.

Appendix A: Product Descriptions

- Decision: accept, reject, defer or grant concession.
- Decision by: the person that made the decision.
- Date of decision.

A.14 LESSONS LOG

A.14.1 Purpose

The purpose of the Lessons Log is to be a repository of any lessons learned during the project that can be usefully applied to other projects. At the close of the project it is formally written up in the Lessons Report. As a minimum requirement, it should be updated at the end of a stage, but sensibly a note should be made in it of any good or bad point that arises in the use of the management and specialist products and tools at the time of the experience.

A.14.2 Composition

- Lesson type:
    - Project;
    - Corporate/programme;
    - Both.
- Lesson detail:
    - Cause;
    - Event;
    - Effect;
    - Whether there were any early warning indicators;
    - Recommendations;
    - Previously identified as a risk: yes or no.
- Date logged.
- Logged by: the person that raised the lesson.
- Priority.

A.15 LESSONS REPORT

A.15.1 Purpose

The purpose of the Lessons Report is to pass on to other projects any useful lessons that can be learned from this project.

The data in the report should be used by an independent group, such as quality assurance, who are responsible for the site Quality Management System, to refine, change and improve project management and technical standards. Statistics on how much effort was needed for products can help improve future estimating.

A.15.2 Composition

- Executive summary.
- Scope of the report: stage or project.
- What management and quality processes:
    - Went well;
    - Went badly;
    - Were lacking.
- An assessment of the efficacy of technical methods and tools used.
- Recommendations for future enhancement or modification of the project management method, including any tailoring done, plus the reasons for the modifications.
- Review of the project strategy documents: how effective were they?
- Measurements on how much effort was required to create the various products.
- A description of any abnormal events causing deviations to targets or plans.
- An analysis of Issue Reports raised, their causes and results.
- Statistics on how effective quality reviews and other tests were in error trapping (for example, the number of errors that were found after products had passed a quality review or test).

A.16 PLAN

A.16.1 Purpose

A mandatory plan which shows at a high level how and when a project's objectives are to be achieved. It contains the major products of the project, the activities and resources required.

It provides the Business Case with planned project costs, and identifies the management stages and other major control points.

Appendix A: Product Descriptions

The Project Board uses this plan as a baseline against which to monitor project progress and cost stage by stage. It forms part of the Project Initiation Documentation.

A.16.2 Composition

- Plan description: level of plan (i.e. Project, Stage, Team and Exception Plans) and the planning approach.
- Plan prerequisites: anything that must be in place before the work begins and remain in place for the duration of the planned work, such as training, workspace, passwords, access.
- Plan assumptions: any assumptions made in creating the plan, such as external events, timings.
- External dependencies: anything outside the project that might affect it, such as completion of products by other projects.
- Tolerances: time, cost and scope.
- Lessons incorporated: any lessons from earlier projects that have been incorporated.
- Monitoring and control: how it is intended to monitor and control the plan's execution.
- Budgets: time and cost, including any change budget and risk analysis allowance.
- Product Descriptions: for the products in the plan.
- Schedule: may be represented in graphical form and contain:
  o Gantt or bar chart;
  o Product Breakdown Structure;
  o Product Flow Diagram;
  o Planning network;
  o Table of resource requirements;
  o Table of requested or assigned resources by name.

A.17 PRODUCT BREAKDOWN STRUCTURE

A.17.1 Purpose

- To show all products to be developed and quality controlled;
- To provide a statement of how and when objectives are to be achieved by showing the products, activities and resources

required for the scope of the plan. In PRINCE2 there are three levels of plan: project, stage and team. Team Plans are optional and may not follow the composition of this Product Description.
- To show the project management activities required to control and report on the plan's work.

A.17.2 Composition

- Top-to-bottom diagram showing a breakdown of all products to be developed during the life of the plan. External products must be included, clearly distinguished from those to be developed.

A.18 PRODUCT CHECKLIST

A.18.1 Purpose

To list the products to be produced within a plan, together with key status dates. It is updated at agreed reporting intervals by the Project Manager and used by the Project Board to monitor progress.

A.18.2 Composition

- Plan identification.
- Product names (and identifiers where appropriate).
- Planned and actual dates for:
  o Draft product ready;
  o Quality check;
  o Approval.

A.19 PRODUCT DESCRIPTION

A.19.1 Purpose

To define the information needed to describe each product to be created by the project.

A.19.2 Composition

- Identifier: a unique key, the basis of which should be defined in the Configuration Management Strategy, that includes the project and product identifiers and version number.
- Title: should be the same as the title used in the Product Breakdown Structure.
- Purpose: An explanation of the purpose of the product:
    o Composition: a list of the various parts of the product, e.g. chapters of the document;
    o Format and presentation: what the product should look like. If it is a document, the name of the template to be used;
    o Development skills required: the skills and resources required to develop the product;
    o Derivation: The sources of information for the product;
    o Quality criteria: what quality measurements the product must meet;
    o Quality tolerance: any range in the quality criteria within which the product would be acceptable, e.g. ±5 per cent;
    o Quality method: the method to be used to check the product's quality and the type of skill required;
    o Quality checking skills required: an indication of the skills required by those who will check the quality of the product.

A.20 PRODUCT FLOW DIAGRAM

A.20.1 Purpose

To show the required sequence of delivery of a plan's products and identify dependencies between those products, including any external products.

A.20.2 Composition

- A diagram showing the product delivery sequence from top to bottom (or left to right), plus the dependencies between those products. Arrows indicate dependencies between products. External products must be clearly distinguished from the products developed by the plan. The PRINCE2 convention is for project products to be shown as rectangles and external products as ellipses.

A.21 PRODUCT STATUS ACCOUNT

A.21.1 Purpose

The Product Status Account provides information about the state of products. For example, the report could cover the entire project, a particular stage or a particular area of the project. It is particularly useful if the Project Manager wishes to confirm the version number of products or confirm that all products within a specific plan have reached a certain status, such as draft, tested or approved.

A.21.2 Composition

The composition will vary but will normally consist of the following information:

- Project Name.
- Date produced.

For each product identified the following additional information may be provided:

- Product identifier.
- Version number.
- Product status.
- Date of last status change.
- Owner: who must be consulted before any changes are made to the product.
- Copy-holders.
- Product location.
- Users.
- Producer and date allocated to producer.
- Planned and actual dates when the Product Description was baselined.

- Date when the product was baselined.
- Planned date for next baseline.
- List of related products.
- Issue that caused this version.
- Any outstanding issues.

A.22 PROJECT BRIEF

A.22.1 Purpose

To briefly explain the reasons for the project, the customer's expectations and any limitations which apply.

A.22.2 Composition

The following is a suggested list of contents that should be tailored to the requirements and environment of each project.

- Project definition, explaining what the project needs to achieve:
  o Background;
  o Project objectives;
  o Project scope;
  o Outline project deliverables and/or desired outcomes;
  o Any exclusions;
  o Constraints;
  o Assumptions;
  o Project tolerances;
  o Users and stakeholders;
  o Interfaces.
- Outline Business Case:
  o Reason for the project;
  o Description of how this project supports business strategy, plans or programmes.
- Project Product Description.
- Project approach:
  o Defines the type of solution to be developed or procured by the project. It should also identify the environment into which the product must be delivered.

- Type of solution, for example:
  - Off the shelf;
  - Built from scratch;
  - Modification of an existing product;
  - Built by one or more external suppliers;
  - Addition to or modification of a product developed by another project;
  - Built by company members of staff;
  - Built by contract members of staff under the supervision of the Project Manager;
  - Reason for the selection of project approach, e.g. part of a programme;
  - Implications on the project.
- Project management team structure.
- Role descriptions.
- References to associated documents or products.

If earlier work has been done, the Project Brief may refer to other documents, such as the outline Project Plan.

A.23 PROJECT INITIATION DOCUMENTATION

A.23.1 Purpose

To define the project and to form the basis for the ultimate assessment of the project's success and the project's management.

There are two primary uses of the document:

- To ensure that the project has a sound basis before asking the Project Board to make any major commitment to the project;
- To act as a base document against which the Project Board and Project Manager assess progress, evaluate change issues and questions about the project's continuing viability.

A.23.2 Composition

The Project Initiation Documentation must answer the following fundamental questions:

- What the project is aiming to achieve.
- Why it is important to achieve it.
- Who is going to be involved in managing the project and what are their responsibilities.
- How and when it is all going to happen.

The following list should be seen as the information needed in order to make the initiation decisions.

- Background: explaining the context of the project and steps taken to arrive at the current position of requiring a project.
- Project definition: explains what the project needs to achieve and might include:
  - Project objectives;
  - Project deliverables and/or desired outcomes;
  - Project scope;
  - Constraints;
  - Exclusions;
  - Interfaces;
  - Assumptions.
- Project approach.
- Business Case: explains why the project is being undertaken.
- Project management team structure: defines the project management team.
- Quality Management Strategy: see *Quality Management Strategy* section A.25).
- Project Plan: explains how and when the activities of the project will occur; see *Plan* section A.16.
- Project tolerances: showing tolerance levels for time, cost, quality, benefit, risk and resources. Tolerances for quality should already be in the Quality Management Strategy and benefit tolerances in the Business Case, so a choice can be made to simply point to their presence in those documents rather than repeat them.

- Project controls: stating how control is to be exercised within the project, and the reporting and monitoring mechanisms which will support this.
- Communication Management Strategy: see *Communication Management Strategy* section A.4.
- Risk Management Strategy: see *Risk Management Strategy* section A.27.
- Tailoring of PRINCE2: a summary of how the method will be tailored for the project.

A.24 PROJECT PRODUCT DESCRIPTION

A.24.1 Purpose

The Project Product Description is a special form of Product Description that defines what the project must deliver in order to gain acceptance. It is used to:

- Gain agreement from the user on the project's scope and requirements;
- Define the customer's quality expectations;
- Define the acceptance criteria, methods and responsibilities for the project.

The Product Description for the project product is created in the *Starting up a Project* process (see chapter 10) as part of the initial scoping activity, and is refined during the *Initiating a Project* process (see chapter 11) when creating the Project Plan. It is used by the *Closing a Project* process (see chapter 16) as part of the verification that the project has delivered what was expected of it, and that the acceptance criteria have been met.

A.24.2 Composition

- Title: name by which the project is known.
- Purpose: this defines the purpose that the project product will fulfil and who will use it. It is helpful in understanding the product's functions, size, quality, complexity, robustness etc.

Appendix A: Product Descriptions

- Composition: a description of the major products to be delivered by the project.
- Derivation: what are the source products from which this product is derived? Examples are:
  - Existing products to be modified;
  - Design specifications;
  - A feasibility report;
  - Project mandate.
- Development skills required: an indication of the skills required to develop the product, or a pointer to which area(s) should supply the development resources.
- Customer's quality expectations: a description of the quality expected of the project product and the standards and processes that will need to be applied to achieve that quality. These will impact on every part of the product development and, thus, on time and cost. The quality expectations are captured in discussions with the customer (business and user stakeholders). Where possible, expectations should be prioritized.
- Acceptance criteria: a prioritized list of criteria that the project product must meet before the customer will accept it; i.e. measurable definitions of the attributes that must apply to the set of products to be acceptable to key stakeholders (and, in particular, the users and the operational and maintenance organizations). Examples are: ease of use, ease of support, ease of maintenance, appearance, major functions, development costs, running costs, capacity, availability, reliability, security, accuracy or performance.
- Project-level quality tolerances: specifying any tolerances that may apply to the acceptance criteria.
- Acceptance method: stating the means by which acceptance will be confirmed. This may simply be a case of confirming that all the project's products have been approved, or may involve describing complex handover arrangements for the project product, including any phased handover of the project's products.
- Acceptance responsibilities: defining who will be responsible for confirming acceptance.

A.25 QUALITY MANAGEMENT STRATEGY

A.25.1 Purpose

The purpose is to define how the supplier intends to deliver products that meet the customer's quality expectations and the agreed quality standards.

A.25.2 Composition

- Introduction: identifies who is responsible for the strategy, plus its purpose, objectives and scope.
- Quality management procedure: any variance to corporate or programme standards should be identified and reasons given. It covers:
  - Quality planning;
  - Quality control: this may include quality standards to be followed and templates and forms to be used (indicate where these may be found);
  - Quality assurance: Project Board quality responsibilities; audits; corporate or programme reviews;
  - Tools and techniques: any tools or techniques that are to be used in quality checking;
  - Records: what records of quality inspections will be kept and where. This includes the format of the Risk Register;
  - Roles and responsibilities: quality responsibilities, including those of corporate or programme management.

A.26 QUALITY REGISTER

A.26.1 Purpose

To issue a unique reference for each quality check or test planned and act as a pointer to the quality check and test documentation for a product. The Quality Register also acts as a summary of the number and type of quality checks and tests held. The log summarizes all the quality checks and tests which are planned/have taken place, and provides information for the End Stage and End Project Reports, as well as the Lessons Report.

A.26.2 Composition

For each entry in the register:

- Quality check reference number.
- Product to be checked or tested.
- Method: what method of quality check is to be used, e.g. quality review, audit, stress test.
- Roles and responsibilities: who will be involved and their roles.
- Planned date of the check.
- Actual date of the check.
- Result of the check.
- Number of action items found.
- Target sign-off date.
- Actual sign-off date.
- Quality records: reference to any inspection documentation, including follow-on action lists.

A.27 RISK MANAGEMENT STRATEGY

A.27.1 Purpose

The Risk Management Strategy describes the risk management procedure, techniques and standards to be applied and the responsibilities for risk management.

A.27.2 Composition

- Introduction: the purpose, objectives, scope and responsibility of the strategy.
- The risk management procedure: a description of (or reference to) the risk management procedure to be used. Any variance from corporate or programme management standards should be described, together with its justification. The procedure should cover the risk activities of:
    o Identifying;
    o Assessing;
    o Planning;

- o Implementing;
- o Communicating.
- Risk tolerance: the threshold levels of risk exposure, which, when exceeded, require the risk to be escalated to the next level of management. (For example, a project-level risk tolerance might be the threatened loss below a tolerance limit of certain workforce skills. Such risks would need to be escalated to corporate or programme management.) The risk tolerance should define the risk expectations of corporate or programme management and the Project Board.
- Risk budget: describing if a risk budget is to be established and, if so, how it will be used.
- Tools and techniques: any risk management systems or tools to be used and any preference for techniques that may be used for each step in the risk management procedure.
- Records: definition of the composition and format of the Risk Register and any other risk records to be used by the project.
- Reporting: any risk management reports to be produced, their recipients, purpose and timing.
- Timing of risk management activities: when risk management activities are to be undertaken; e.g. at end stage assessments and issue impact analysis.
- Roles and responsibilities: the roles and responsibilities for risk management activities.
- Scales: the scales to be used for estimating probability and impact of a risk; e.g. to ensure that the scales for cost and time are relevant to the cost and time frame of the project.
- Proximity: how the proximity of a risk is to be assessed. Typical proximity categories will be: imminent, within a month, within the stage, within the project, beyond the project.
- Risk categories: the risk categories to be used (if any).
- Risk response categories: definition of the risk response categories to be used.
- Early warning indicators: indicators to be used to track critical aspects of the project, so that if predefined levels are reached, corrective action will be triggered.

… Appendix A: Product Descriptions

A.28 RISK REGISTER

A.28.1 Purpose

The purpose of the Risk Register is to:

- Allocate a unique number to each risk;
- Record the type of risk;
- Be a summary of the risks, their analysis and status.

A.28.2 Composition

- Risk identifier: a unique number by which to refer to the risk within the project.
- Risk type (business, project, stage).
- Author.
- Date risk identified.
- Date of last risk status update.
- Risk description: given in terms of cause, event and effect.
- Likelihood: probability of the risk occurring.
- Impact: a valuation of the impact in terms of time, cost, scope, quality, benefits and people.
- Proximity: when the risk is likely to occur.
- Countermeasure(s): these should be aligned to the risk categories (for threats – avoid, reduce, fallback, transfer, accept, share; for opportunities – enhance, exploit, reject, share).
- Status.
- Risk owner: the person responsible for monitoring the risk.
- Risk actionee: the person who will carry out the countermeasure(s) – this may or may not be the risk owner.

A.29 WORK PACKAGE

A.29.1 Purpose

A set of instructions to produce one or more required products that is given by the Project Manager to a Team Manager or team member.

A.29.2 Composition

Although the content may vary greatly according to the relationship between the Project Manager and the recipient of the Work Package, it should cover:

- Date: date of the agreement between Project Manager and the Team Manager or person to whom the work is allocated.
- Team Manager or person authorized: with whom the agreement has been made.
- A summary of the work to be done.
- Product Description(s) of the products to be produced.
- Techniques, processes and procedures: standards, tools and techniques to be used in the production of the products.
- Development interfaces: interfaces that must be maintained during development of the product(s) – people providing or receiving information or products from the team or individual.
- Operations and maintenance interfaces: identification of the products with which the products of the Work Package will have to work in their operational life. These may be other products from the same project, other projects or may be already in the operational environment.
- Configuration management requirements: this covers the interaction required with the project's configuration management system, covering the use of version control, the submission of copies to the configuration library, obtaining copies of other products, product security requirements and advice of any change in the product's status.
- Joint agreements: these cover the agreements on start and end dates, amount of effort, cost and any key milestones.
- Tolerances: agreed tolerances for the work in terms of cost and time. Scope and risk should also be reviewed in case tolerances should be made for these.
- Constraints: any limitations on the use of people to create the product (for example, how much time is available from an Information Technology expert); the level of staff to be capable of using the products (for example, current staff, the untrained public or a university physics graduate); rules to be followed (for example, security and safety); charges, etc.

- Reporting arrangements: usually Checkpoint Reports, stating their expected content and frequency.
- Problem handling and escalation: this should cover the procedures to be followed to raise issues or risks.
- Extracts or references: any documents or correspondence that will be helpful. These should include:
    o An extract from the Stage Plan that shows where the Work Package fits in;
    o Copies of the relevant Product Descriptions.
- Approval method: identifying the person, role or group who will approve the completed product(s) and how the Project Manager is to be informed of completion of the Work Package.

Appendix B

Project Management Team Roles

This section gives a description for each role in the project management structure. These can be used as the basis to discuss an individual's job and tailored to suit the project's circumstances. The tailored role description becomes that person's *job description* for the project. Two copies of an agreed job description should be signed by the individual: one for retention by the individual, the other to be filed in the project file.

B.1 PROJECT BOARD

B.1.1 General

The Project Board is appointed by corporate or programme management to provide overall direction and management of the project. The Project Board is accountable for the success of the project, and has responsibility and authority for the project within the limits set by corporate or programme management.

The Project Board is the project's 'voice' to the outside world and is responsible for any publicity or other dissemination of information about the project.

B.1.2 Specific responsibilities

The Project Board approves all major plans and authorizes any major deviation from agreed Stage Plans. It is the authority that signs off the completion of each stage and authorizes the start of the next stage.

It ensures that required resources are committed and arbitrates on any conflicts within the project, or negotiates a solution to any problems between the project and external bodies. In addition, it approves the appointment and responsibility of the Project Manager and any delegation of its Project Assurance responsibility.

The Project Board has the following responsibilities. This is a general list and will need tailoring for a specific project.

At the beginning of the project:

- Assurance that the Project Initiation Documentation complies with relevant customer standards and policies, plus any associated contract with the supplier.
- Agreement with the Project Manager on that person's responsibility and objectives.
- Confirmation with corporate or programme management of project tolerances.
- Specification of external constraints on the project, such as quality assurance.
- Approval of accurate and satisfactory Project Initiation Documentation.
- Delegation of any Project Assurance roles.
- Commitment of project resources required by the next Stage Plan.

As the project progresses:

- Provision of overall guidance and direction to the project, ensuring it remains within any specified constraints.
- Review of each completed stage and approval of progress to the next.
- Review and approval of Stage Plans and any Exception Plans.
- 'Ownership' of one or more of the identified project risks as allocated at plan approval time; i.e. the responsibility to monitor the risk and advise the Project Manager of any change in its status and to take action, if appropriate, to ameliorate the risk.
- Approval of changes.
- Compliance with corporate or programme management directives.

At the end of the project:

- Assurance that all products have been delivered satisfactorily.
- Assurance that all acceptance criteria have been met.
- Approval of the End Project Report.
- Approval of the Lessons Report and the passage of this to the appropriate standards group to ensure action.
- Decisions on the recommendations for follow-on actions and the passage of these to the appropriate authorities.
- Arrangements, where appropriate, for one or more benefits reviews.
- Project closure notification to corporate or programme management.

The Project Board is ultimately responsible for the assurance of the project and that it remains on course to deliver the desired outcome, of the required quality, to meet the Business Case defined in the project contract. According to the size, complexity and risk of the project, the Project Board may decide to delegate some of this Project Assurance responsibility. Later in this chapter Project Assurance is defined in more detail.

One Project Board responsibility that should receive careful consideration is that of approving and funding changes. *Change control* (section 9.2) should be read before finalizing this responsibility of approving and funding changes.

The responsibilities of specific members of the Project Board are described in the following sections.

B.2 EXECUTIVE

B.2.1 General

The Executive is ultimately responsible for the project, supported by the Senior User(s) and Senior Supplier. The Executive has to ensure that the project is value for money, ensuring a cost-conscious approach to the project and balancing the demands of business, user and supplier.

Throughout the project the Executive 'owns' the Business Case.

B.2.2 Specific responsibilities

- Ensure that tolerances are set for the project by corporate or programme management in the project mandate.
- Authorize customer expenditure and set stage tolerances.
- Approve the End Project Report and Lessons Report.
- Brief corporate or programme management about project progress.
- Organize and chair Project Board meetings.
- Recommend future action on the project to corporate or programme management if the project tolerance is exceeded.
- Approve the sending of the notification of project closure to corporate or programme management.

The Executive is responsible for overall business assurance of the project; i.e. that it remains on target to deliver products that will achieve the expected business benefits and the project will complete within its agreed tolerances for budget and schedule. Business Project Assurance covers:

- Validation and monitoring of the Business Case against external events and against project progress.
- Keeping the project in line with customer strategies.
- Monitoring project finance on behalf of the customer.
- Monitoring the business risks to ensure that these are kept under control.
- Monitoring any supplier and contractor payments.
- Monitoring changes to the Project Plan to see if there is any impact on the needs of the business or the project Business Case.
- Assessing the impact of potential changes on the Business Case and Project Plan.
- Constraining user and supplier excesses.
- Informing the project of any changes caused by a programme of which the project is part (this responsibility may be transferred if there is other programme representation on the project management team).
- Monitoring stage and project progress against the agreed tolerance.

If the project warrants it, the Executive may delegate some responsibility for the above business Project Assurance functions.

B.3 SENIOR USER

B.3.1 General

The Senior User is responsible for the specification of the needs of all those who will use the final product(s), user liaison with the project team and for monitoring that the solution will meet those needs within the constraints of the Business Case.

The role represents the interests of all those who will use the final product(s) of the project, those for whom the product will achieve an objective or those who will use the product to deliver benefits. The Senior User role commits user resources and monitors products against requirements. This role may require more than one person to cover all the user interests. For the sake of effectiveness the role should not be split between too many people.

B.3.2 Specific responsibilities

- Ensure the desired outcome of the project is specified.
- Make sure that progress towards the outcome required by the users remains consistent from the user perspective.
- Promote and maintain focus on the desired project outcome.
- Ensure that any user resources required for the project are made available.
- Approve Product Descriptions for those products which act as inputs or outputs (interim or final) from the supplier function, or will affect them directly, and ensure that the products are signed off once completed.
- Prioritize and contribute user opinions on Project Board decisions on whether to implement recommendations on proposed changes.
- Resolve user requirements and priority conflicts.
- Provide the user with recommended follow-up actions.
- Brief and advise user management on all matters concerning the project.

The Project Assurance responsibilities of the Senior User are to ensure that:

- Specification of the user's needs is accurate, complete and unambiguous.
- Development of the solution at all stages is monitored to ensure that it will meet the user's needs and is progressing towards that target.
- Impact of potential changes is evaluated from the user's point of view.
- Risks to the users are constantly monitored.
- Testing of the product at all stages has the appropriate user representation.
- Quality control procedures are used correctly to ensure products meet user requirements.
- User liaison is functioning effectively.

Where the project's size, complexity or importance warrants it, the Senior User may delegate the responsibility and authority for some of the Project Assurance responsibility.

B.4 SENIOR SUPPLIER

B.4.1 General

Represents the interests of those designing, developing, facilitating, procuring, implementing, operating and maintaining the project's products. The Senior Supplier role must have the authority to commit or acquire the required supplier resources.

If necessary, more than one person may be required to represent the suppliers.

B.4.2 Specific responsibilities

- Agree objectives for specialist activities.
- Make sure that progress towards the outcome remains consistent from the supplier perspective.
- Promote and maintain focus on the desired project outcome from the point of view of supplier management.
- Ensure that the supplier resources required for the project are made available.

Appendix B: Project Management Team Roles

- Approve Product Descriptions for specialist products.
- Contribute supplier opinions on Project Board decisions on whether to implement recommendations on proposed changes.
- Resolve supplier requirements and priority conflicts.
- Arbitrate on, and ensure resolution of, any specialist priority or resource conflicts.
- Brief non-technical management on specialist aspects of the project.

The Senior Supplier is responsible for the specialist Project Assurance of the project. The specialist Project Assurance role responsibilities are to:

- Advise on the selection of technical strategy, design and methods.
- Ensure that any specialist and operating standards defined for the project are met and used to good effect.
- Monitor potential changes and their impact on the correctness, completeness and assurance of products against their Product Description from a technical perspective.
- Monitor any risks in the specialist and production aspects of the project.
- Ensure quality control procedures are used correctly so that products adhere to technical requirements.

If warranted, some of these Project Assurance responsibilities may be delegated. Depending on the particular customer/supplier environment of a project, the customer may also wish to appoint people to specialist Project Assurance roles.

B.5 PROJECT MANAGER

B.5.1 General

The Project Manager has the authority to run the project on a day-to-day basis on behalf of the Project Board within the constraints laid down by the Board. In a customer/supplier environment the Project Manager will normally come from the customer organization.

B.5.2 Responsibility

The Project Manager's prime responsibility is to ensure that the project produces the required products, to the required standard of quality and within the specified constraints of time and cost. The Project Manager is also responsible for the project producing a result that is capable of achieving the benefits defined in the Business Case.

B.5.3 Specific responsibilities

- Manage the production of the required products.
- Direct and motivate the project team.
- Plan and monitor the project.
- Agree any delegation and use of Project Assurance roles required by the Project Board.
- Produce the project contract.
- Prepare Project, Stage and, if necessary, Exception Plans in conjunction with Team Managers and appointed Project Assurance roles, and agree them with the Project Board.
- Manage business and project risks, including the development of contingency plans.
- Liaise with programme management if the project is part of a programme.
- Liaise with programme management or related projects to ensure that work is neither overlooked nor duplicated.
- Take responsibility for overall progress and use of resources, and initiate corrective action where necessary.
- Be responsible for change control and any required configuration management.
- Report to the Project Board through Highlight Reports and end stage assessments.
- Liaise with the Project Board or its appointed Project Assurance roles to assure the overall direction and assurance of the project.
- Agree technical and quality strategy with appropriate members of the Project Board.
- Prepare the Lessons Report.
- Prepare any follow-on action recommendations required.
- Prepare the End Project Report.

- Identify and obtain any support and advice required for the management, planning and control of the project.
- Be responsible for project administration.
- Liaise with any suppliers or account managers.

B.6 TEAM MANAGER

B.6.1 General

The allocation of this role to one or more people is optional. Where the project does not warrant the use of a Team Manager, the Project Manager takes the role.

The Project Manager may find that it is beneficial to delegate the authority and responsibility for planning the creation of certain products and managing a team of technicians to produce those products. There are many reasons why it may be decided to employ this role. Some of these are the size of the project, the particular specialist skills or knowledge needed for certain products, the geographical location of some team members and the preferences of the Project Board.

The Team Manager's prime responsibility is to ensure production of those products defined by the Project Manager to an appropriate quality, in a timescale and at a cost acceptable to the Project Board. The Team Manager reports to and takes direction from the Project Manager.

The use of this role should be discussed by the Project Manager with the Project Board and, if the role is required, planned at the outset of the project. This is discussed in the *Starting up a Project* (chapter 10) and *Initiating a Project* (chapter 11) processes.

B.6.2 Specific responsibilities

- Prepare plans for the team's work and agree these with the Project Manager.
- Receive authorization from the Project Manager to create products (the Work Package).

- Manage the team.
- Direct, plan and monitor the team work.
- Take responsibility for the progress of the team's work, and use of team resources, and initiate corrective action where necessary within the constraints laid down by the Project Manager.
- Advise the Project Manager of any deviations from plan, recommend corrective action and help prepare any appropriate Exception Plans.
- Pass products which have been completed and approved in line with the agreed Work Package requirements back to the Project Manager.
- Ensure all Issue Reports are properly reported to the person maintaining the Issue Register.
- Ensure the evaluation of Issue Reports that arise within the team's work, and recommend action to the Project Manager.
- Liaise with any Project Assurance roles.
- Attend any stage assessments as directed by the Project Manager.
- Arrange and lead team checkpoints.
- Ensure that quality controls of the team's work are planned and performed correctly.
- Maintain, or ensure the maintenance of, team files.
- Identify and advise the Project Manager of any risks associated with a Work Package.
- Ensure that such risks are entered on the Risk Register.
- Manage specific risks as directed by the Project Manager.

B.7 PROJECT ASSURANCE

B.7.1 General

The Project Board members do not work full time on the project, therefore they place a great deal of reliance on the Project Manager. Although they receive regular reports from the Project Manager, there may always be questions at the back of their minds: "Are things really going as well as we are being told?"; "Are any problems being hidden from us?"; "Is the solution going to be what we want?"; and "Are we suddenly going to find that the project is over budget or late?", etc. In addition, the supplier may have a quality assurance function

Appendix B: Project Management Team Roles

charged with the responsibility to check that all projects are adhering to the quality system. This means that there is a need in the project organization for an independent monitoring of all aspects of the project's performance and products. This is the Project Assurance function.

To cater for a small project, we start by identifying these Project Assurance functions as part of the role of each Project Board member. According to the needs and desires of the Project Board, any of these Project Assurance responsibilities can be delegated as long as their recipients are independent of the Project Manager and the rest of the project management team. Any appointed Project Assurance jobs assure the project on behalf of one or more members of the Project Board.

It is not mandatory that all Project Assurance roles be delegated. Each of the Project Assurance roles that is delegated may be assigned to one individual or shared. The Project Board decides when a Project Assurance role needs to be delegated. It may be for the entire project or only part of it. The person or persons filling a Project Assurance role may be changed during the project at the request of the Project Board. Any use of Project Assurance roles needs to be planned at initiation stage otherwise resource usage and costs for Project Assurance could easily get out of control.

There is no stipulation on how many Project Assurance roles there must be. Each Project Board role has Project Assurance responsibility. Again, each project should determine what support, if any, each Project Board role needs to achieve this Project Assurance.

For example, an international standards group, such as ISO may certificate the supplier's work standards. A requirement of the certification is that there will be some form of quality assurance function that is required to monitor the supplier's work. Some of the Senior Supplier's Project Assurance responsibility may be delegated to this function. Note that they would only be delegated. The Project Board member retains accountability, and any delegation should be documented. The quality assurance could include verification by an external party that the Project Board is performing its functions correctly.

Assurance covers all aspects of a project, including business, user and supplier.

Project Assurance has to be independent of the Project Manager, therefore the Project Board cannot delegate any of its Project Assurance responsibility to the Project Manager.

B.7.2 Specific responsibilities

The implementation of the Project Assurance responsibility needs to answer the question "What is to be assured?" A list of possibilities would include:

- Maintenance of thorough liaison throughout the project between the supplier and the customer.
- Customer needs and expectations are being met or managed.
- Risks are being controlled.
- Adherence to the Business Case.
- Constant reassessment of the value-for-money solution.
- Fit with the overall programme or company strategy.
- The right people being involved in writing Product Descriptions, especially for the quality criteria.
- The right people being planned to be involved in quality checking at the correct points in the product's development.
- Ensuring that staff are properly trained in the quality checking procedures.
- Ensuring that quality checking follow-up actions are dealt with correctly.
- Ensuring that the quality checking procedures are being correctly followed.
- An acceptable solution is developed.
- Project remains viable.
- The scope of the project is not 'creeping up' unnoticed.
- Focus on the business need is maintained.
- Internal and external communications are working.
- Applicable standards are being used.
- Any legislative constraints are being observed.
- The needs of specialist interests, e.g. security, are being observed.
- Adherence to quality assurance standards.

It is not enough to believe that standards will be obeyed. It is not enough to ensure that a project is well set up and justified at the outset. All the aspects listed above need to be checked throughout the project as part of ensuring that it remains consistent with, and continues to meet, a business need, and that no changes to the external environment have affected the validity of the project. This includes monitoring stage and team planning, Work Package and quality review preparation.

B.8 PROJECT SUPPORT

B.8.1 General

The provision of any Project Support on a formal basis is optional. It is driven by the needs of the individual project and Project Manager. Project Support could be in the form of advice on project management tools and allocating administrative services, such as filing or the collection of actual data, to one or more related projects. Where set up as an official body, Project Support can act as a repository for lessons learned, and a central source of expertise in specialist support tools.

One support function that must be considered is configuration management. Depending on the project size and environment, there may be a need to formalize this, and it quickly becomes a task with which the Project Manager cannot cope without support. See *Configuration management* (section 9.1) for details of the work.

B.8.2 Main tasks

The following is a suggested list of tasks.

Administration:

- Administer change control.
- Set up and maintain project files.
- Establish document control procedures.
- Compile, copy and distribute all project management products.
- Collect actual data and forecasts.

- Update plans.
- Administer the quality review process.
- Administer Project Board meetings.
- Assist with the compilation of reports.

Advice:

- Specialist knowledge; e.g. estimating, management of risk.
- Specialist tool expertise; e.g. planning and control tools, risk analysis.
- Specialist techniques.
- Standards.

Appendix C

Product-based Planning

C.1 THE BENEFITS OF PRODUCT-BASED PLANNING

PRINCE2 recommends Product-based Planning. There are two reasons for this. First, a project delivers products, not activities, so why begin at a lower level? The second reason is quality. We can measure the quality of a product, but the quality of an activity can only be measured by the quality of its outcome (the product). Other benefits include:

- A consistent and unambiguous way of describing each product.
- A discipline to think of the purpose(s) of each product before creating it.
- A discipline to think of the quality required by a product before creating it.
- A visual way of defining the scope of a plan.
- The involvement of users in defining the products.
- The identification of products required by the project that either already exist, or are to be created by projects outside the Project Manager's control (called external products).

C.2 PRODUCT-BASED PLANNING RULES

PRINCE2 uses two graphical symbols (Figure C.1).

A rectangle contains a product (or an idea of a group of products) to be created by the project. An ellipse indicates an external product.

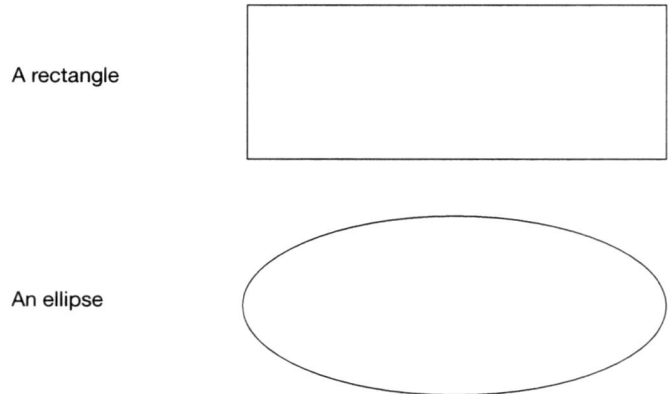

FIGURE C.1 PRINCE2 product symbols

C.2.1 External products

There are times when you may wish to show that the plan is dependent on a product that already exists or over whose delivery you have no control. For example, you might have to create a product 'packaged disks'. Before you can create this product you have to receive the plastic disk box from the stock of an external supplier. To show that the development of the plastic disk box is outside your control you would use a different symbol on the plan; PRINCE2 uses an ellipse. The Product Flow Diagram for this example would be as shown in Figure C.2.

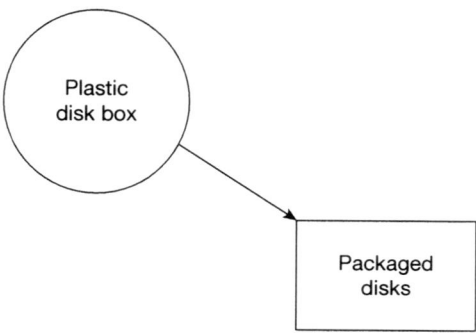

FIGURE C.2 Product Flow Diagram

Appendix C: Product-based Planning

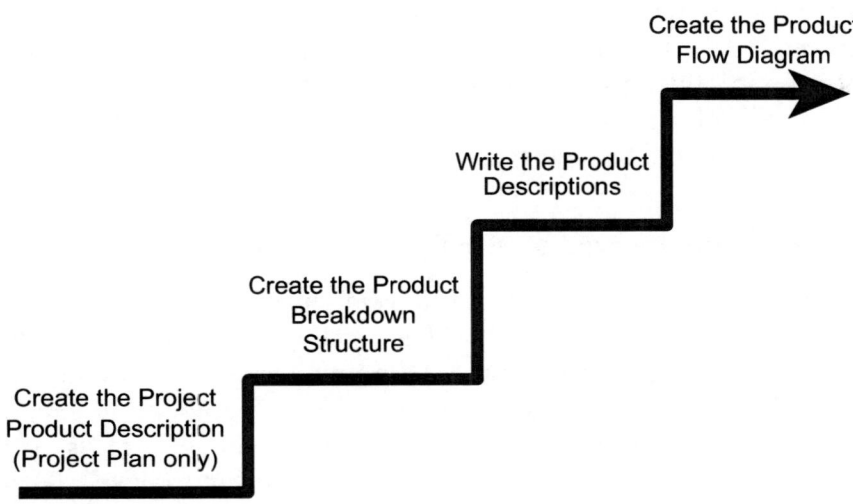

FIGURE C.3 Product-based Planning steps

To summarize, an external product contains a single product that either already exists or will be provided by another project.

C.3 PRODUCT-BASED PLANNING STEPS

Product-based Planning has four steps (Figure C.3):

- Write the Project Product Description;
- Create the Product Breakdown Structure;
- Write the Product Descriptions;
- Create the Product Flow Diagram.

C.3.1 Write the Project Product Description

The first step in Product-based Planning is actually to write a special format of a Product Description for the final product. This is a summary of the project's final product. It defines what the project must deliver in order to be accepted by the customer. This helps establish if the customer actually understands, and can describe, the required final product and helps establish the customer's quality expectations (and therefore needs to be done during the *Starting up a Project* process – chapter 10). A Product Description of a Project Product Description is given in Appendix A.19. Its creation is officially the responsibility of the Senior User(s), but usually the Project Manager writes it in consultation with the Senior User(s) and Executive.

C.3.2 Create the Product Breakdown Structure

A Product Breakdown Structure is a hierarchy of the products whose creation is to be planned. (As well as creating products, there might be some that you purchase or obtain from other sources.) At the top of the hierarchy is the final end product; e.g. a computer system, a new yacht or a department relocated to a new building. This is then broken down into its major constituents at the next level. Each constituent is then broken down into its parts, and this process continues until the planner has reached the level of detail required for the plan. Let's look at a really simple example (Figure C.4):

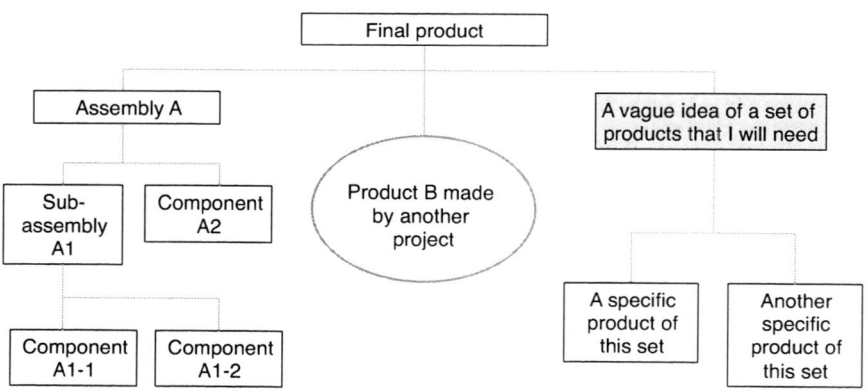

FIGURE C.4 Product Breakdown Structure

Figure C.5 is an example of a Product Breakdown Structure as a hierarchical top-down structure.

The left-hand side is pretty easy to understand. Our final product needs assembly A. This consists of component A2 and a sub-assembly A1. The sub-assembly consists of component A1–1 and component A1–2. So we have three simple products – the three components. Two

Appendix C: Product-based Planning

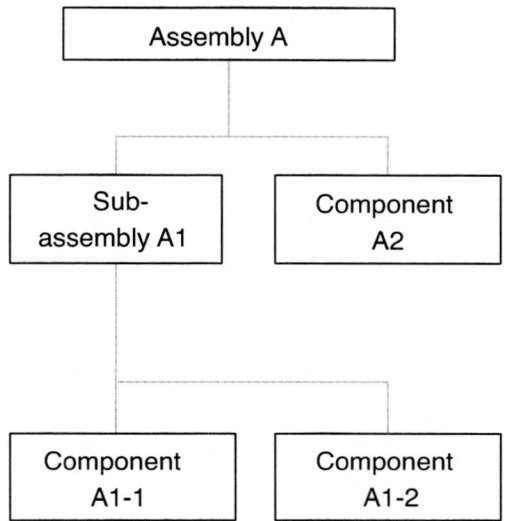

FIGURE C.5 A hierarchical top-down structure

of these make up our sub-assembly A1, which then joins component A2 to make up assembly A, which becomes part of our final product.

Each of these requires a Product Description to be written for them.

The lowest level on a Product Breakdown Structure is not fixed. It depends on the level of detail required in the plan to allow the Project Board, Project Manager or Team Manager to exercise an appropriate level of control.

The ellipse, shown in Figure C.6, is a bit different. As we can see from the words, the creation of product B is the work of another project, so we have no work to do in its creation and it should arrive fully tested. We will have to test its connection to our final product, but, if it has any quality problems off it goes, back to the other project. To indicate that it is not our responsibility we use a different symbol, traditionally an ellipse. While the Project Manager is not accountable for the creation of external products, the project does need the product(s) in order to achieve its objectives. A plan must therefore include any external products required to achieve the plan's objectives, plus any dependencies on these external products. *We do not write a Product Description for external products.*

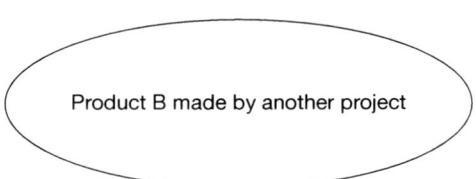

FIGURE C.6 An ellipse to indicate a product made by another project

The third part of our final product is another 'oddity' (Figure C.7). It's not a *real* product in itself, but later, as we think about it, we realize that it consists of two specific products. These are real products, but the box with the vague idea was a temporary measure until we got round to working out of what products it would consist.

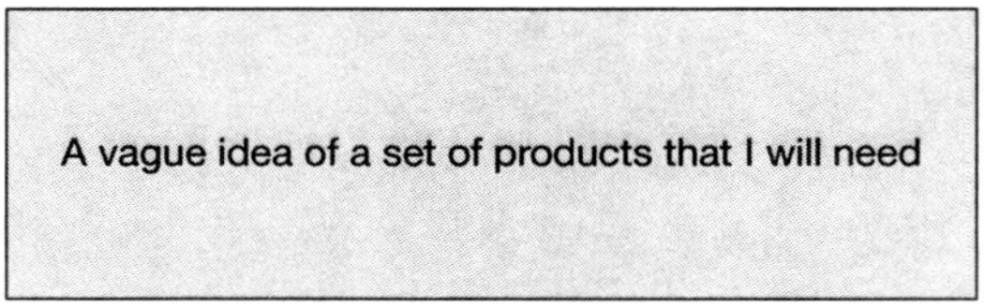

FIGURE C.7 A box indicating a temporary Product Description

Let's take an example: our final product is a new mobile phone. We know that we will have to produce some instructional material, but at the start we haven't made up our mind about what kind of material this will be. When we come back and think about the 'vague idea' we decide that it will consist of two products: a diagram of the phone and a set of instructions. We will need to write Product Descriptions for the two specific products, but not for the 'vague idea'.

A hierarchical diagram is just one version of how to create a Product Breakdown Structure. If you are used to drawing mind maps, you might have drawn our example like the one in Figure C.8.

C.3.3 Write the Product Descriptions

For each significant *real* product to be created by the project, a Product Description is produced. Its creation forces the planner to consider

Appendix C: Product-based Planning

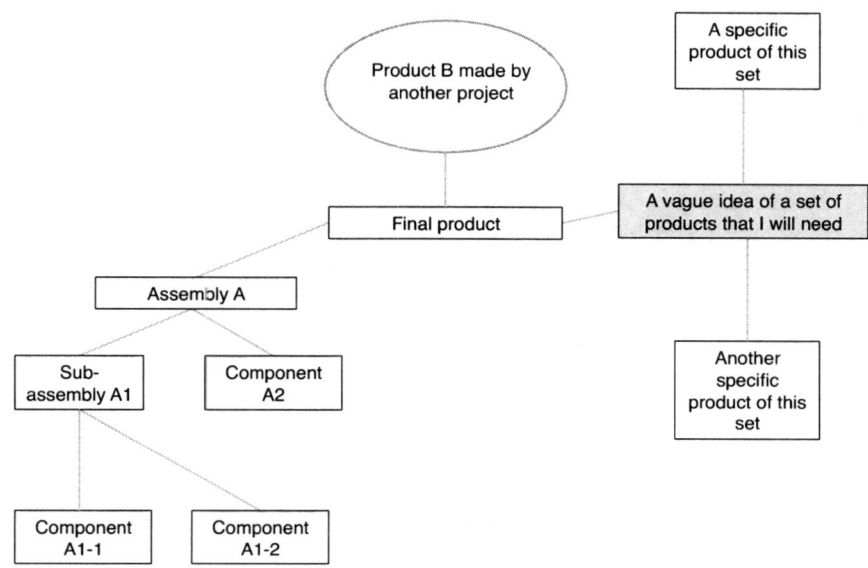

FIGURE C.8 Product Breakdown Structure mind map

whether sufficient is known about the product in order to plan its production. It is also the first time that the quality of the product is considered. The quality criteria should be measurable statements on the expected quality of the product and what type of quality checking will be required. As an example, 'faster' and 'better' are not measurable and would therefore not be useful quality criteria. 'Able to bear a weight of 10 tons' and 'maximum response time of 3 seconds' are examples of measurable criteria.

The purposes of writing a Product Description are, therefore, to provide a guide:

- To the planner on how much effort will be required to create the product;
- To the author of the product on what is required;
- Against which the finished product can be measured.

These descriptions are a vital checklist to be used at a quality check of the related products.

The description should contain:

- The purpose of the product;
- The composition of the product;
- The products from which it is derived;
- Any standards for format and presentation;
- The quality criteria to be applied to the product;
- The quality verification method to be used.

The Product Description is given to both the product's creator and those who will verify its quality.

C.3.4 Create the Product Flow Diagram

The Product Flow Diagram is a diagram that shows the sequence in which the products have to be produced and the dependencies between them. The products are those shown in the Product

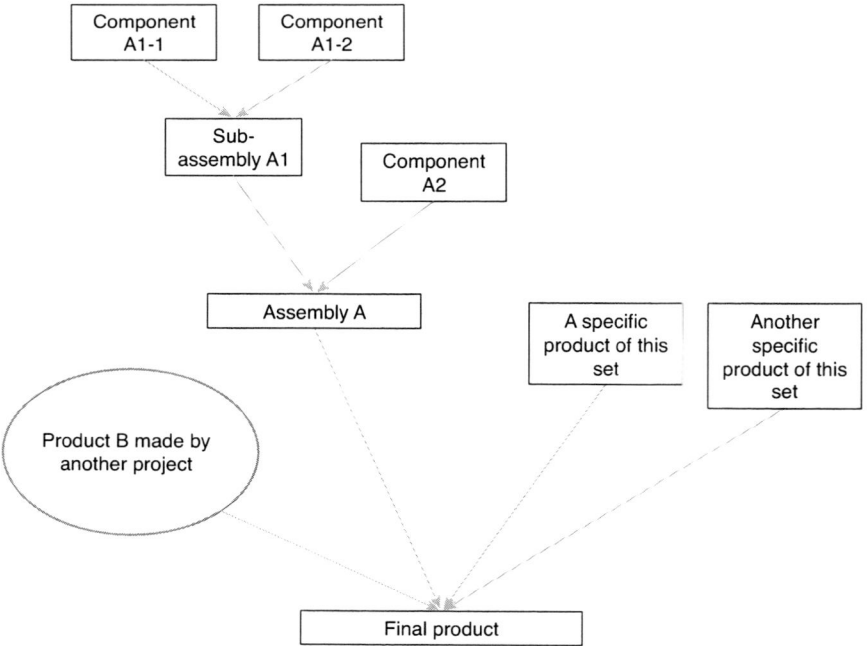

FIGURE C.9 Product Flow Diagram

Breakdown Structure and care should be taken to ensure that the same names are used for products in the two diagrams.

It uses the same rectangle and ellipse symbols plus arrows to show the dependencies. Figure C.9 is a Product Flow Diagram for the simple Product Breakdown Structure with which we started.

Not all 'products' in a Product Breakdown Structure may need to be transferred to the Product Flow Diagram. Some of them may not be products in their own right, but thoughts for a series of products that will be needed. For example, if the project is to create a training manual, one 'product' may be 'translations'. You are not going to produce a product called 'translations', but it will trigger you to think of real products, such as making translations of product literature into German, French, etc. 'Translations' would not be transferred to the Product Flow Diagram. So, only *real* products in the Product Breakdown Structure are transferred to the Product Flow Diagram.

C.4 PRODUCT-BASED PLANNING EXAMPLE

You are a garden designer. You are approached by a local businessman. He has had a new house built at the edge of town and he wants you to design and construct his back garden. You are invited to meet him at the house.

The garden area is large with a good fence round the perimeter. Inside the fence, the area is the typical mess that you might expect from a reclaimed area: builder's rubble, old prams, weeds, brambles, etc.

He tells you that he hasn't much idea about gardening, but he has a few ideas. He wants a large patio, large enough to be able to entertain about fifty guests. Since his childhood he has had a dream of himself cooking at a barbecue and he wants a brick-built barbecue on the patio.

For the rest of the garden he envisages plenty of lawn with a few flower beds.

He doesn't intend to do the gardening himself, so he wants a garden shed in some corner filled with the tools that a gardener will need to maintain the garden.

C.4.1 The Product Breakdown Structure

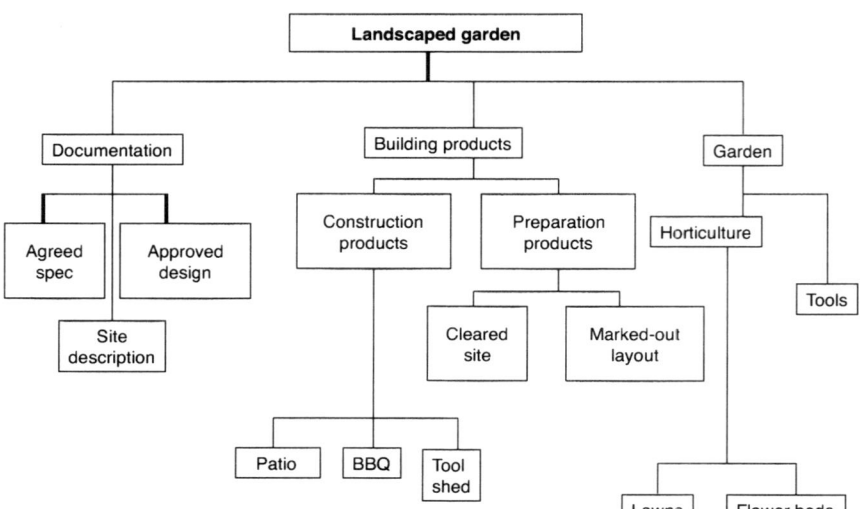

FIGURE C.10 Example of a Product Breakdown Structure

We can see in Figure C.10 that below the final product – Landscaped Garden – we have put in three 'ideas' products just to separate the types of product – documentation, building products and garden.

Below 'documentation', this has been broken down into three real products. For 'building products' more separation is still required, so we break this down into 'construction products' and 'preparation products' – still not *real* products in their own right. Both of these now break down into the products that we will need.

'Garden' consists of tools and another non-product 'horticulture', which consists of lawns and flower beds. We could have omitted 'horticulture' and just had the three products directly below 'garden', but writing the plan like this allows us to drop its two products down into the bottom layer to make the diagram look neater.

Appendix C: Product-based Planning

C.4.2 Key points about the Product Breakdown Structure

- Consider products not activities (especially at lowest level).
- If a box is broken down to a lower level, this means "This product consists completely of the products below" not "This is followed by".
- Do not include one-to-one breakdowns.
- Different branches of the hierarchy do not join up at a lower level.
- Do not use arrows.
- Keep lowest level relevant to the level of the plan.

C.4.3 The Product Flow Diagram of our landscaped garden

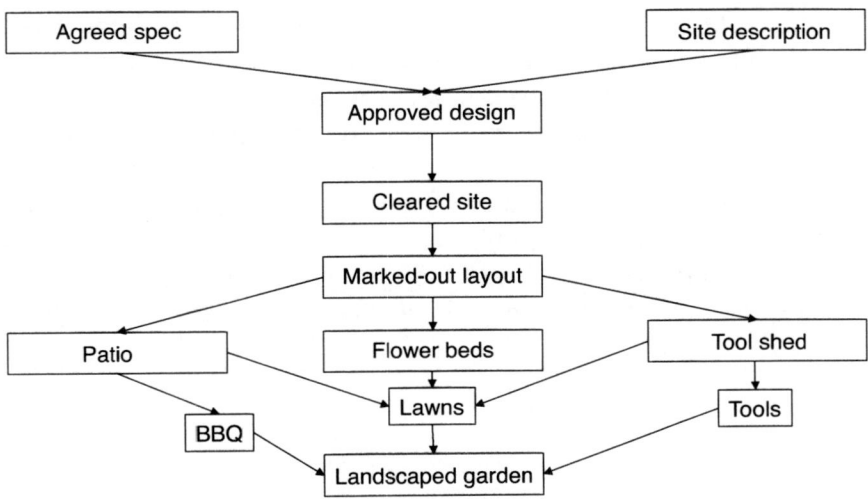

FIGURE C.11 Example of a Product Flow Diagram

In Figure C.11 we can see how only the real products have been transferred across from the Product Breakdown Structure. We can see how the diagram shows the dependencies and this information will be easy to transfer to a Gantt chart.

C.4.4 Key points about Product Flow Diagrams

- Must contain all the lowest level products from the Product Breakdown Structure.
- May contain some higher-level products *if* there is still work to be done to assemble or test them.
- Must use the same names as in the Product Breakdown Structure.
- Uses arrows to show the development sequence of the products of the plan.
- Can be drawn in a top-to-bottom or left-to-right orientation.

C.5 PRODUCT STATES

One subject that causes debate is whether a product that passes through several states should be shown as one product or as a product for each state. For example, if in relocating a factory you have 'dismantled machinery', 'transported machinery' and 'reassembled machinery', there may be good reasons for treating these as three products; there would be different purposes, quality criteria and quality checks, and different teams may be used for each state. On the other hand, a document will have several states, such as draft, reviewed, proofread and published. Do you really need to write a Product Description for each of these states? It can usually be done by one Product Description with quality criteria for each of these 'states'.

Appendix D

Quality Review

This is a team method of checking a document's quality by a review process. The purpose of a quality review is to inspect a document for errors in a planned, independent, controlled and documented manner and ensure that any errors found are fixed.

The quality review technique is a structured way of reviewing documents to ensure that all aspects are properly covered. It needs to be used with common sense to avoid the dangers of an over-bureaucratic approach but with the intent to follow the procedures laid down (to ensure nothing is missed).

The major aim is to improve product quality. There are several subordinate objectives. These are to:

- Trap errors as early as possible;
- Encourage the concept of documents as team property rather than belonging to an individual;
- Enhance product status data; e.g. not only has the creator declared a product finished, but others have confirmed that it is of good quality;
- Monitor the use of standards;
- Spread knowledge of the document among those whose own products may interact with it.

Quality review documentation, when filed in the quality file, provides, together with the Quality Register, a record that the document was inspected, that any errors found were corrected and that the corrections were themselves checked. The knowledge that a document has been checked and declared error-free provides a more confident basis for use of that document as the basis of future work than simply taking the word of the creator.

D.1 ROLES AT THE QUALITY REVIEW

D.1.1 Roles

The roles involved in a quality review are:

- The *presenter*: who is normally the author of the document being reviewed. This role has to ensure that the reviewers have all the required information in order to perform their job. This means getting a copy of the document from the Configuration Librarian to the reviewers during the preparation phase, plus any documents needed to put it in context. Then the presenter has to answer questions about the document during the review until a decision can be reached on whether there is an error or not. Finally, the presenter will do most, if not all, of the correcting work. The presenter must not be allowed to be defensive about the document.
- The *chair*: who needs an open, objective attitude. The chair requires the following attributes:
  o Sufficient authority to control the review;
  o Thorough understanding of the quality review process;
  o Chairmanship experience.
  The chair is responsible for ensuring that the quality review is properly organized and that it runs smoothly during all of its phases. For the preparation phase this includes checking that administrative procedures have been carried out and that the right people have been invited. This needs consultation with any appointed Project Assurance roles and reference to the Stage Plan.
- The *reviewers*: who must be competent to assess the product from their particular viewpoints.
- An *administrator*: someone who will note down any required actions resulting from the review. This role may be taken by one of the other attendees, but if the review has several attendees it is sensible to give this role to someone other than the chair, so that the chair can concentrate on controlling the review.

It must be remembered that all these are roles. They must all be present at a quality review, but a person may take on more than one role.

D.1.2 People involved

The interests of parties who should be considered when drawing up the list of attendees are:

- The product author;
- Those with Project Assurance responsibilities delegated by the Project Board;
- The customer;
- Staff who will use the document as a basis for further work;
- Other staff whose work will be affected by the product;
- Specialists in the relevant product area;
- Standards representatives.

D.2 PHASES

There are three distinct phases within the quality review procedure: preparation; review; and follow-up.

D.2.1 Phase 1 – Preparation

The objective of this phase is to examine the document under review and to create a list of questions for the review.

The chair checks with the presenter that the document will be ready on time. If not, the Project Manager is advised. This will lead to an update of the Stage Plan and the Quality Register. The chair ensures that the team of reviewers is agreed, that they will all be available and that the venue for the review has been arranged. Project Assurance may wish to be involved in confirming that the team of reviewers is satisfactory to them.

An invitation is sent out, giving the time and place for the review with copies of the document, the relevant Product Description and any checklist available. This should be done with sufficient time before the review to allow the reviewers time to examine the document and to provide a question list to the presenter (Figure D.1).

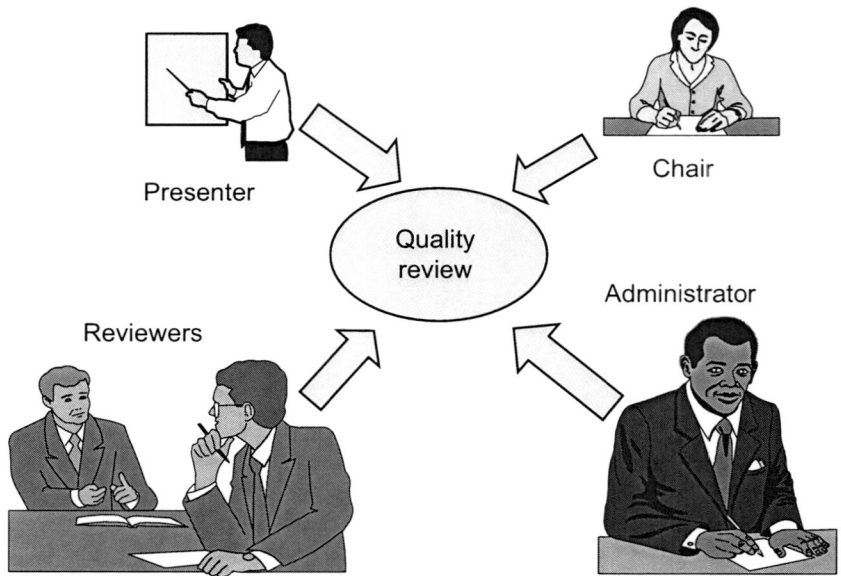

FIGURE D.1 Quality review

Each reviewer will study the document and supporting documents (including the quality criteria in the Product Description), annotate the document with any spelling or grammatical errors and complete a question list.

A copy of the question lists will, wherever possible, be sent to the presenter before the review. The presenter and chair should review these to allow the chair to set up an agenda, prioritize the questions and roughly allocate time to each point. To save time at the review, the presenter can acknowledge questions that identify agreed errors.

D.2.2 Phase 2 – Review

The objective of the review is to agree a list of any actions needed to correct or complete the document (Figure D.2). The chair and the presenter do not have to reconcile these actions at the meeting – it is sufficient for the chair and reviewers to agree that a particular area needs correction or at least re-examination. Provided that the action is logged, the reviewers have an opportunity in the next phase to confirm that action has been taken.

Appendix D: Quality Review

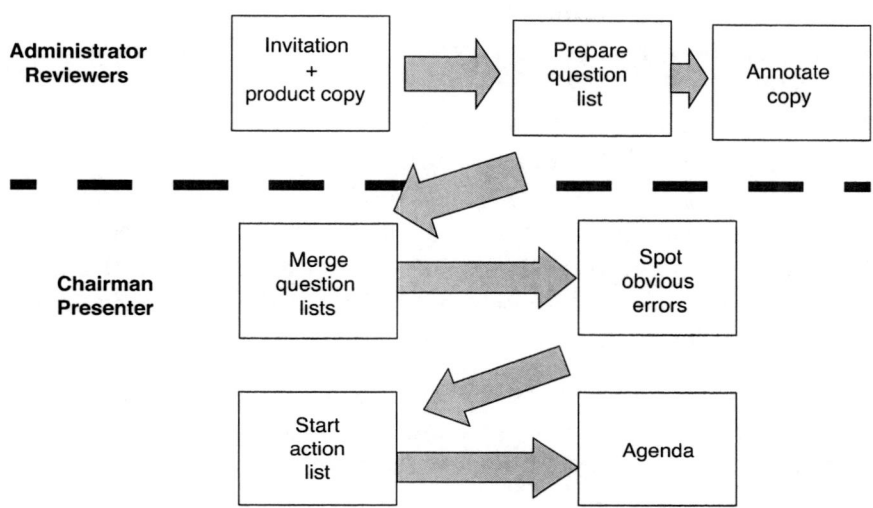

FIGURE D.2 Quality review preparation

The chair opens the meeting and, if necessary, introduces those present. Timing (suggested maximum of two hours) is announced.

The presenter then 'walks through' the questions in detail. This will be determined by the reviewers' question lists already sent to the presenter. If it is found that any part is understood and accepted, there is no point in walking through it.

The chair controls the discussion during the review, ensuring that no arguments or solutions are discussed (other than obvious and immediately accepted solutions!). The administrator notes actions on a follow-up action list. No other minutes are taken of the review.

At the conclusion of the walk-through, the chair asks the administrator to read back the actions and determines responsibility for correction of any points. A target date is set for each action, and the initials of the reviewer(s) who will sign off each corrective action as it is completed and found acceptable are recorded on the follow-up action list by the administrator.

The chair, after seeking the reviewers' and presenter's opinions, will decide on the outcome of the review. There can be one of three outcomes:

- The document is error-free;
- The document will be acceptable on completion of the actions noted;
- There is so much corrective work to be done that the entire document needs to be re-reviewed.

In the latter case, the chair will advise the Project Manager so that the Stage Plan can be updated. The Quality Register is updated. A result notification will be completed and the documents attached. These forms will be filed in the quality file.

The reviewers' question lists, copies of the document (probably containing the reviewers' annotations) and any other relevant documentation is collected by the chair and passed to the presenter to assist in the follow-up.

D.2.3 Phase 3 – Follow-up

The objective of the follow-up phase is to ensure that all actions identified on the follow-up action list are dealt with (Figure D.3).

The presenter takes the follow-up action list away from the review and evaluates, discusses and corrects, if necessary, all the errors.

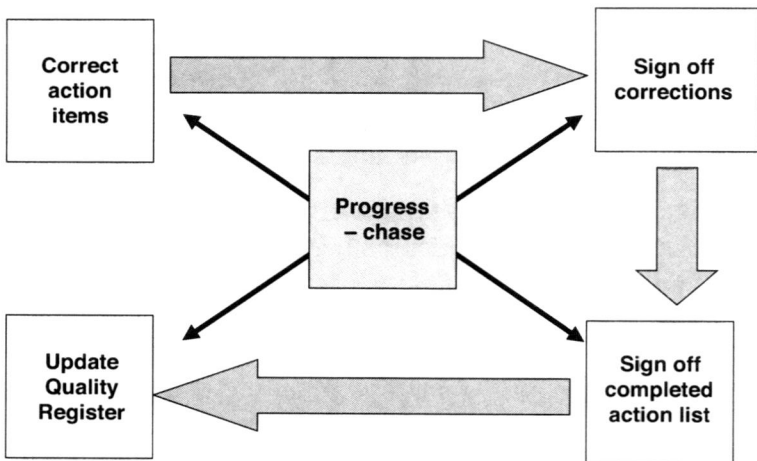

FIGURE D.3 Quality review follow-up

When an error has been fixed, the presenter will obtain sign-off from whoever is nominated on the follow-up action list. This person may be the reviewer who raised the initial query, but other reviewers have the option of checking the correction.

When all errors have been reconciled and sign-off obtained, the chair will confirm that the document is complete and sign off the follow-up action list. The documents will be filed in the Quality Register and the Stage Plan updated.

D.3 QUALITY REVIEW RESPONSIBILITIES

D.3.1 Chair's responsibilities

Preparation Phase:

- Check with the presenter that the product is ready for review.
- If the product is not ready for review, update the Stage Plan; e.g. a revised completion date.
- Consult with the presenter and those performing Project Assurance roles to confirm appropriate reviewers.
- Agree the amount of preparation time required with the presenter (and reviewers, if this is appropriate).
- Arrange a time, location and duration for the review in consultation with the presenter and reviewers.
- Advise the Project Manager if there is to be any delay in holding the review.
- Arrange for copies of any relevant checklist or standard to be provided.
- Ensure the Configuration Librarian provides Product Descriptions and product copies for all reviewers.
- Send an invitation, Product Description, document copy, blank question list, Product Checklist (if there is one) to each reviewer.
- Send a copy of the invitation to the presenter.
- Decide if a short overview presentation of the document to the reviewers is required as part of the preparation, and arrange if required.
- Arrange with the reviewers for collection of their question lists prior to the review.

- Create an agenda for the review from the question lists in consultation with the presenter. Agree any obvious errors in the document with the presenter. Prioritize the questions and roughly allocate time.
- Confirm attendance with each reviewer shortly before the review. If a reviewer cannot attend, ensure that the reviewer's question list is made out and submitted. If too many reviewers cannot attend, reschedule the review and inform the Project Manager of the delay.
- If necessary, rehearse the review with the presenter.

Review:

- Provide a copy of the agenda to all attendees.
- Open the review, stating objectives and apologizing for any non-attendees.
- Decide whether the reviewers present and the question lists from the non-attendees are adequate to review the document. If not, the review should be stopped, rescheduled and the Project Manager advised.
- Identify any errors in the document already agreed by the presenter and ensure that these are documented on the follow-up action list.
- Step through the agenda, with the appropriate reviewer giving further information, where necessary, on each question.
- Allow reasonable discussion on each question between presenter and reviewers to decide if action is required.
- Ensure that the administrator documents any agreed actions required on a follow-up action list.
- Prevent any discussion of possible solutions or matters of style.
- Ensure that reviewers are given a chance to voice their comments.
- Where agreement cannot be reached on a point in a reasonable time frame, declare it an action point and note the reviewer(s) concerned.
- Where necessary, decide on the premature close of the review in the light of the comments made.
- If faults are identified in documents not under review, ensure that an issue is raised and sent to the Configuration Librarian.

Appendix D: Quality Review

- Collect any annotated documents detailing minor or typographical errors.
- Read back the follow-up action list and obtain confirmation from the presenter and reviewers that it is complete and correct.
- Identify who is to be involved in working on each action item. Obtain a target date for completion of the work.
- Agree with the reviewers who is to approve the work done on each action item and note this on the follow-up action list.
- Pass the follow-up action list and all copies of the annotated document to the presenter. Lodge a copy of the follow-up action list in the Quality Register.
- Decide with the reviewers what the status of the review is. It can be:
  o complete with no errors discovered;
  o complete with some rework required;
  o in need of rework and another review.
- If the review is incomplete, recommend a course of action to the Project Manager. There are five possible courses of action. The last two of these are not recommended:
  o The document should be reworked prior to another review;
  o The review should be reconvened to finish with no interim need for rework;
  o The review should be reconvened without rework with a different set of reviewers;
  o The review should be declared complete, the errors found so far corrected and the rest of the document accepted as is;
  o The review should be abandoned and the document used as is, i.e. none of the errors corrected, but noted in an issue.

Follow up:

- Monitor the correction of errors and sign off the follow-up action list when all corrections have been approved.
- If an action cannot be taken within the time agreed, the chair and presenter may decide to transfer it to an issue as a possible error. This requires the agreement of the Project Manager. The follow-up action list is updated with the Issue Register number and those waiting to sign off the action item informed.

- On completion and sign-off of all action items, sign off the follow-up action list as complete and file it in the Quality Register, with copies to all reviewers. Update the Quality Register.
- Supervise the passage of the error-free document to the Configuration Librarian.

D.3.2 Producer's responsibilities

Preparation:

- Ask the Project Manager to nominate a chair if none is identified in the Stage Plan.
- Confirm with the chair that the document is ready for review. This should occur several days prior to the planned review date to allow for preparation time.
- Confirm the attendees with the chair and those holding Project Assurance responsibilities.
- Agree with the chair and reviewers the length of preparation time needed and review location.
- Assess the question lists from the reviewers, identifying any errors in the document that can be agreed without further discussion.
- Agree the agenda with the chair in the light of the question lists.

Review:

- Answer any questions about the document.
- Offer an opinion to the chair on whether a question has highlighted an error in the document.
- If the review is judged to be complete, collect from the chair the follow-up action list and any annotated copies of the document from the reviewers.

Follow-up:

- Resolve all allocated action items.
- Obtain sign-off for each action item from the nominated reviewers.
- If an action item cannot be resolved within a reasonable time frame, then decide with the chair to transfer it to an issue. An alternative is to agree new target dates.

- Pass the follow-up action list to the chair on resolution of all the action items.

D.3.3 Reviewer's responsibilities

Preparation:

- Consult the Product Description and any pertinent checklists and standards against which the document should be judged.
- Allow sufficient time to prepare for the review.
- Consult any necessary source documents from which the document is derived.
- Annotate any spelling or typographical mistakes on the document copy, but do not add these to the question list.
- Check the document for completeness, defects, ambiguities, inconsistencies, lack of clarity or deviations from standards. Note any such items on the question list.
- Forward the question list to the chair in advance of the review. If possible, this should be done early enough to give the presenter time to digest the points and prepare an agenda with the chair.
- Forward a question list and the annotated document copy to the chair if unable to attend the review.

Review:

- Ensure that the points noted on the question list are raised at the review.
- Restrict comments to faults in the document under review.
- Avoid attempting to redesign the document.
- Avoid 'improvement' comments if the document meets requirements and standards.
- Verify and approve the follow-up action list as complete and correct when read back by the chair.
- Agree to assist in the resolution of any action items if requested by the chair.
- Request to check and sign off any action items either raised personally or which impact the reviewer's area of expertise or interest.

Follow-up:

- Work with the presenter to resolve any allocated action item.
- Check and sign off those action items where allocated as reviewer.

Quality reviews can be either formal (i.e. a scheduled meeting conducted as described above) or informal (i.e. a get-together between two people to informally walk through a document). A variation on a formal review is to have the reviewers forward their follow-up action lists, but only the chair and the presenter do the actual review.

D.4 INFORMAL QUALITY REVIEWS

Informal quality reviews will follow a similar format to the formal quality review – the paperwork emerging from both meetings is similar. The main difference will be the informality of the proceedings during the three phases and the overall time required.

For informal quality reviews two people can be given the task of checking each other's work on an ongoing basis. Alternatively an experienced person can be asked to regularly hold reviews of an inexperienced person's work as it develops.

Factors in deciding whether a formal or informal review is needed are:

- The importance of the document;
- Whether it is a final deliverable;
- Whether it is the source for a number of other documents;
- The author's experience;
- Who the document's consumer is;
- Whether it is a review of a partial document.

Appendix E

Risk Categories

The following categories can be used as a starting point for identifying your organization's main areas of risk in relation to projects or programmes.

E.1 STRATEGIC/COMMERCIAL RISKS

- Underperformance to specification.
- Management will underperform against expectations.
- Collapse of contractors.
- Insolvency of promoter.
- Failure of suppliers to meet contractual commitments; this could be in terms of quality, quantity, timescales or their own exposure to risk.
- Insufficient capital revenues.
- Market fluctuations.
- Fraud/theft.
- Partnerships failing to deliver the desired outcome.
- The situation being non-insurable (or cost of insurance outweighs the benefit).
- Lack of availability of capital investment.

E.2 ECONOMIC/FINANCIAL/MARKET

- Exchange rate fluctuation.
- Interest rate instability.
- Inflation.
- Shortage of working capital.

- Failure to meet projected revenue targets.
- Market developments will adversely affect plans.

E.3 LEGAL AND REGULATORY

- New or changed legislation may invalidate assumptions upon which the activity is based.
- Failure to obtain appropriate approval, e.g. planning, consent.
- Unforeseen inclusion of contingent liabilities.
- Loss of intellectual property rights.
- Failure to achieve satisfactory contractual arrangements.
- Unexpected regulatory controls or licensing requirements.
- Changes in tax or tariff structure.

E.4 ORGANIZATIONAL/MANAGEMENT/HUMAN FACTORS

- Management incompetence.
- Inadequate corporate policies.
- Inadequate adoption of management practices.
- Poor leadership.
- Key personnel have inadequate authority to fulfil their roles.
- Poor staff selection procedures.
- Lack of clarity over roles and responsibilities.
- Vested interests creating conflict and compromising the overall aims.
- Individual or group interests given unwarranted priority.
- Personality clashes.
- Indecision or inappropriate decision-making.
- Lack of operational support.
- Inadequate or inaccurate information.
- Health and safety constraints.

E.5 POLITICAL

- Change of government policy (national or international); e.g. approach to nationalization.
- Change of government.

- War and disorder.
- Adverse public opinion/media intervention.

E.6 ENVIRONMENTAL

- Natural disasters.
- Storms, flooding, tempests.
- Pollution incidents.
- Transport problems, including aircraft/vehicle collisions.

E.7 TECHNICAL/OPERATIONAL/INFRASTRUCTURE

- Inadequate design.
- Professional negligence.
- Human error/incompetence.
- Infrastructure failure.
- Operation lifetime lower than expected.
- Residual value of assets lower than expected.
- Increased dismantling/decommissioning costs.
- Safety being compromised.
- Performance failure.
- Residual maintenance problems.
- Scope creep.
- Unclear expectations.
- Breaches in security/information security.
- Lack or inadequacy of business continuity.

Index

B
Baseline: 108
Benefits Review Plan: 21, 227
Benefits: 4
BUS: 7, 25
Business Case: 17–24, 228; business options 19; continued business justification 68; expected benefits 20; investment appraisal 21; negative consequences 20; refine the Business Case 154–6

C
Change: 103–19; Change authority 41, 113–14; change control 40, 113–19; issue and change control procedure 115–19
Checkpoint Report: 72, 229
Closing a Project: 16, 211–20; evaluate the project 217–19; hand over products 215–17; prepare planned closure 213–14; prepare premature close 214–15; recommend project closure 219–20
Communication Management Strategy: 147–150, 230, 232
Configuration Item Record: 121, 231
Configuration management: 103–13; baseline 108; configuration auditing 109–110; Configuration Item Record 107; Configuration Management Strategy 107–8, 144–7; Product Status Account 108; release package 110–12
Controlling a Stage: 15; 171–88; authorize a Work Package 172–4; capture and examine issues and risks 177–180; escalate issues and risks 186–8; report highlights 182–4; receive completed Work Packages 176–7; review stage status 180–2; review Work Package status 174–6, take corrective action 184–6;
Controls: event and time-driven controls 73–5; set up project controls 152–4
Corporate or programme management: 38

D
Daily Log: 233, 131, 138, 143, 144, 177
Directing a Project: 14, 159–70; authorize initiation 160–2; authorize the project 162–4;

authorize project closure 168–9; authorize a Stage or Exception Plan 164–6; give ad hoc direction 166–8;

E
Early warning indicators: 89
End Project Report: 233, 217–19
End Stage Report: 234
Event-driven controls: 73–5
Exception Plan: authorize a Stage or Exception Plan 164–6; produce an Exception Plan 206–9
Exception Report: 236, 186
Executive: 22, 32, 259
External products: 272

H
Highlight Report: 69, 101, 182–4, 236

I
Initiating a Project: 14, 139–58; assemble the Project Initiation Documentation 156–8; create the Project Plan 150–2; prepare the Communication Management Strategy 147–150; prepare the Configuration Management Strategy 144–7; prepare the Quality Management Strategy 140–2; prepare the Risk Management Strategy 140–4; refine the Business Case 154–6; set up project controls 152–4
Issue Register: 71, 115, 145, 237
Issue Report: 115, 238
Issues: 114–15; escalate issues and risks 186–8; issue and change control procedure 115–19; off-specification 114–15; problem or concern 115; request for change 114

L
Lessons Log: 125, 239
Lessons Report: 6, 205, 218, 239

M
Management by exception: 8, 65–6, 186
Managing a Stage Boundary: 16, 197–210; plan the next stage 198–200; produce an Exception Plan 206–9; report stage end 204–6; update the Business Case 202–4; update the Project Plan 201–2
Managing Product Delivery: 15, 189–95; accept a Work Package 190–2; deliver a Work Package 194–5; execute a Work Package 192–4

O
Organization: 25–45; changes 41; Executive 32; four layers of management 26; Project Assurance 35–7; Project Board 31; Project Manager 33–4; Project Support 37; Senior Supplier 33; Senior User 33; tailoring the organization 223; Team Manager 34–5

P
Plans: 47–62; approach to planning 52–3; Exception Plan 52; hierarchy of plans 48; plan narrative 50; plan prerequisites 51; Project Plan 49; Stage Plan 49–50; external dependencies 51; Team

Index

Plan 52; create the Project Plan 150–2; update the Project Plan 201–2;plan Product Description 240; tailoring plans 224
Post-project benefit review: 22
PRINCE2 approach to planning 52–62; analyze the risks 58–9; define and analyse products 55–6; design a plan 54–5; document the plan 59–60; identify activities and dependencies 56–7; prepare estimates 56–7; prepare the schedule 57–8;
Principles: 4–9; continued business justification 5; defined roles and responsibilities 6; focus on products 9; learn from experience 6; manage by exception 8; manage by stages 7; tailor to suit the project environment 9
Processes: 12; tailoring processes 225–6
Product Breakdown Structure: 241, 274–6
Product Checklist: 242
Product Descriptions: 242, 84, 227–55; 276–8
Product Flow Diagram: 243, 278–9
Product Status Account: 108, 244
Product-based Planning: 271–82, product states 282
Progress: 63–75; management by exception 65–6; management by stages 63–5
Project approach: 98, 121, 132–6
Project Assurance: 266, 35–7; Project Assurance versus quality assurance 83
Project Board: 257, 31–3, 38; Project Board controls 68–71; Senior Supplier 33; Senior User 33

Project Brief: 132, 245
Project closure: 211–20
Project Initiation Documentation: 246; assemble the Project Initiation Documentation 156–8; tailoring the PID 226
Project management team roles: 257–70
Project Manager: 263, 33–4, 39; Project Manager controls 71–3
Project performance aspects: 3
Project Product Description: 81, 248, 273–4
Project Support: 269, 37

Q

Quality: 3; 77–86; acceptance criteria 80–1; customer's quality expectations 78–9; quality path 77–8; Quality Management Strategy 81–2, 140–2; quality review 85; stage quality plan 84; tailoring quality 224
Quality Management Strategy: 250, 81–2; prepare the Quality Management Strategy 140–2
Quality Register: 83, 250
Quality review: 85, 283–94; chair responsibilities 289–92; follow-up 288–9; informal quality reviews 294; preparation 285–6; producer responsibilities 292–3; quality review roles 284–5; review 286–8; reviewer responsibilities 293–4

R

Release package: 110–12
Risk: 87–102; early warning indicators 89; ; prepare the Risk Management Strategy 140–4; risk actionee 94; risk analysis

questions 95–7; risk budget 95; risk categories 295–7; risk management procedure 89–95; Risk Management Strategy 87, 140–4; risk owner 94; Risk Register 88, 253; risk tolerance 88; summary risk profile 92

Risk management procedure: 89–95; assess 91; communicate 95; escalate issues and risks 186–8; identify risks 90–1; implement 93–4; plan 92–3

Risk Management Strategy: 87, 143–4, 251

Risk Register: 71, 88, 143, 253

S

Scope: 3
Senior Supplier: 33, 262
Senior User: 22, 33, 261
Starting up a Project (SU): 14, 121–38; appoint the Executive and Project Manager 122–5; capture previous lessons 125–6; design and appoint the project management team 126–9; plan the initiation stage 136–8; prepare the outline Business Case 130–2; select the project approach and prepare the Project Brief 132–6

T

Tailoring PRINCE2: 221–6
Team Manager: 265, 34–5, 39
Themes: 10–11
Time: 3
Time-driven controls: 73–5
Tolerance: 186–7

W

Work Package: 253; accept a Work Package 190–2; deliver a Work Package 194–5; execute a Work Package 192–4